ENDORSEMENTS FOR *THE PRODIGAL ROAD*

Gary Ward, Multi-published Author and Retired Pastor of Living Word Church, Manhattan, KS

A powerful testimony of a life of endurance with the result being victory! The author's life story should be an encouragement to anyone who is facing repeated times of difficulty. See how victory can be yours if you don't give in or give up.

Gerald Deaton, Deliverance Ministries, Inc., Oklahoma City, OK

God's Word, His power, His love, and His faithfulness bring about victories for those who believe Him to be Who He is as revealed in His Word. *The Prodigal Road* is a testimony of God's amazing grace poured out as one man humbled himself, drew near to God, warred against the enemy of his soul and stood firm in his faith! Prayerfully read my wonderful friend's personal story of struggle, torment, hurt, and pain and his Good Shepherd's pathway to healing, deliverance, and victories unlimited! You will want to share this story with your loved ones and friends who need God's encouragement to never give up!

Bobbie Hightower, Christian Counselor/Pastor's Wife, La Grange, NC

The Prodigal Road is a must read from a threefold aspect: 1. The one who has done battle with the enemy will relate well to this book. That one knows the truth of Christ's deliverance and will give praise to God. 2. The ones who are in the midst of the battle will gain insight into what is happening to them and be relieved to know there is help in the person of the Lord Jesus Christ, that they are not crazy. 3. It also should be read by those who have no clue of Satan's wiles, such as those that Richard Miller experienced. *The Prodigal Road* will help these readers understand others who are under attack. They will gain knowledge of how to pray with more wisdom and earnestness. Satan is real. His desire is to keep people from coming to Jesus Christ and experiencing the healing He offers. Satan's goal is to destroy. If he cannot destroy, then he desires to defeat believers. He plays mind games—oppressing and attacking through the thinking process—convincing many that they are deranged and not worthy of God's great love.

I am amazed at this story because of the ability of the human spirit to function in the throes of such vicious attacks from the evil one and still be such a successful man. Equal in amazement is the love of God that will not let go until His dear ones are on solid ground and in His safe harbor. That harbor is receiving Jesus Christ and beginning the journey God has mapped out before them. They learn the truth that the enemy (Satan) has no place in their lives unless they give him a foothold. Just as Richard anchored himself to the Word of God and found deliverance, his readers too will find deliverance when they follow his example.

Hugh Emrich, Inventor/Builder, Manhattan, KS

This is the amazing story of God's unequivocal love for and rescue of one of His prodigals. Dick Miller and I have walked through life together for the past 35 years. Other than my wife of 58 years, Dick is my most trusted friend. When I received the draft manuscript, I was so fascinated by his whole story, I could not put it down; I read it completely through in one night.

This book documents Dick's victory over PTSD after his service in Vietnam and it will help you to know that you are not alone in your own invisible war. Through pain and struggles and sometimes joy, God brings us progressively to Himself. This is a real-life story of such a journey anchored in the supremacy of Jesus Christ.

THE
PRODIGAL
ROAD

My Journey up the Mountain

Dr. Richard L. Miller
U.S. Army, Retired

Table of Contents

Acknowledgments. 7

Introduction 9

Part One: Halfway from Hell. **11**

Chapter 1: Encounter with Destiny 13

Chapter 2: Reflections in a Dark Mirror 35

Chapter 3: New Places, New Friends .49

Chapter 4: Silver Linings and Dark Clouds 63

Chapter 5: Welcome to the United States Army. 73

Chapter 6: Surviving in Life's Crucible 91

Chapter 7: Through the Valley of Shadows 109

Chapter 8: Purging Begins 127

Chapter 9: Spiritual Warfare 143

Chapter 10: Gregory Hayward 157

Chapter 11: Rays of Hope, Clouds of Fear 173

Chapter 12: Family on the American Highways. 193

Part Two: Out of the Ashes, New Life **205**

Chapter 13: On the Trail with the Master Trainer 207

Chapter 14: Frontal Attack 223

Chapter 15: The Journal of a Wandering Pilgrim 239

Chapter 16: Time for a Break 255

Chapter 17: Home at Last 269

Chapter 18: Amazing Journey with Jesus .289

Chapter 19: Wrapping It Up 309

Tables and Figures 329

Bibliography 341

Notes 345

Acknowledgments

This book began on a mountain in Colorado more than forty years ago. It may never have been written except for the urging of friends and family members who persisted in reminding me that other people could be helped by reading about "My Journey up the Mountain."

Jesus tracked me down, rescued me, guided me, guarded me, and loved me from the beginning. In retrospect, it is an amazing pattern of making sure I didn't go over the cliff and enabling me to perform the tasks set before me in the military and corporate world.

Jenny, my partner for life, is now my closest friend. God knew I needed her because of her strength and absolute devotion to our relationship. This book is as much about her as it is about me. I would never have finished this book had she not often said, "You have to finish it! We have too much invested in this story!"

Our son Greg gave our family a new life. He absorbed two lines of ancestral sins and in his death terminated the curse of those sins upon us.

Our daughter, Deb, was the first to say, "Dad, you have to write your story!" Her family, Tod, Anson, and Tate, have accepted me and loved me without reservations.

Our son Doug taught me about determination and forgiveness. His family, Connie, Luke, Logan, and Levi, love me and add an exciting variety to my life.

My dad, Harry, set the course for a better life and sold the family farm so I could finish college. The prayers of my mother, Zelia, gave Heaven a reason to rescue me. My sister Irene gave me my first real pigskin football. My brother Donal taught me to swim and took us into his heart and home when tragedy came. My sister Norma gave me the first adventure of my life on a bus ride to her home. My sister Lorena has been my physical and spiritual protector for all of life. My brother John is my very close friend, confidant, and walking partner.

Stan Nuzum, my best man and friend for more than fifty years, gave me a great sacrifice of love with his painting that is the foundation of the cover of this book. Stan is a gifted and successful artist whose painting dexterity is now severely hampered by painful nerve damage. This painting is framed and on my wall; I shall cherish his gift for the remainder of my life.

Hugh Emrich is a close friend and inventor who helped me build my first house upon retirement. Hugh was the first to read the draft manuscript of this book and provided encouragement and valuable editorial advice. He is a beginning artist, and it is his painting of the ponderosa pines growing out of the burned-out stump in Oregon that is the separator between Part One and Part Two of this book.

Introduction

This book is a story about change. And for most of us, change comes hard. Two events come to mind when I think about changes with useful and beautiful results. The first involved a summer job in the open hearth of a steel mill where the purifying temperature of the metal was in excess of 2,500 degrees Fahrenheit. The end results were car bodies and stainless steel refrigerators.

The second event involved thousands of migrating monarch butterflies obscuring the view of the lake nestled among the rolling Flint Hills in Kansas. The dainty creatures wafted by, wave after wave, carried along on a gentle breeze until the last straggler fluttered by. One has to appreciate the genius of the Creator who set in motion the metamorphic phases that transform iron ore into shiny steel and ugly larvae into beautiful creations.

This two-part book describes such a metamorphosis in my life as one of God's prodigals. Part One of this story, "Halfway from Hell," received its title on Sheep Mountain, a towering crag west of Buena Vista, Colorado, in 1972. This encounter is illuminated further in Chapter 9, which chronicles the actions of the Shepherd searching the rocky cliffs on a rescue mission for one of His sheep that had gone astray.

Part Two received its title from a hilariously joyful encounter with Destiny in a burned-out forest in the shadow of Oregon's Three Sisters Mountains on Easter Sunday morning, 2002. This encounter reversed the polarity of the prodigal and triggered a metamorphic phase titled "Out of the Ashes, New Life."

My story is that of an ordinary traveler who has experienced a wide range of successes and failures, along with the vacillating emotions as a result of being harassed by a tenacious enemy grappling to recapture an escaping prisoner. Sometimes I experienced exhilarating joy; other times I felt excruciating agony. Sometimes there was a glimpse of a destination so majestic it dwarfed the significance of the vacillating emotions. Other times an insidious fog obscured the future. Sometimes the journey led through mountain meadows with sparkling rivulets, other times through swamps of darkness infested with spiritual leeches that tried to suck the life out of me.

Perhaps in reading this account, some traveler will be comforted that a fellow traveler successfully navigated the dangerous terrain. Perhaps another will be given hope when there is no apparent reason for hope. For another, a load, which has become intolerably heavy, will be lifted. By exposing the operating tactics and nature of the satanic operatives, a stepping-stone may be placed for some weary traveler whose footing has become tenuous by the slippery mire of a misdirected life tangled in the deceptive web of the destroyer. To the person being invited to become a participant in the eternal governance of God's renewed kingdom, it could be valuable in lighting the path to the Savior.

This book also has value for the researcher looking for empirical data on the role of psycho-cybernetics in personal success or failure. Imbedded in this writing are the contents of personal journals and empirical data from scientific research to determine the correlation between self-efficacy and spiritual development. The results of this research are contained in the dissertation for a Doctor of Strategic Leadership degree from Regent University in 2003.

There are two Appendices at the end of the book, as follows:

Appendix A contains excerpts from *Tools for Transformation* © (TFT), a seminar I wrote upon completion of my doctoral program in 2003. Of particular interest is the empirical data collected during the beta test of the seminar.

Appendix B is titled "Spiritual Warfare" and contains excerpts from articles and books listing the Characters in Spiritual Warfare and defining the various levels of demon activity.

PART ONE

HALFWAY FROM HELL

CHAPTER 1

Encounter with Destiny

Premonition

I walked the fifty yards in the bitter cold December wind to the plane that would carry me from the small Appalachian town on the first leg of a journey of no return. The first stop would be Fort Lewis, Washington, for training prior to reporting for duty with the United States Army in Vietnam. That fifty yards seemed like forever. Flying had become an emotional nightmare for me, and I *knew* I was walking to my eventual death in combat, final punishment from an angry God for my rebellion.

Just before entering the door of the small, two-engine passenger plane, I turned for one last look at Jenny, my wife of eight years, who was shivering in the cold morning air, but would not go inside until the plane was out of sight over the mountains. No one knew about the tears running down my face and freezing in the bitter wind, nor of the fear running through my aching heart. I did not want to go, but I was a soldier and a soldier does what he has to do.

To make matters worse, things were not good between Jenny and me. I wished our goodbye had been more pleasant. For a fleeting moment I had an urge to run back down the ramp, hold her close and say, "I love you, I want our last goodbye to be a gentle time to remember," but there was no time. One engine was already running, and they were waiting on me to enter so they could close the door and start the other engine. We exchanged waves and then I was inside the plane and into a world that would seem suspended in time.

Through a foggy window I watched the small, lone figure getting smaller and smaller, then out of sight as we climbed over the mountains.

I don't think I can handle this, I thought to myself. There had been separations before, but there had always been the anticipation of coming home. Now there was only the gut-wrenching belief that I would never see Jenny again.

Do Not Kick the Can!

The trip to Fort Lewis was a blur, and the two weeks of intensive training were not much better. But these were clear: "Don't kick a can on the road unless you want a chest full of poison spikes." "Wear your flak vest at all times and don't assume anything." "A tray in the mess hall could be booby-trapped." "When you shoot, shoot to kill!"

There were other people there, lots of them, but I had no interest in getting to know any of them. After the training was complete, we received a twenty-four hour pass before departure to Vietnam. I rode a bus into Tacoma early in the morning, a bright sunny day. I rambled around Tacoma, no place to go in particular. I just needed to get away from the inevitable future.

Then I heard singing. I walked in the direction of the music and found myself standing in front of a small church. The music felt happy. I realized it was Sunday, went in, and took a seat near the back. The people seemed genuinely glad to be there, and the preacher talked about everyone having an eternal purpose. The heavy cloud of hopelessness lifted. For a while.

Several people gathered around me after the service to welcome me and find out what I was doing in Tacoma. When they found out I was headed for Vietnam, one family insisted I come home with them for lunch, an invitation I graciously accepted. It was a pleasant afternoon and the pot roast that had been simmering in the crock pot felt like home. That was Jenny's favorite way to prepare Sunday dinner. I felt a promise of peace infiltrating my life and, at the moment, my troubled soul was quiet.

During the trip back to Fort Lewis, I recalled the family's parting words: "Your name will be on our prayer list for the entire time you are over there." Somehow I knew that it would be, and this offered temporary comfort for a soldier in Destiny's grip.

If only there were someone I could share this haunting premonition with. To have shared with my family would have inflicted only fear. It would be better to share with these friendly strangers. Yet the thought was held captive by the fear that verbalizing would bring it to pass. So I kept it to myself and the fear of dying became obscured in the greater fear of flying.

* * *

The terminal in Seattle was the beginning point of the flight to Vietnam. A young unkempt soldier with a strange look in his bloodshot eyes came up to me and asked, "Headed to 'Nam, Major?"

I answered in the affirmative.

"I hope you got your stuff together. Where I just come from officers who don't got their stuff together got fragged!"

"What's fragged?" I asked.

"You know, fragmentation grenade," the soldier said, throwing his arms up in the air. "Boom! No more officer!" I thought the soldier was just spaced out on drugs and passed it off as nonsense.

The public address system came alive. "Attention in the terminal! All military personnel scheduled for Flight 897 proceed to Gate 7 for immediate boarding."

Confirmation

On December 23, 1968, I thought, *This begins my ride to eternity.* I felt suspended in space. I was terrified, but soldiers go where orders tell them to go. It never crossed my mind to find a way out of going, so I picked up my duffel bag and followed the crowd to the plane. If my mind recorded anything about boarding the plane, the record is hidden. My head didn't hurt but my mind was in excruciating pain, interfering with the cognitive recording function of my mind. Yet now, in recollection, the smell of fumes fills my nostrils, and the vibrations from the four engines as they accelerated down the runway send a shudder through my body.

I searched for an empty aisle seat because I couldn't bear looking down through the window. I took a seat as far away from the emergency door as possible so I would not attempt to open it and jump out.

During the flight, I became aware of another officer in the seat beside me who sat staring out the window. Obviously neither of us felt much like talking, so I closed my eyes and began to focus on the days ahead, rehearsing the training I had just received.

Suddenly, a thought flooded over me like hot gas. In twenty-four hours, I may have to kill other human beings. For more than ten years I had trained to be a soldier, and the mission of a soldier is to kill enemy soldiers. The reality was shattering.

Could I do it? I wondered. It had been one thing to watch John Wayne in Sands of Iwo Jima and be there as this hero cleared the island of the enemy in strange uniforms. This was different, and I began to ask myself questions. *What will it be like to pull the trigger and watch another human fall? What will it be like to feel the bullet from the enemy's rifle? Will I panic? Will I scream with pain? Will I be brave enough to honor my country and my family?*

The officer next to me broke the silence, and we exchanged histories and geographic information. As time passed we talked about possibly seeing each other again in-country and exchanged duty assignments. He was the mortuary officer for the morgue in Saigon. There was the confirmation! "I'm sure I will visit you. I hope you remember me," I said, trying to make it sound like a joke.

Battle Zone—Strange Sounds, Strange Aromas

I have almost no memory of those first few days in Vietnam, except for the pungent odor, which burnt the inside of my nose, and the sounds in the distance, like heavy denim ripping and the constant high-speed *whop, whop, whop* . . .

Bob Hope put on a show for the troops Christmas Eve at Cameron Bay. I went but could not remember any of the details.

The chefs in the dining facility did a great job for Christmas dinner. The troops feasted on succulent turkey and all the trimmings, including shrimp cocktail, nuts, and pumpkin pie. The Army does take care of its own. The food was ok, but not like home. Home. I glanced around the room at all the soldiers in the dining facility. There was no laughter. Of the four hundred soldiers in the room, how many would not see home again? Forty? I wondered who the other thirty-nine would be. After dinner, I walked. Then it was dark and *whop, whop, whop* . . .

On December 26, 1968, I went to the transfer point to check the manifest for my flight out. I was assigned as the Battalion Executive Officer to a Field Artillery battalion somewhere in the central highlands but was not on the list. I went to Personnel. They didn't know why, but my name had been taken off the list. I was told to come back the next day—still no orders.

Finally, the fourth day, my name appeared on a manifest to Bien Hoa. The transportation to Bien Hoa was a Lockheed C-130 Hercules military transport aircraft. We all sat on the floor facing the rear, using the man's legs behind for a backrest.

A lieutenant colonel met me at the airport in Bien Hoa. He said he was the Personnel Officer (G1) for II Field Force Artillery, which was located at Long Binh. "Sir, do you know what my new assignment is?" I asked.

"You'll find out soon enough," he said.

Zero Tact, Too Dumb to Quit

At Long Binh, the G1 ushered me immediately to the II Field Force Artillery Commanding General's office. "Sir, Major Miller reporting for duty!" I said as I saluted with drill team precision.

"At ease, Miller. Have a seat." The general looked at me for a long time, sizing me up. Finally he said, "Well, Major, I guess you're wondering what's going on."

"Yes, Sir, that's a fact," I said.

The general scowled and leaned forward. "Miller," he said. "I've got a problem. I called Branch and told them I wanted a major who had very little tact and was too dumb to know when to quit. Do you fit that bill?"

The challenge and the general's direct approach began to make me feel alive again. "Could be, General. I'll let you be the judge."

The problem was with the 8th Target Acquisition Battalion (TAB). The line batteries had been deactivated, and in their place, thirteen counter mortar and personnel radar detachments had been strung all over the II Field Force area of operation (AO). In addition there were two meteorological sections, one at Can Tho, the other at Tan An, in the Mekong Delta with the 9th Infantry Division. The previous TAB commander was a major who was under an Article 32 investigation for breach of conduct as prescribed by the Uniform Code of Military Justice (UCMJ).

"I need those radars operating!" the general exclaimed. "Any resemblance the TAB has to a military unit is purely coincidental! The discipline is non-existent, the equipment doesn't operate, and it takes a week to move a radar! I want the unit straightened out and I want to be able to call you at 0800 any morning after staff briefing and have any one of the radars operational anywhere in our AO by sundown! You want the job?" The general slammed his open palm on the desk.

"Sir, I appreciate your courtesy of asking," I said. "But I assume I have no choice. Before you change your mind, I'll accept the job on one condition."

"OK, what's the condition?" the general asked.

Leaning forward and meeting the general's eyes, I said, "If I need help, I come directly to you and you give me what I need."

The challenge was stirring a renewed bravado in me.

The general said, "Fair enough" and pounded the desk with his fist. "You come to me and if it is within my power to give what you ask, you will have it. You will be assigned as the Assistant S2 for thirty days so you can size up the TAB unit, then you'll take over as commander. Good luck and welcome to Vietnam!"

I came to attention, saluted, and said, "Thank you, Sir. I'm sure I will be forever grateful."

The general smiled for the first time and reached across the desk to give a handshake to match his bold demeanor.

* * *

The officer's quarters (BOQ) were one-story wood frame structures with individual rooms. Each had a three-quarter bed, a dresser, a clothes closet, and the ever-present footlocker. That first night welcomed me with the same *whop, whop, whop* sounds along with a sinus headache so intense my vision blurred.

A war zone is a strange place. Things that were once important don't matter much there. I learned to function within the reality that this would be my last assignment. I had a strong desire to do the very best I could for my country. I hoped my family would be proud of their soldier. During those first thirty days, I spent several hours at night sitting on the bank near the BOQ listening to the *whop, whop, whop,* and the *rrrrrrrrup, rrrrrrrrup.* I discovered the whopping sound was from the blades of Huey helicopters and the ripping denim was from Spooky, a C-130 aircraft equipped with a Gatling gun. Every fifth round in the belt of the Gatling gun ammunition was a tracer, and as the plane twisted and turned to stay on target, the tracers looked like a lighted rope curving along underneath the plane.

The thirty-day indoctrination proved to be a prelude to a most amazing assignment. Many of the fears, anxieties, and foreboding thoughts that followed me to this war zone were ever so slowly being swallowed up in my new excitement and determination to accomplish the job I had trained for since my college days as an ROTC student at West Virginia University. I spent the first week learning the organization and where the detachments were located. I visited some of the closer radar detachments with the Intelligence Officer (S2). The AN/MPQ-4 (Q4) counter mortar radars were located around Tonsonut Air Force Base (AFB) for the purpose of locating enemy mortars firing on the AFB. The AN/TPS-25 (TPS25) personnel radars were located out in the base camps at various locations to detect enemy troop movement. A good TPS25 operator could tell the difference between a man and a woman walking at a distance of ten kilometers and could count the number of people in a group plus or minus three or four. So the TAB became the eyes and ears for the Artillery at night.

My first visit to the TAB headquarters was unannounced. I walked into the orderly room and realized I was the only one in uniform. Matter of fact, from the looks I received, everyone seemed surprised to *see* a uniform. I asked to see the commander, and a soldier in a drab, olive T-shirt came alive and pointed to a room behind his desk.

Seated behind the desk in that room was a young man I presumed to be a soldier, feet on the desk, wearing cutoffs, no shirt, reading a magazine not of military origin. He greeted me with, "Hey, Maj. Draw up a chair."

There was a real soldier! He recognized my rank. After confirming the man was a captain filling the vacancy left by the major who was relieved of duty, I held a brief counseling session. I explained my next visit would be the following morning at 0600 hours with expectations of recognizing everyone by the name and insignia on their uniform.

Headaches continued to plague me to the point they affected my ability to function. One night before I hit the sack, I knelt beside my bunk and voiced a simple request: "Please remove this headache so I can do my job here in Vietnam." The next morning I awoke refreshed and totally free of any headache or pain.

Mission: Boot Camp 101

The Headquarters Battery of the 8th TAB was located at the neck of a gourd-shaped compound known as Long Binh. To the front and across the road was Widows Village, a killing zone from Tet '68, a major Viet Cong (VC) offensive kicked off at the Tet holiday season in February 1968. To the rear was the vast ammunitions dump, which the VC set on fire during Tet '68. Documents from captured VC stated the ammo dump was again a primary target. And it turned out the shortest distance from Widows Village to the ammo dump was through the TAB's segment of the perimeter.

On February 1, the day I assumed command of TAB, I confirmed the general's assessment of the TAB—there was no resemblance to a military unit. That a military unit could deteriorate to this level was beyond my comprehension. The first week in command, I observed several shortfalls, any one of which could have had a deadly effect on the compound and mission—not to mention all the violations of the Uniform Code of Military Justice.

1. No one carried their M-16 as their primary weapon. Everyone tried to see how exotic a weapon they could find.

2. There were zero spare parts in the motor pool to support over one hundred vehicles. Vehicles were kept running by scrounging.

3. The survey plot for the final protective fires, a nonstop barrage of friendly artillery fire in the event the position is about to be overrun, was two hundred yards *inside* the TAB perimeter. A call for final protective fires would have wiped out the entire compound.

4. None of the equipment at the detachments was properly accounted for on property books. Therefore no support for maintenance was authorized.

On my third day in command, the entire compound went on red alert. Tet '69 had begun. The first night was chaos. There were bunkers on the front and rear perimeters. When the alert sounded, I grabbed my weapon and combat gear and dashed for the command bunker. I asked the first sergeant, often respectfully called Top, to get on the phone and get a report of all the other bunkers and who was in charge at each one. Blank stare. I grabbed the field phone, but it wasn't connected to anything!

"Top, you go to the rear perimeter and get it organized; I'll take the front perimeter," I said. On my way, I went past the day room. The red alert had little effect on the pool game going on. But I had a serious effect on the pool game!

Four bunkers lined the front perimeter, each to be manned with soldiers and automatic weapons. Everybody was in one bunker, trying to get as comfortable as possible for a long summer night's dream. I had a serious effect on their comfort level.

I climbed up on one of the bunkers to get a better view of Widow's Village using binoculars to scan the dim terrain. When my eyes adjusted to the darkness, I was amazed to see Widow's Village crawling with figures clad in black pajamas, the uniform of the VC. I reported this to the Artillery Command Center, and then asked the supply sergeant if there were any Claymore mines, the directional anti-personnel mines used for perimeter defense. He thought there were some in the ammo bunker.

"Get them and find someone who knows how to set them out!" I said.

Thirty minutes later he was back with the mines in unopened boxes and reported he could find no one who could remember how to arm them.

I grabbed the first box of mines and headed for the road that ran between the TAB perimeter and Widow's Village. My Jeep driver, a sharp PFC, grabbed the other box and followed. We crawled along the road on our bellies and set up and armed the mines.

In the meantime, Command Center had activated Spooky and notified a column of Light Infantry Brigade troops to block any retreating VC while Spooky hosed down the area with its 20 mm Gatling gun. It was quite a fireworks display and Widow's Village added another validation of its name.

The next morning, I ordered a commander's call with all personnel present to share my observations for the past thirty days and the events of the preceding night. I laid my authorized pistol on the podium and looked over the group slowly, making eye contact with each soldier. There was one soldier who stared back with hate-filled eyes and I made note of the name on his fatigue jacket.

The briefing was short. "I have been observing this outfit for thirty days and in many respects this unit does not meet military standards," I said. "I am well aware of the lack of leadership in the past and I will allow for that. During the next thirty days, you will be given a great opportunity to become soldiers and complete the mission you were sent here to do.

"I also understand you have a drug ring operating within the unit and that there is a contract on anyone who interferes. I am an expert with this pistol and will not hesitate to use it on either a VC or a traitor attempting to harm me or any of our men. Our next exercise will be a shakedown inspection during which I will confiscate all unauthorized weapons and reissue authorized weapons. Then we will begin learning how to be soldiers. That is all! Report to your bunk and prepare for inspection. Dismissed!"

During the shakedown inspection we collected a trailer full of every kind of personal weapon ranging from pearl-handled revolvers to WWII grease guns with one clip of ammo to AK-47s, the Russian-made weapon the VC used. We hooked up telephones, located automatic weapons, issued the authorized personal M-16s with ammo, and learned passwords and how to say, "Halt or I will shoot!" three times in Vietnamese. By noon the troops were dead on their feet.

That evening, a newly assigned maintenance warrant officer came to my office and asked for a closed-door session. He explained that he had been an investigator for a police department and specialized in breaking up drug rings. He had one request: "Give me free reign for the next ten days and I will identify the drug ring and its leaders for you."

I granted his request. Seven days later he placed the list of names on my desk. I recognized the name of the leader—it was the soldier with the hate-filled eyes. I also recognized I needed help and knew exactly where to get it.

First Sergeant Ronald R. Tolson

I believed first sergeant was the most important rank in the Army and the dearest to my heart because it is the enlisted soldiers like these who ultimately do the work, and the cohesion and operation of a unit depends on the experience and knowledge of the first sergeant. I had to have a new one. Let's just say it was time for a change. And the change had to be *now*, so I headed for the general's office. "Sir, I've come to collect your promise. I need a new first sergeant immediately."

"OK, Major, do you have one in mind?"

"Yes, sir. First Sergeant Ronald R. Tolson."

"You know this man?"

"Yes, sir, served with him in Germany. He's one of the best I know and he has target acquisition experience."

"Okay, Major, tell G1 to get him. By the way, where is he?"

"Sir, he's with the 9th Infantry Division Artillery [DivArty]."

"Not the 9th! I can't move a key man out of the 9th without a replacement! You'll just have to find someone else!"

"Sir, you gave me your word that you would give me the help I needed to straighten out this route step outfit. I need Tolson."

"Well, I've got to think about this one. I'll let you know."

The entire compound went on red alert again at dark. I made the rounds of all positions, checking gear and weapons. Everything seemed in order and all positions were properly manned. Around midnight, I went to the TAB operations bunker to try to get some rest. I heard a chopper land on the DivArty pad and wondered who was out this time of night. A few minutes later there was a knock on the bunker door.

I heard the guard issue a challenge: "Who's there?"

"Tolson. I'm looking for Major Miller."

The general came through as promised. He sent his personal chopper to pick up the requested man that night. I will be forever grateful to First Sergeant (1SGT) Ronald R. Tolson, for he gave up a certain promotion to sergeant major and many combat awards to help a friend and the Army he loved. And help he did! Within fifteen days, the outfit was a military unit again. He took care of the enlisted men, and I took care of the officers. And the men left a lot of sweat on the running trails in the dim light of dawn every morning.

* * *

One morning Top came to me and said, "Sir, the word is tomorrow morning when you give the command to double time they are going to lay down."

"Who is the one in charge of rebellion?"

"Major, I'll give you three guesses and the first two don't count," Top said.

"Okay. Don't say anything to him beforehand. Have him in position so he will be right by me on the front row when I give the command to double time for the morning run around the inside of the compound."

The next morning after doing calisthenics, and just before I gave the command to double time, I stood very close to the identified soldier and presented him with options. It is truly amazing what effect a brief counseling session can have on the mental attitude of a rebel, if the words and sounds are chosen carefully and delivered appropriately. Suffice it to say, there was no more trouble during PT.

I gave the list of names in the drug ring provided by the maintenance warrant to 1SGT Tolson and coordinated a pretrial confinement for any on the list with the Staff Judge Advocate (JAG) and the Military Police (MP). Top identified two of his best NCOs and assigned them the duty of monitoring the ringleader with hate-filled eyes' every move and gathering evidence of his activities. A few days later the ringleader got suspicious, pulled a gun on one of the sergeants, and was disarmed by the other sergeant and taken to the MP station. The ringleader went immediately to pretrial lockup, was tried by court martial, and was sentenced to prison at Fort Leavenworth, Kansas. Cleansing the unit of the drug ring did wonders for the morale of the unit.

Angels Unaware

A few days later the general summoned me to headquarters.

"Major, we captured a VC who had papers saying a VC division will be infiltrating through the banana plantation between here and Bearcat beginning tonight," he said. "I would like a TPS25 radar out there to locate that unit. I don't have a security unit to give you, so you could be sitting there with no protection except the Artillery Battery at Bearcat. It could be very risky, but if that division gets through, they could destroy the entire ammo dump. Do you have enough personnel to set up a fire support base and be operational by dark today?"

"Sir," I said. "I'll need a chopper to go on recon and I know where there is a Twin 40[1] that would make a mighty good defense in that jungle. I'll also need the engineers to build a tower to get the TPS25 up out of the trees."

The general's response was brief: "Roger that, and I'll have a light fire team ready for you in half an hour to escort you on the recon. Take an engineer officer with you. Good luck."

The recon team was airborne in thirty minutes and over the jungle in fifteen. The two Huey gunships broke away and went down on the deck to clear a landing area. For the first time since the general's call, I had time to think. This was my first mission and the premonition of being killed rushed in, gripping me with fear I hadn't experienced since arriving in country. A heat wave started at my feet and rose to set my face blazing. I felt a sudden urgency to pray, yet was hesitant to bow my head. I half-bowed my head and whispered, "God, I ask for courage to do the job I've been given."

Do not fear. I have set a thousand angels to watch over you.

Where did that come from? I first thought the voice had come through the headset in my flight helmet, and that the pilot had heard me pray and was joking with me. This was not a time for joking, but just in case, I keyed my mic to ask the pilot where he would get a thousand angels. When the mic crackled, I realized the "voice" had not come through my headset.

The next few seconds were dazzling, incomprehensible. Moments before, I was shaking with fear. Now I was filled with total peace.

"OK," I said. "Let's take her down; land in that clearing over there."

Chopper pilots in Vietnam were a rare breed. They could make those machines do unbelievable things. Instantly the team was on the ground and possibly in the middle of a large enemy unit waiting for darkness to move upon the ammunition dump. Amazingly, I was walking around like it was a Sunday picnic. I staked out the location

---

1 * A Twin 40 is a 40 mm, track-mounted, two-barreled air defense weapon that is also lethal cutting through the jungles.

for the tower and the support vehicles and fields of fire for the Twin 40. Then I marked out a perimeter for the security force being assembled by 1SGT Tolson.

The professionalism of the helicopter pilots cannot be underestimated. They stayed alive by getting in and getting out before the VC could react. I glanced at my watch. We had been on the ground more than twenty minutes. The pilot said, "Major, let's get out of here! Enemy rockets could rip this thing to shreds any minute!"

"Not to worry," I said. "There will be no harm to us today."

While I was making the recon, 1SGT Tolson held a formation of all the cooks, mechanics, and anyone else who happened to be in the TAB area.

"Men, we have a mission to install a TPS25 radar in the jungle between here and Bearcat," Tolson said. "It could be very risky. We may be in the path of an entire VC division. I need twenty volunteers as a guard force for the radar section. If you are willing to go, please step forward."

Every man stepped forward. What a difference a good first sergeant and a few days made.

A chopper picked up the radar at a distant location, and the engineers delivered the tinker toy tower to be erected on sight. The radar arrived before the tower was anchored. Lowering the radar onto a weaving six-foot square platform sixty feet in the air was a real challenge. A crew member and I climbed the sixty-foot tower, grabbed the radar, and braced against the tower rigging to stabilize the tower long enough for the pilot to set the radar down and release it. The down-wash from the chopper blades caused the tower to weave violently. The next five seconds made a tight-rope walk across the Grand Canyon seem like child's play. But that was only the beginning of the sacrifice by the crew.

Transport damaged the device that permitted the alignment of the radar antennae so the direction and range of the target could be determined. The antenna was under a dome and could not be seen from the outside. The chief warrant officer (CWO), who was the section leader, said, "Major, I think I can get this thing pointed in the right direction."

With that he climbed the tower and directed the radar operator to turn the radar to full power and hold the antennae stationery. The crew on the ground watched curiously as the CWO on the tower faced the dome and began side-stepping a few steps then stopping as if listening to something. Then he would side-step a few steps and listen, moving around the dome.

Finally he yelled, "I got it!"

It turned out the CWO moved around the dome until his head began to ache, and then moved until it no longer ached. By locating the direction of maximum pain from the radiation, he was able to ascertain the direction the antenna was pointing. Using a navigation compass, he was able to orient the radar so the operator could report the direction and range to the personnel target. The high morale of the troops in the face of danger and the CWO's knowledge of the system and his sacrificial performance ensured that the radar was operational by dark as requested by the general.

The operator picked up the leading elements of the VC units on the TPS25 radar and directed the fire from the Bearcat artillery battery so effectively that the VC apparently abandoned the plan to infiltrate through the banana plantation.

When I returned to base camp, I got a Bible and looked for the quote, "I have set a thousand angels to watch over you." It was not there!

Then where did those words that brought total peace and confidence come from? Does God speak to men these days? Why me? And a thousand angels?

I will never know the mystery of the number of angels assigned, yet after four decades the promise I heard is as clear as it was then. Recently the thought occurred to me that to the best of my knowledge there were no fatal casualties in the units stationed at our location during the time I was there. Is it possible the promised protection extended to the others as well, thereby accounting for the number of angels assigned?

Angels Versus Claymore Mines

The incident in the chopper had an impact. When we were in base camp, 1SGT Tolson and I began to meet early in the morning and took turns reading from the Bible and praying for the men in the unit, especially for the isolated detachments and the survey crews that were continuously in the jungles surveying all critical locations within the II Field Force AO. The prayers seemed to work. But early one morning, I got a call that one of the radar sections had been hit, and one of the men had been taken to the hospital. By the time I got to the hospital, the injured soldier had been released. I drove to the radar site and received a briefing from the section chief about the incident.

Their radar had stopped operating during the night and two of the soldiers had taken it upon themselves to drive to another radar site for a spare part even though the roads were closed to military traffic during the hours of darkness. That kind of courage and dedication was typical of many American soldiers in a very unpopular war. After picking up the critical part, the two soldiers were about halfway back to their site when the VC detonated an American Claymore mine just as the Jeep passed.

"Major, are you a believer?" the section chief asked. "Look at this Jeep they were riding in!"

Hundreds of pellets from the Claymore mine had riddled the passenger side of the Jeep, tearing the Jeep's skin to shreds. The section chief asked me to bend down and look at the Jeep from the angle the mine would have been at when it detonated. The Jeep had obviously just passed the mine, and there on the dash was the outline of a man where there were no holes. Yet the only injury to the soldier was a goose egg on his right thigh from a piece of shrapnel that had penetrated a book in his fatigue pocket but had not broken the skin.

Again the section chief asked, "Major, can you explain this?"

I studied the pattern on the dashboard and said, "I have read of similar incidents with George Washington and in the Six-Day War in Israel, but I never expected to see it firsthand."

I stared at the shattered Jeep for a long time and imagined what that smiling soldier standing beside me should have looked like. I straightened up and said, "Yes, I am a believer and this just reinforces it."

I praised the men and made a mental note to reward them for their acts of bravery.

Angels versus AK-47s

A few days later, the general directed the movement of another TPS25 radar to a remote site along the route of suspected VC penetration. The radar became operational just after dark. I received a radio message that the general wanted another radar moved the following morning.

"Man, this is becoming routine!" I exclaimed. The roads in that region were off limits at night, but I had no choice. If we were to make the move on schedule, I had to get back to base camp immediately. I asked 1SGT Tolson to get my Jeep and driver ready for the trip. Tolson objected, but when he reported the Jeep ready, he and another crew-member were in the back seat with enough weapons to hold off a small army. We decided the best thing to do was to pretend to be a recon party, hoping the VC would hesitate to fire on us and give away their position.

So we drove along searching the route with large flashlights. Why not? You can't hide a Jeep anyway. We were passing through the last of a banana thicket when two AK-47's opened up with automatic fire less than ten feet away and the driver started to stop. I jammed his foot on the accelerator and jumped the Jeep out of there.

When out of range, we stopped to assess the damage. No one was hit and there was not a scratch anywhere on the vehicle. When Top asked the driver why he started to stop he said, "First Sergeant, with all that firepower in the back, I figured you wanted to take the VC under fire!" I commended the driver for his courage. 1SGT Tolson said, "I wonder what those two VC gunners are thinking right now," and began laughing hilariously.

Another Strange Sound

There are many strange sounds in a combat zone. I woke up about 0300 one morning to a sound like a person shoveling gravel using a shovel covered with burlap. The next night I heard the same sound, and again on the third night. It began about the same time and lasted about two hours. After walking around the area and doing strange things like lying down with my ear pressed against the floor and against the ground near the BOQ, I determined it was coming from beneath the BOQ. I reasoned that if I reported my suspicions to Operations, they would send me for a psychiatric evaluation. So I got a large two-and-a-half-ton truck differential bell housing, borrowed a stethoscope from the doctor, stretched a tight membrane over the small end of the bell housing, buried the bell housing halfway in the ground, and waited for the burlap shovel to begin again.

The sound began the same time that night, so I grabbed the stethoscope, plugged it into my ears, and placed the sound piece against the taunt membrane. The makeshift device worked; the sound was coming from somewhere underground. The logical conclusion was that the VC was trying to tunnel under the compound to get to the huge ammo dump on the rear perimeter. The shortest distance from Widow's Village to the ammo dump was right under my bunk.

The next morning I borrowed a backhoe with an auger from the engineering unit and plugged the area with several holes. No tunnel was discovered. If there was a tunnel it would likely be only big enough for one small VC to crawl through dragging a bag of explosives to start the detonation in the ammo dump. The sound stopped so I considered the interdiction a success.

Recovering Discipline

Restoring military discipline and physical fitness within the TAB was a priority after taking command. I initiated physical training (PT) every morning before breakfast consisting of the Army Daily Dozen calisthenics and a progressive run inside the compound. One of the soldiers wrote his mother that I was exposing him to enemy fire along the perimeter. His mother wrote her congressman. Her congressman wrote the general. I wrote the response. The general's aide sent it back for rewrite.

Then, as a result of confiscating all the worthless personal weapons and issuing each man his assigned M-16 with full ammo allocation, a soldier wrote his mother that I had taken his weapon and he had no way to defend himself. His mother wrote her congressman. Her congressman wrote the general. I wrote the response. The general's aide sent the response back for rewrite. The general thought it was inappropriate to tell the congressman to take care of his business and let me take care of mine. Oh, well.

One morning the Inspector General (IG) and his crew showed up for the annual unannounced inspection of everything from spare parts in the motor pool to the quality of food in the dining hall. He also listened to any complaints. The line to talk to him looked like the first showing of *Rear Window*! The report with all the complaints was ten pages long. 1SGT Tolson and I had a riot answering the allegations. They sent it back for rewrite.

Halt or I'll Shoot!

The night after the IG visit, as I was making the rounds of the front and back perimeters, I saw a figure duck into the shadows. I dropped to the ground and yelled "Halt or I'll shoot" three times in Vietnamese. No response. I chambered a round, and then drew a bead on the figure in the shadows. Microseconds before the hammer dropped, the figure yelled, "Don't shoot!"

The man was one of the IG inspectors checking out some of the reports, including one from two of the medics who told him of an incident that happened a few days earlier.

The medics were on their way back to their barracks late one night after an emergency at the hospital when they saw a figure in the shadows near the door to my sleeping quarters. They slipped up behind the figure and pinned his arms to his side. It turned out to be one of the TAB soldiers with two hand grenades. The soldier had already pulled the pin on one of the grenades, which they somehow wrestled away from him, miraculously keeping it from detonating. They told the IG they had not reported the incident to me for fear of what I might do.

I called the soldier into my office the next day, explained his rights under the Uniform Code of Military Justice (UCMJ), and asked him if he would care to explain what he was intending to accomplish. He claimed he was "popping pills," and when he was high, he heard voices yelling at him, "Kill the Major then Sergeant Tolson!" He had pulled the pin on one of the grenades and was ready to toss it into my bedroom. The other grenade was for 1SGT Tolson.

I did not mince words. "Soldier, you have two choices. Continue to pop pills, try the hand grenade trick again and you will expose yourself to a possible trip home in a body bag. The other choice is to forget the pills, straighten up, become a good soldier, and go home a hero."

He chose the latter and turned out to be one of the best soldiers in the outfit.

A Quiet Respite

The days and weeks flew by quickly. Eventually, Tet '69 seemed to be over and there were no radars to move. The general must have been out of country. 1SGT Tolson and I decided it was time to spruce up the barren compound and add some revetments around the sleeping quarters for protection from incoming mortar rounds. We initiated a contest with prizes to the sections with the greatest improvement in safety and beauty. The activity was amazing.

The Maintenance Section won first prize, an all-expenses paid weekend to the Rest and Recreation (R&R) Center, with four-foot high revetments with a variety of flowers in the top of the walls and flower beds all around their area. Then 1SGT Tolson rotated himself and the other TAB members through the R&R Center. It got quiet around the compound. I was planning a week of R&R in Hawaii with Jenny later, so I stayed to hold down the fort.

Boiling Clouds

During the quiet pause, I just wanted to be alone to try to sort out what had been happening. I came here to die, but it seemed as if I was encased in a bubble that bullets could not penetrate. I walked the perimeter as far away as I could. I not only walked for hours around the compound but also walked back through my life and then climbed out on a chronological stairway.

Most of the trip was unpleasant. I realized I was recalling mostly painful events. *Were there never happy moments in my life?* I asked as I turned to watch a rapidly building cloud with billowing white and grey foam rolling and boiling, rising upward rapidly. *This is a picture of my life in turmoil,* I thought, recalling a recent chopper flight.

The pilot had been dubious about taking off. "We'll give it a go, but those clouds are already building," he explained.

With full power and full pitch on the blades, the chopper shuddered upward, but it soon became evident the cloud was winning, and we could not get over the top. The pilot nosed the chopper down and slid back down the boiling cumulous giant and returned to base.

I wonder if that is the story of my life; I gave it all I had but it was too little, I mused.

I returned to my room and plopped down on my bunk, staring at the ceiling, letting the events of the day and my life float through my mind. In the span of a few hours of relaxed walking, a voluminous amount of data transferred from its buried depth into my conscious mind. Amazingly, the memories came with their associated emotions, smells, sounds, and pictures as if they had happened yesterday. I could even recall the smell of my horse, Bess, after a sweaty day's work, and the pungent odor of the plastic housing of the old battery-powered Zenith radio on which I listened to Sky King, Tennessee Jed, and the Hit Parade. Some of the memories are pleasant, some are unpleasant. I have recorded some of both that shaped my life as a boy growing up in a rural Appalachian area.

CHAPTER 2

Reflections in a Dark Mirror

The Young Years

They tell me I was born March 9, 1935, at home in Big Springs, West Virginia. My first memory is of a shanty up in the "holler" from Grandpa Jarvis's house when I was two or three years old. The shanty was made of slabs from a nearby sawmill where my dad worked. We carried water from a deep ravine below the house. I hated to go there because of the horrible stench from dead cows. An epidemic had totally wiped out my uncle's herd of cattle, and dead animals were dumped in the ravine just below the spring. I still smell that putrid odor.

Just above the little shack, we cleared an area of trees for a small garden. I was excited when Mom let me help her plant peanuts in the garden. I checked on them every day to see if they had come through the ground. One day I saw the little leaves all along the row and ran to tell Mom that our peanuts had come up. A few days later I went to check on them again and our milk cow was in the garden and had eaten all the peanuts. I felt very sad.

When I was four years old, we moved from the shack to a community called Minora, where we lived in a little house by Otis Brannon's store. One day a lot of chewing gum spilt off a delivery truck on the road in front of the store. The driver let my sister and me pick it up and keep some clove and teaberry. That was my first chewing gum. I liked the taste of the teaberry best, but I like the smell of the clove best because it reminded me of the smell in Mom's kitchen at Christmas time.

Sometimes Mr. Brannon let me help pump gas into people's cars. Both of us pumped that big handle back and forth, and red gas began to fill a tank above our heads. Then we hooked up a hose to the car and the gas drained into their tank. I felt real important helping at a gas station.

Mom spent a lot of time working on a thing they called a switchboard. One day I was helping her, and a scary man with a big voice, a big beard, and a red and white suit came in the room and tried to grab me. I escaped and hid behind the switchboard until he was gone. Everyone thought it was funny. I thought it was scary.

Then we moved down the road to a big house. One day it began to rain and rain and rain. Then it got dark and was still raining. I remember being carried out because of a big flood that was coming into our house. My uncle picked me up and jumped over the muddy water that was already past the back porch. The floodwaters didn't smell good, and the water roared as it went by. The next day we came back and the water was still around our house and the car was mostly under water.

Soon after the flood we moved to Grandpa Miller's house because Grandma Miller died. Grandpa's heart stopped soon after we got there. I don't remember him, just the funeral with women screaming and falling down. From then on I didn't like funerals.

There was one thing that happened soon after Grandpa's heart stopped that really scared me. My older brother, Donal, and I shared a room at the top of the stairs and there was no light in the room because we did not have electricity. I went to bed before Donal and one night as I crawled into bed, I felt something scary come into my room, like a ghost or something. I couldn't see anything, but the room got so cold I was freezing even though it was summer. I crawled under the feather tick to try to get warm and stayed there all night. I didn't tell anyone because I was afraid they would make fun of me, but from that time on I was afraid in the dark.

Later that summer we went to a neighbor's house to visit. I had a friend there who was also four and we played all around the house. Then we chased each other around a telephone pole and he fell down. I tried to help him up and there was blood running out of his head. I got his blood all over my hand. The older people came running out and his mother screamed at me: "You killed my boy! You killed my boy!" Then they all left, and I just stood there shaking. I didn't mean to hurt my friend. I expected I would get a spanking for doing it, but nobody said anything about it. At the funeral they had flowers that had a smell I had never smelled before and I didn't like the smell.

Soon after that Mom and Dad told us that some crazy man was loose over in Grantsville. Everybody was talking about this little boy the man had kidnapped and they found him all cut up in pieces and put in a bag. That made me feel awful. I was scared and hoped I would never have to go to Grantsville.

The next summer we put up hay at a neighbor's house. I was about five and I went along to tromp the hay back in the hayloft. There was an older girl there. I guess she liked me. She hugged me a lot and when we were alone, she always wanted to "play house." I didn't know what that was all about, but I enjoyed the hugs.

Our car was ruined in the flood, so we walked everywhere. We often had to walk past a barn where we were told a woman without a head carried her baby around in the loft at night. I never saw her because I turned my head and ran past the barn at night. But there was something scary about that place. One day coming home from school we found a man lying in the pigpen across from the barn. The hogs had eaten part of his face off. I guess he had been feeding the pigs when he died and fell in the mud.

The next year I started school. The school was one room and all the kids in the White Oak community went to school there. One day my sister, Lorena, and I were walking home from school. My dog had come to meet us and was jumping around. Lorena said it was our dog, but everyone knows that dogs belong to boys. Then for no good reason, some man drove his car clear off the road to hit my dog and sped off. I picked my dog up and held him until he quit whimpering. I cried for a while, then carried him home and buried him.

When I was six or seven Uncle Doc Jarvis came home from the war. He was a big Marine in uniform! He knelt down so I could see all the buttons and ribbons on his uniform, then he put me on his shoulder and carried me around the yard. He was my hero. From that day I wanted to be a Marine.

The Big War

In the winter of 1944 everybody was talking about the bomb that was going to destroy the world. One night the sky lit up with all kinds of wavy colors. I thought the bomb had gone off and the world would burn up. Then someone said it was the Northern Lights, but nobody explained what that was. That night we had to turn off all the lights and listen to lots of planes drone on and on forever. In later years, we found out we were on a flyway path from an Air Force base in Ohio, and those were bombers headed for the European war.

When I was about nine, my Uncle Gordon also came home from the war. Other soldiers with guns escorted him in a big box. They took him up on the hill to the cemetery. The soldiers fired their guns and I jumped and hid behind a big cedar tree, afraid the soldiers were going to attack us. The soldiers put their guns down. Another soldier up in the edge of the woods played a horn. I didn't like the way it made me feel, all lonesome inside or something like that. A lot of other people didn't like it either because they cried. I didn't cry because I didn't know what I would be crying for, but I had never felt like that before. They covered Uncle Gordon up and we all went home.

I Didn't Mean to Hurt These People

One day Lorena and I got into trouble. I guess Mom and Dad blamed me, for they made me get in the car and go with them. Lorena got to stay and play with the other kids. Somebody stopped us and told Mom something real bad because she began to cry something awful, even shaking the car! I wanted to run away.

Then we drove down the road to where a car was turned upside down. There was the smell of gas and smoke. This was exactly the same place where the mom said I killed her baby at the telephone pole. I felt like they thought I caused this bad thing also, but I didn't mean to do this. I didn't mean to hurt my mom. Everyone cried a lot for a few days and later we went on the hill to another graveyard. I smelled the same flowers again that I didn't like. No one said a word to me and I felt confused and scared. It was years later that I found out it was Mom's sister who was killed in the accident.

No Chance to Explain

That summer we went blackberry picking. We filled every bucket in the house with big, juicy blackberries. I filled my bucket and my tummy also. That evening, Dad and I went to the barn to take care of the cows and horses. Dad sent me back to the house to get the milk buckets.

When I asked Mom where the buckets were, she said, "Richard, they are still full of berries. You go play in the yard 'til I get them empty and I will call you when they are ready." So I went out in the yard and lay down under the apple tree and watched ants. Next thing I knew my dad was yelling at me for not minding him and whipping me with a limb off the apple tree. It hurt, but mostly I was really mad because I was just doing what Mom told me to do and he didn't even give me a chance to explain. After that, I used to dream he was dying. Sometimes I would get really scared and come downstairs and pretend I was sick just to make sure Dad was okay. Then when he cut my hair, stood close, and touched me, I would get a headache. I didn't want him to touch me.

Blood Everywhere

When I was eight or nine we were hauling hay on a sled. The sled had stakes about three feet tall along each side to hold the hay on. I was riding on the front of the sled, and Donal was driving. The horses crossed the little creek, and the sled dived down one side and jammed against the far side, jerking the horses back. The one on my side fell back on the front stake right under its tail. Blood flew everywhere and splattered all over me. The horse made a lot of loud noises and died right there.

Floods, Fingernails, and Friends

We had another big flood that year. Water was everywhere. They called it a gully washer, and said it was caused by a cloudburst up the holler. We played in the raging muddy water in our front yard. It was really scary, but

I felt sad when the water started going down. When we went down the road later to see what damage was done, we found our one-room schoolhouse lodged way down by the church. I thought that was good because we wouldn't have school for a long time. Turned out, I was wrong about that. I don't know to this day how they got it back up there, but when it was time for school to start, there it was—big as everything!

When I was ten, my dad let me stay over at Jack's house. Jack was my best friend. His mom always fixed burnt sugar syrup for breakfast. I liked everything about staying over with Jack except the stories his dad told us every night. They were stories about ghosts and wild animals. The worst one was about a wild, crazy woman who lived up in the holler. She had wild eyes that shined in the dark and long fingernails as sharp as razors. Sometimes you could hear her scream. Then Jack's dad would lean over real serious like and whisper, "She likes to catch little boys and cut them up with her fingernails!" The side of my face got real hot around my ears, and I could feel something crawling up the back of my neck. We had to sleep in the dark, but I didn't sleep much because every noise I heard was that wild woman trying to get in the house.

Preachers and a Pig's Squeal

Every winter we had a revival meeting with a preacher from Grantsville. They always stayed at our house and we always had pie and milk after church. My favorite preacher was Fell Kennedy. He bought my 4-H Club Fattening Pig. We butchered the pig and sent it to him and he sent the money back in an envelope with a note saying he kept a dollar because I didn't send all the pig. I would get the dollar when he got the tail and the squeal. Well, I found the tail easy enough, but I looked all over for a squeal and didn't find one. Fell Kennedy just about doubled over when I told him. He gave me the dollar anyway.

My dad was a preacher. One time he was preaching and some of us boys were whispering in the back. He came down out of the pulpit and headed for us. I knew we were in trouble. He grabbed me by the right ear, pulled me out of the pew, marched me down front, and made me sit on the platform in front of the pulpit facing the people. I didn't like church or my dad much after that. But later on, I used to beg him to take me when he went to other churches. I was afraid he would not come back or maybe die.

Grown Up

It seems like a lot of things happened the year I was twelve, some good, some bad. Playing house with Donna continued until she got interested in some older boys and wanted nothing to do with me. It hurt to be rejected after all those years, but I did not cry. That fall my dad let me start hunting. We had a Crackshot 22, a .22 caliber rifle with a lever action that held one shot. I had one box of shells, and I practiced and got real good. When squirrel season came in, Dad told me I could take the gun and go hunting by myself. I was under that big beechnut tree before daylight. Just as it got light, a big ol' red squirrel came out of his hole and started up the limb. I could hardly breathe and was shaking so much I couldn't keep the sights lined up. Finally I pulled the trigger and the squirrel didn't move. I tried to reload, but I was so nervous I kept dropping the shells. Then I looked up and that big red squirrel was hanging by one foot. Then, *kerplunk*, he hit the ground. I grabbed him by the tail and ran all the way to the house as fast as I could. I was so proud! Then Dad said I had to skin him. I hadn't thought about this part and didn't enjoy skinning it, but when Mom whipped up a batch of biscuits and squirrel gravy, that was a different story!

I was considered the best shot in the family, so I was given the job of shooting the hogs in the head on butchering day. That stunned the hog, and the men hooked up a rope to the hog's hind legs and pulled it up until it hung upside down. I didn't like killing the animals I had fed all year. But the very worst part was sticking the hog's throat with a butcher knife to let the blood out. I had nightmares about it, but that's what we had to do. I couldn't tell anybody I hated it.

The Thing

When I was twelve, my dad let Jack and me go possum hunting at night to catch animals with fur to sell for money. One night we borrowed our neighbor's hunting dog, a big, black dog named Night. There was a wet snow on the ground, and we lit the old kerosene lantern and took off up the holler and over the ridge above where the wild woman was supposed to be—but we were all grown up and not scared. Our feet got wet so we stopped and built a fire to dry out. Just when we started to put the fire out, there was this blood-curdling squall just over the hill. I wasn't scared at first, but as the squalls got closer, I looked over at Jack and every time the thing squalled, his hair would stand straight up and raise his cap. Then I got scared!

By this time we could see a big pair of eyes shining at the edge of the lantern light. Maybe this was the wild woman coming to get us. I started to run but my feet wouldn't move. Ol' Night had wandered off while we were drying out. After my mind began to work again, I remembered that Night would come to Jack's shrill whistle, so I whispered, "Whistle for Night!" Instead of a whistle, Jack let out a yell that echoed in the hills, "Hyar Night!" Night came running and scared the thing that was squalling at us. We felt safe with him there. However, it was short-lived because the thing came back and let out another squall from a different direction. Night dove between my legs, and I could not get him to move. Now I was really scared! That had to be that wild woman crawling toward us.

When I got a voice back, I whispered, "Jack, what are we gonna do? If we run, she will catch us for sure. So the only thing to do is grab a club and attack her!"

Jack said he saw one he could grab, and there was a sassafras sapling I figured I could break off.

"On the count of three, grab and attack. One, two, three, grab!" The sapling snapped like a matchstick. Jack grabbed his club, and we attacked yelling at the top of our voices. That frontal attack worked. The thing took off. Later we checked the tracks in the snow and it turned out to be a lynx.

We decided that was enough excitement for one night so we headed for home. We went to my house first. Jack called his dad on the party line phone hanging by the front door to see if he could stay the night.

"No," his dad said. "You get right home."

That was that, and he headed down the holler in the pitch-black dark with just the carbide light that the coal miners used. It wasn't long until we heard the chain of the gate rattle and Jack came crashing through the front door and collapsed on the couch just inside the door. He was white as a sheet and gasping for breath.

He stammered, "I . . . I . . . got down . . . to that deep holler where . . . where those big hickory trees are . . . and . . . that thing let out a sq . . . squa . . . squall . . . like up on the ridge!" He paused. "I think I peed my pants. Anyway, I got out of there as fast as I could, feeling like that thing was gonna jump on my back at any minute! I'm not going back down there by myself."

Jack was afraid to call his dad again, so my dad finally said, "Alright, you boys can take the .22 and Richard can stay the night."

He handed me the Crackshot 22, and I got my shells, loaded one, and set the safety, and off we went brave as everything now that we had protection. When we got to the deep holler, a fox barked up on the bank. I didn't say anything, but I figured that was what Jack heard. But, hey, sound gets amplified down in those deep hollers at night when you are alone.

The Greatest Gift of All

We didn't know we were poor because everyone else was about like us. Our house was about a quarter of a mile off the paved road. From our front porch, when there were no leaves on the trees, you could see down by the road where the mailbox was. Once a year we got an order from the Sears and Roebuck catalog. I usually got one pair of shoes, a pair of overalls, and a new shirt. It took about two weeks for the order to get there, and after the order was mailed we watched that road every day for the mail truck to come. When we saw the driver set a package down we would run all the way down to get it. Usually by spring the soles of our shoes were coming loose, and to keep the soles from flapping when we walked, we'd put a rubber jar ring around our shoes and the sole until it was warm enough to go barefoot.

Christmastime was special. We got two gifts each year. The first was from school, where we drew names. We'd get a comb or a pencil or a new eraser. At home we got one gift. Us kids would try to figure out the hiding place and sneak a look if we could. One time I found the hiding place under Dad and Mom's bed. One day when they were both gone I crawled under the bed, found the one I suspected was mine, and tried to figure out how it worked. Best I could tell it was a cork-shooting rifle. When you cocked it with a level and pulled the trigger, a piece of metal like the end of a screwdriver jumped forward and knocked the cork out. Somehow I managed to get my finger stuck in the barrel. I tried to shoot it out. The spring sunk that piece of metal into my finger and blood flew everywhere. Lorena bandaged me up.

When I was thirteen, my other sister, Irene, went to Arizona. She came home for Christmas and brought me the best present I ever got: a real pigskin football! I carried that treasure everywhere and slept with it. I loved to play football and thought Coach Underwood over at Calhoun County High School was great.

A Dream Come True, Almost

When I was in the eighth grade, we had Regional Field Day at Orma. The field was a farmer's field he had mowed so the grass would be short and easy to run in. My favorite race was the hundred-yard dash. They had three grown-ups at the finish line to catch the top three places. Coach Underwood was the catcher for first place.

"On your mark, get set, GO!"

Man, I burned the grass and finished way ahead of the others! I will never forget what a wonderful feeling it was for Coach Underwood to put his arm around my shoulder and walk me back to the winner's area. He called me Miller just like the big boys. "Miller, I'll be looking for you in the fall," he said. I don't remember a thing about the rest of the day. I could hardly wait for August and football camp.

Then we went to the county finals. I was sure Coach Underwood would be there again, and I knew I'd see him at the finish line. Well, I had some things to learn about people. One of the star runners from Grantsville, a big school, looked me up just before the race.

"They say you're the fastest in the county," he said. "Here, I got you a big RC, thought you might be thirsty. And here's a Babe Ruth candy bar in case you're hungry."

I was and it sure tasted good and I had to eat and drink fast because they called for the boy's hundred-yard dash.

"On your mark, get set, GO!" I sprang forward, but felt like I had rocks around my legs and even the slow runners passed me. I began cramping so bad I didn't make it to the fifty-yard line. I was so humiliated I just snuck off and hid down by the river where I vomited up the RC and the Babe Ruth. My dream was over. I never saw Coach Underwood again because we moved.

Goodbye, Bess

The Miller homestead in Calhoun County consisted of about eighty acres of hillsides and thirteen acres of flat land. That was the acreage remaining from the original parcel homesteaded by my great-grandfather. It was on that farm on the branch of Lower White Oak that Dad and Mom managed to raise a family of eight and implanted in us a positive work ethic and a powerful sense of patriotism. In those years just about everything we ate came from the earth on that ninety-three acres. Groceries either came from Mom's garden with soil enriched by years of plowing in the barnyard waste or from Otis Brannon's store, traded for with eggs we hauled there every week.

In the early years we hauled the eggs on a horse-drawn sled with hickory sapling runners. I liked to smell the scorched wood when the runners were pulled over sharp rocks in the road. Dresses for the girls and shirts for the boys were mostly hand made out of the flowered feed sacks the chicken feed came in. Mom also made sheets by sewing sacks together. If there were not enough eggs to cover everything she needed that week, the remainder was added to her bill.

We had two horses to till the land; Bess was an English Sire, as gentle as a pet and smart as a whip. She had a colt Dad named Billy. Bess and Billy worked side by side, and Donal trained Bess to guide the team around the field so the harrow overlapped the rough ground and what the harrow had just smoothed over. He would start them out and go sit in the shade while they harrowed the freshly plowed field.

In those days I had two books, both by Zane Gray: *Riders of the Purple Sage* and *Roping Lions in the Grand Canyon*. Roping lions sounded okay, but I dreamed of being a cowboy. Specifically, I dreamed of riding Bess into that boxed canyon to rescue my sweetheart! I didn't have a saddle, but with Bess it didn't matter. She had a nice round back, and when she broke into a lope it was like she just floated through the air. Jack rode our other horse, Billy, and one summer we built a shack back up in the head of one of the hollers. It became our secret hiding place. After two or three times of riding Bess there all I had to do was jump on and say, "Shack," and she would take off like going for sugar and would not stop until we got to the shack.

One day I was riding Bess and we got into a hornet's nest by the old sawmill. The hornets began stinging both Bess and me. We fought them while Bess pranced like a dancer. In the process I fell off and landed between Bess's legs. That horse stopped prancing immediately and stood stark still until I got out from under her! She turned her head to make sure I was out of the way and began fighting the hornets again. That was my friend Bess.

In August that year Dad called us all together to give us the news: "We're moving to Auburn over in Ritchie County in two weeks."

The bottom just dropped out of my stomach and I didn't hear what else he said.

"Ritchie County!" I thought, "Who wants to play football for Ritchie County?!" I went to the barn, got Bess, and rode up the holler to the shack. I stayed there a long time, but the pain didn't go away. I sat by the shack crying. Bess knew there was something wrong. She came over and nuzzled me with her nose. I laid my face on her face and she stood very still until I moved. That was the last time I got to ride Bess. We wouldn't need her over in Ritchie County.

Saying goodbye to Bess was hard, but saying goodbye to Jack was harder. He came by to help me load my stuff on the moving truck Dad borrowed. We didn't talk much during the loading time because we didn't know what to say. We had never thought about a time we wouldn't be together. When the loading was complete, Jack and I hopped on the back of the truck and rode together down to his house. When Dad stopped to let him off, we just waved goodbye. I climbed in the cab of the truck and felt tears running down my face as Dad drove the truck down the road. I have seen Jack only once since then because his family moved to Ohio. But the memories of the fun we had as two boys growing up in the country linger still.

CHAPTER 3

New Places, New Friends

Moving Day

We spent the night at Aunt Mary's and headed for Auburn in Ritchie County early the next morning. We were unloaded by noon in the parsonage. It had running water and inside toilets. Some neighbors came by to help and to tell us who we should not associate with, like that one boy who is always in trouble, not fit company for the preacher's boy.

After lunch I went out in the yard and lay down by the road. I was pretty lonely. A boy rode up on a bike and asked, "Wanna go play some football?"

"Sure, why not," I said, and yelled into the house, "Hey, Mom! I'm going down the road to play some football."

The boy asked, "Where's your bike?"

"I don't have one," I told him.

"OK, get on," he said. We rode double on that bicycle for twenty miles from Auburn to Harrisville, over two big hills. Actually we walked up the hills and flew down the other side at break-neck speed. Anyway, when we got there, we were at the football field at Harrisville High School. I found out the coach's name was Mr. Vance Vanarie, and the boy with the bike was Don "Runt" Cornell, the boy I was supposed to avoid. We practiced all afternoon then took turns pushing the bike home. We never tried that again.

A Perfect Place

With football season and school starting, the pain gradually faded and Auburn—a small town of three hundred people at the edge of the county—turned out to be a perfect place to grow up. There were lots of kids my age in town and we had great times playing football and kick the can. But most of those years were spent hunting and fishing with "Runt" Cornell. I didn't like the name Runt, so I told everyone to stop calling him that. From that time on he was Don. We had the run of all the streams, and all the farmers trusted us to hunt anywhere we wanted to. Don had a double barrel 20-gauge shotgun. All I had was a .22 rifle, but I could burst bottles in the air with the .22.

One day Don wanted to go quail hunting, so I got my .22 and a box of shells. Don fell down laughing. Well, my neighbor heard the commotion and came out to see what was going on. When he found out, he said I could borrow his shotgun. It was a single-barrel 12-gauge Iver-Johnson. I shot three quail with three shots that day. This was easier than bursting bottles with a .22, so I traded my .22 for the shotgun. Later I ordered a WWII Springfield 30-06 from The National Rifle Association. Don and I rebuilt the stock out of walnut knots from Bill Gross's cabinet shop.

Ole Brindle

Ole Brindle was a legendary buck with a rack that looked like a tree. We used to see him way back on the hill meadow in the evenings. One fall we hunted for Brindle until midafternoon but never saw him, so we came in for lunch. After eating, I stretched out on the couch and went to sleep. Don woke me up and said, "Get your gun, we're going to go find Brindle."

Half-heartedly I got my 30-06 and one clip of shells and squeezed in the front seat of our boss's pickup. About five miles down the road, the boss slammed on the brakes and yelled, "Look at that!"

I didn't know what he had seen, but knew it had to be big!

I rolled out of the pickup loading my rifle and ran around behind the pickup in time to see Ole Brindle leap the creek and head up the hillside. I dropped to one knee and fired three times and every time kicked up dirt under his belly. Then he was gone. I stayed kneeling, initially disappointed. But as my mind replayed those last few bounds of that magnificent buck with great muscles rippling and that awesome rack defiant in the air, I was relieved he escaped.

I looked to see why no one else had fired. The boss was standing there holding a shattered 30-30 rifle. Well, it turned out that Brindle was standing broadside to him about seventy-five yards away when he jumped out of the truck, but his gun jammed, so he wrapped it around the front bumper of the truck! By the time Don got out of the truck and loaded, Brindle had vanished.

Oops

The boss liked fried rabbit, so he would come by with his flatbed truck and Don and I would shoot rabbits as he drove down the country road. One time a rabbit suddenly darted across the road in front of the truck and the boss reacted by hitting the brakes just as Don pulled the trigger. He didn't get the rabbit, but he made shredded metal out of the pickup's hood. Last time for that!

Tree Hugger

During football practice when I was a freshman, another player crashed down with his knees on my back. The pain was deep, but I tried to ignore it. That night I had blood in my urine, but I figured it would go away and I managed to make it through the season.

However, the pain got worse and the bleeding continued. One winter day I was out in the backyard and the pain was so bad I hugged a tree to stand up, but I guess I passed out and fell to the ground. The next thing I knew I was on the way to the hospital. It turned out that my kidney and bladder were both infected and my bladder had to be flushed out every two or three hours. The trauma and pain aside, it was an interesting experience for a fourteen-year-old boy to be so exposed every day to nurses who thought my shyness was becoming. The doctor said I could not play sports for several months, so I didn't play basketball or baseball that year.

Beavers

One fall three of us went bear hunting in the mountains with a tent and sleeping bags. We camped by a small branch of Cheat River and built a big fire. As we started to crawl into the sleeping bags, we heard a blood-curdling squall on the mountain.

"Man, what was that?" Don yelled. Then one on the other side of the valley answered back. I knew the squall well, so I said, "That is two wild cats attracted by the fire."

A rifle shot in the air stopped their convergence, and we finally crawled into our bags and went to sleep to the wonderful melody of a careening mountain stream.

Sometime in the night the tent suddenly crashed in on us. We just about tore the tent flap off getting out. Without saying a word, we all knew the wild cats had attacked us and we came out ready to start shooting. When we regained our senses, we found the beavers had cut a tree down across our tent. We had invaded their space and they were showing their objection.

Rebellion Begins

When I was a junior in high school, I was selected to have the lead male role in our school play. The role called for a dance with the female star. I told the teacher I could not accept the role since my religious beliefs did not permit me to dance. So I could stay in the role, the teacher modified the dance so that all I did was take the girl by the hand and sorta twirl her around in a half-circle. I was surprised and pleased that my parents came to the play. We received a rousing ovation at the end of the play, and when I saw my dad coming backstage, I expected him to say, "Good job."

Instead, in front of everyone, he bawled me out for dancing. Everyone was shocked and embarrassed. I just stood there, frozen in place.

My relationship with Dad was obviously not good. We had very little quality one-on-one time together and apparently were content to keep it that way. Rebellion seeped into my life without recognition and things only went downhill from there.

Later that year a visiting preacher was at our church in Auburn. After he preached, he invited anyone who wanted to "surrender to full-time Christian service" to come forward. I got a burning sensation in my chest and felt I should go down. But I was not going to be a preacher! It was hard, but I didn't budge. After that, I became afraid God would punish me. Soon after that I heard about a man whose heart exploded because he rebelled against God. Even though I worried God would punish me with a heart attack, I was not going to be a preacher!

My rebellious heart manifested itself in other ways. Dad bought a 1949 Ford with overdrive. In second gear overdrive, that thing ate up those mountain roads. I had the reputation of the fastest driver in the area, and I used every opportunity I could find to maintain my standing.

On moonlit nights my friends and I used to turn out our lights and play hide and seek in our cars. If Dad had known, he would have grounded me for life. Was I flirting with death to spite Dad or God—or both?

A Marine Aviator?

This time in my life was also the beginning of another dream's failure. When I was eight or nine, I got a cardboard airplane cockpit for Christmas that I flew for hours. I dreamed of being a fighter pilot. A Marine recruiter came to our school at the beginning of my senior year. I told him of my dream to fly and to be a Marine.

He said, "Richard, you are the kind of man we are looking for!" I filled out the application to volunteer for officers training and flight school in the Marine Corps upon graduation. Since I would not be eighteen for several months, my parents had to sign the application. I took it home for Dad's signature and he said, "No. You need to go to college."

Pro Baseball Material?

Well, let's see: Field and track star—dead in the water. Playing football for the Coach Underwood—never happened. Marine aviator—the view from my rear view window. I'd say at this point I was batting zero.

And speaking of baseball, when I was a senior, I did have one moment that will live in infamy for me. We were playing our archrival one bright afternoon in May. It was one of those days when everything clicked. I was catching, Ira was pitching, and Joe was playing second base. Ira's first pitch was an out-drop that curved so much it caught my second finger head on and cracked the first knuckle. It began to swell, but I continued to play and no one noticed.

It was the best game I ever played—at bat and at catcher. On one play, an opposing batter bunted a nice lay-down toward third base and the player on first headed for second base. I tore off my mask, scooped the ball up on the run, and threw to Joe who was headed for second base with his back toward first base. My peg was on target and he caught the ball in full stride, hit the base with one foot, spun around in the air and threw the runner out at first base. It was a perfectly executed double play.

After the game, Coach Vanarie told Ira, Joe, and me that a man wanted to meet us. It turned out to be a scout from a major league team whose car had broken down on the way to another game. The mechanic told him about our game so he decided to come watch us play. The scout offered the three of us an invitation to attend a tryout the following August. He followed up with a written invitation. Ira did go and played semi-pro for a while. But I was working at Republic Steel in Massillon, Ohio, making more money than I thought possible. The money I would lose by quitting two weeks early to attend the tryout would pay for my tuition and books for the entire year, so I declined. Joe was working in the steel mill and also declined. Still batting zero, but this time it was by my own choice.

When I was a senior, I was selected for the Little Kanawha Conference All-Star football team and my parents came to the game. The coach assigned me to the left end position. The right end and the quarterback were from the same high school—guess who got all the passes and who got none. And so four, mostly wonderful years at Harrisville High came to a close. Despite all the disappointments, there were some achievements I can place on the plus side of my résumé. I had been captain of the football team, president of the student body, salutatorian, and president of the honor society. And I was engaged to a majorette.

Right to Work

My parents instilled in me that all work was honorable and to do it as "unto the Lord." The summer job at Republic Steel was a blessing financially and a real-world learning experience. Since I was a summer employee, I was assigned to the labor gang and worked at various jobs. After the first week I was assigned to the baling machine. The task included feeding all the remnants from the slitter machines and baling them for recycling. These remnants were continuous strands of steel shaved off the edges of the rolls of steel and had razor-sharp, jagged edges. I wore out a pair of leather palmed work gloves every shift and my boots and pant legs looked as if I had been in a fight with a pack of jackals.

When I started the job, I was asked to join the union, but I turned it down because the dues would buy my food for a week. Nobody wanted the baler job, and the foreman kept me on it because I didn't complain. I didn't know I was supposed to.

Thirty days before I was to return home to begin college at West Virginia University, the foreman called me into his office. This didn't happen often, and on the way I made mental notes of the days' activities looking for something I might have done wrong.

"You are going to college in about a month, right?" he asked.

I answered in the affirmative.

"Okay, Miller, I have a challenge for you," he said. "We have a one-of-a-kind high carbon rolling mill that is operated by one lead operator and one assistant operator. The assistant operator has accrued thirty days of vacation and will be leaving this coming Monday. The operators on this mill can make more in bonus than base wages, and the lead operator insists I provide him an assistant who can hustle. I've watched you hustle for two months and I am offering you the job.

"Here is the challenge: you are not a member of the union and I will be elevating you over union members who have more seniority than you. There will be a complaint filed, but it will take more than thirty days to process the complaint and by that time you will be gone. So what do you say?"

It seemed too good to be true.

I said, "Sir, if you think I can do it, I am ready."

For two days that week I worked with the assistant learning the job and came in Monday morning ready to hustle, and hustle I did. One evening after work I noticed a group of workers from the labor gang lingering at the gate. As I walked toward my car, they began to follow. I suspected foul play, so I made a mad dash for my car and jumped in and, fortunately, my trusty '47 Ford fired the first revolution. By this time the gang was rocking the car in an attempt to turn it over. I slammed the Ford in low and tromped the peddle to the metal. When I glanced in the rearview mirror, most of the gang members were strung out on the ground.

From then on, I came early and parked near the guard shack and was not bothered again. The union did file a complaint, which the foreman was able to delay until I was gone. Financially, I made more in that one month than the two previous months combined. On the last day at work, I went by the foreman's office and thanked him for helping me.

"Miller, thank me by hitting those books and get back here next summer." I did hit the books and I did go back to Republic Steel the next summer.

The Prodigal

September 1953. I entered West Virginia University (WVU) majoring in Electrical Engineering. I enrolled in nineteen hours of core courses and washed pots and pans in the cafeteria for my meals. I also was required by law to enroll in ROTC for the first two years of college. It was very lonely to look out the window over the sink and see all the other students playing ball and having fun, so I closed the curtain and quit looking. I was in my room by 8:00 P.M. and studied until one or two in the morning. I couldn't sleep anyway because I believed God was going to kill me for not being a preacher. I kept a constant vigil by pressing a finger on the artery along my neck, as if that would help.

When I went home for Christmas, one of the guys from high school told me he had caught my fiancée making out in a pickup truck after a basketball game. I went to her house, verified the rumor, got my ring, and walked away from the relationship. I am not sure what hurt the most—my heart or my pride. The boy she chose was on my list as the one most likely to *not* succeed.

April 1954. One night during mid-semester exams, after a long study session, I decided to try to get some sleep. Almost immediately my heart began to beat erratically. This was it! God was finally going to take my life. I jumped out of bed and ran all the way up the side of a mountain to the dispensary. They ran some tests, kept me in the clinic overnight, and called my dad the next day. He took me to Myers Clinic in Philippi where the doctors ran even more tests, then called Dad in for the results.

"Harry," they said. "We found nothing organically wrong with Richard. Our conclusion is that Richard is suffering from near complete exhaustion and it is affecting his neurological system causing his heart to beat erratically. Obviously his heart is strong or the run up the mountain in Morgantown would have killed him."

I had enough hours already banked to pay for my meals for the remainder of the year, so I gave up my job washing pots and pans. I decided to talk to a pastor, hoping he would shed some light on what was happening to me. He was nice, but, unfortunately, offered no help, so I made an appointment with a more senior pastor. The mental pain was so great I essentially blacked out sitting in the chair in his office. He had not even noticed. I left and never went back to that church. I thought maybe if God was not going to kill me, He would have me go insane. I had heard a preacher tell about a man who had rejected God and went stark raving mad.

Incredibly, I completed all course work that semester with As and Bs. As soon as school was out, I headed back to Massillon, Ohio, and reported to Republic Steel. Although Massillon was almost two hundred miles from my home in West Virginia, it was where a lot of people from West Virginia went to get a job because there were few jobs around home. When I reported into personnel I was assigned to the Open Hearth as a lab technician to gather samples and analyze the molten steel to ensure it met the specifications. I was not required to join the union, and the summer passed without incident. It was also a nice break from the oppressive fear of a heart attack or insanity.

In September I reluctantly reported back to the boarding house in Morgantown and met my new roommate, a veteran returning from the Korean War who was going to school on the GI Bill. He was quite a ladies' man, and I seldom saw him except late at night.

My First Mentor

My roommate flunked calculus. Because he was really smart and still bombing out, I figured I couldn't pass either. My professor called me in just before finals. He told me he had reviewed my past records and entrance scores and that I should be making an easy "B" in calculus. It was amazing how good that felt and what a difference it made to hear someone express his confidence in my abilities! I scored in the high 90s on the final, enough to bring my grade to a D. I took the course over the next semester and made an easy B and made As and Bs in all math courses after that.

Cherry Pink and Apple Blossom White

Fall 1956. After recovering from the pain of the experience with my high school girlfriend, I had made it a point to avoid serious relationships. Then Lorena, who attended Alderson Broadus College in Philippi, West Virginia, asked a favor. There were more girls than boys in their school, so for the big fall dance, she asked me to round up some guys to come even things out a bit, which I was able to do. We waited in the receiving room at the women's dorm for the girls to come down. After a bit, Lorena and another girl came down the stairs. Lorena pointed to the girl, and then at me meaning this was my "date" for the evening. When I looked at her, my date beamed with personality and beauty.

Lorena explained that Rene was part of the Queen's Court and needed an escort just for the evening, nothing more. We had a lovely time—even though I am not a good dancer. What was happening to me must have been very obvious because, during the break, one of the guys who came with me rained on my parade with, "Richard, you better take it easy. Have you noticed her left hand?" My response was, "No, I haven't," and I didn't like the sinking feeling in the pit of my stomach.

Hoping it wasn't true, but somehow knowing it was, I bridged the short distance between us. She saw me coming and the expression on her face told me she knew that I knew. Without a word, I took her hands and there it was: a small diamond ring! Rene looked at me with tears welling up in her eyes. "I am so sorry. I thought this would be just a nice social thing and I needed an escort for the ball. My fiancé, Fred, is in the military and could not be here. I have never dated anyone else and I didn't mean for this to happen."

By now her voice was quivering. I managed to say something like, "It's okay. We can get through this."

We did get through it, painfully for me, but unnoticed by anyone else. After the ball was over and all activities complete, I escorted Rene back to the dorm. She thanked me for coming, turned, and ran up the stairs. I don't remember much about the next few days. I finished the semester, went home for Christmas, and buried my thoughts in hunting and roaming the hills.

I settled into the next semester and focused on studies and ROTC activities. In late spring, I got a call from Lorena. "I'm almost afraid to ask, but Rene has been selected as Maid of Honor to the Strawberry Festival Queen in Buchanan, and they insist she have an escort. She is planning to decline the honor, but I thought maybe you could do me one more favor and be her escort. I know this is a lot to ask, but Rene is a special friend."

I thought about it for a couple days, then called Lorena and said I thought I could handle it, but to make it clear to Rene that I would only be there to carry out my official role as her escort. I showed up for the event that lasted three days, and I was the perfect gentleman. Always on time then vanishing when not needed. Everything was going just fine until the final dance with the Queen and her Court. The music was the tune to "Mister Wonderful," and Rene began singing softly as we danced. Her voice was beautiful. It was so beautiful that it caught me by surprise and penetrated my shield. Okay, so I'm a sentimental guy.

I was to take her home after the festival, so we loaded up her belongings and headed that way. At the first intersection, one road led to her home, the other led to the mountains. On impulse I whipped the car to the right and Rene fell over against me. "We aren't going home are we," she stated, more than asked.

So we went up into the mountains. At a state park we both changed into blue jeans and spent the night just laughing and roaming around the mountains, shutting out the rest of the world and reality. It was wonderful, just holding hands, running through the pine-scented forest, sitting by a sparkling brook and climbing upon the gigantic boulders placed there by a glacier long past. It was spring and the moon was full and for a while we were alone in our own perfect world.

As the first rays of dawn penetrated the forest, Rene suddenly exclaimed, "Oh, my goodness! My mother will be frantic! We have to go home." She took my hand and kissed my cheek, and we headed for her home. After convincing her mother that "nothing had happened" and her dad that there was nothing to be gained by shooting me or having me thrown in jail, we were served a wonderful country breakfast. As I was leaving, Rene said she was going to write her fiancé and tell him she was not ready to go through with the wedding and ask him to give her some time to sort things out.

I went back to Morgantown in a cherry-pink-and-apple-blossom-white frame of mind to finish out the semester, then home to work until summer camp. Rene wrote almost every day, and it appeared that Fred had agreed to her request for time to sort things out. In June I headed for ROTC Summer Camp at Ft. Meade, Maryland.

I came to an intersection—one road led to Ft. Meade, the other led to Rene. You guessed it. I headed my '47 Ford south instead of east. I had not alerted her that I was coming and my timing was not good, because Fred was there also. It was pretty awkward and Fred took her by the arm and led her to his car and they took off. I went in to say good-bye to her parents and her mother asked me to stay.

"Richard," she said, "Rene did write and ask for more time, but he was not willing. She has cried every day since and did not go back to summer school. I believe she truly loves you and I believe you may be the right one for her."

It took a while for it to sink in what she was saying. I have always respected other peoples' space and told her it looked as if I had already interfered too much. "Rene has to decide this for herself," I protested. "Besides, I have to be at Ft. Meade by 0800 tomorrow, and it is already getting dark."

With a very heavy heart I headed for Ft. Meade, but a few miles down the road my Ford overheated, and I had no idea where to find a mechanic. I knew Rene's dad was a mechanical supervisor and had a workshop, so I limped back to their house. Fred was not there when I pulled up to the house.

Rene's dad had the tools and a spare radiator hose that worked. I thanked him and told him I would be on my way. He said, "I think there is someone there on the porch who wants to talk to you." Rene came to my car dressed in a light blue, flowing robe—a sight to behold! She explained that Fred had rejected her request for more time, had rented an apartment, and had everything ready for the wedding. She was crying.

"I don't know what to do," she said. "I wish you would just take me with you like you did in the mountains."

I held her until the sobbing stopped. "Rene, I have to go or I will be AWOL," I said. "If you decide not to go through with the wedding I will be back. If I don't hear from you by the end of the month, I will know you married Fred."

I held her face in both my hands and kissed her ever so lightly, turned, got in my car, and headed for Ft. Meade. Seemed like I was always the one walking away with a heavy heart. Would I ever get it right?

I didn't hear from Rene, but about three weeks later Lorena wrote to tell me she heard Rene had married Fred and gone with him to the fort where he was stationed. My heart ached as never before, but I was now a soldier and I had a job to do, so I committed my life to being the best soldier I could be.

Recovery

ROTC summer camp was another decision point for me. As Yogi Berra said, "When you come to a fork in the road, take it!" Prior to summer camp, my interest in ROTC was the twenty-nine-dollar-per-month stipend that provided enough food to keep my belt buckle in front of my back pockets. The activities at summer camp brought to life aspirations that had been latent. The dream from childhood of being a Marine came alive. The patriotic desire to serve my country surfaced. The designation of Distinguished Military Student brought to life the belief that I was capable of making things happen. I also saw for the first time a life course that combined an engineering and military career. So in the fall of 1956 I returned to school with a view of the future and began to initiate action rather than react. I applied for various summer jobs during the university's job fair week. One company really caught my attention with their claim that they gave young engineers the opportunity to chart their own course.

CHAPTER 4

Silver Linings and Dark Clouds

Kaiser—Stan and Big Jake

Sometimes we get so focused on the silver lining that we do not see the dark clouds. My story contains such an episode. It began on Monday after the end of the 1957 spring semester. I reported to the personnel office at Kaiser Aluminum in Ravenswood, West Virginia, and accepted the position as an electrical engineer in training for the summer. Stan Nuzum, another summer hire, also reported the same day. During the in-processing, we had a lot of time to get acquainted and, by the end of the day, had formed a friendship that would last a lifetime. Together we found a mini-apartment in Ripley to share for the remainder of the summer.

Kaiser management, true to their claim, assigned me to a section of the plant in which I would be responsible for all electrical engineering projects. My first job was to redesign the control circuitry of a rolling mill relocated from Kaiser Steel that was tearing the softer aluminum as it started to pull the rolled aluminum through the mill. My new boss said, "The blueprints are on your desk. Let me see your final design for the modification and have the work ready to be done while the mill is shut down over the July 4 weekend. Any questions?"

I didn't know enough to ask questions.

The blueprint on my desk was daunting to say the least. I sat there staring at the thick packet wondering what I would find when I lifted the cover page. It was Greek to me. The symbols were not even close to the textbooks at school. One of the old timers caught me mesmerized by the blueprints. Sam came over, introduced himself and offered to help. Between the two of us, I mastered the schematics, completed the modification design, got it approved, and ordered the parts. As Sam departed on Friday evening before the modification was to be installed, he stopped by my desk and said, "OK, you can do this. Good luck."

The office was now empty and a flock of butterflies erupted in the pit of my stomach. In one hour, I would brief the electrical crew on the project.

I had been coordinating with Big Jake, the electrical foreman. He was not impressed with an "upstart college student." Under his watchful eye, the modification was installed within forty-eight hours, and we were ready for the big moment.

"Okay, Big Jake," I said. "Throw the switch!"

Nothing, not a sound! My heart sank!

We began troubleshooting, tracing every wire. After an hour, I came across a wire that was not on the correct post of a control rheostat.

"Jake, this wire appears to be connected wrong," I said.

Caught up in his own moment of triumph, he responded, "Naw, the schematic was wrong so I corrected the connection."

I retraced the entire circuit and came up with the same answer: the schematic was correct. "Jake, I respect your experience," I said. "But I am asking you to reconnect the device according to the schematic."

Jake shrugged his shoulders, made the connection, and defiantly threw the switch to prove his point. Circuits immediately lit up! The big machine began to whir, picking up speed as it stepped through the new acceleration process and the big roll of aluminum began to feed through the rollers without ripping.

I'll say this for Big Jake: he was also a big man.

"Well, I'll be! How do you like that?"

He came over, shook my hand vigorously, and about knocked the breath out of me with a slap on the back. Turning to his crew, he said, "OK, boys, shut 'er down and let's go shoot some fireworks!"

From that time on Big Jake and I were an unbeatable team, and the summer flew by with one completed project after the other. At the end of the summer the boss offered me a permanent position upon graduation the following spring. My guess is Big Jake played a big role in the decision.

The Roses Do Bloom Again

I was making big money with Kaiser and traded my noisy '47 Ford with twin glass pack mufflers for a '52 Oldsmobile. After my last two experiences with women I decided to be footloose and fancy free. Love? It doesn't work very well for me. So my goal was to see how many women I could date during the summer. I even made a score sheet. That was going pretty well the first couple of weeks, and one evening on the way out of the plant, Ray and I were walking behind a cluster of women I was sizing up for my next venture. "Ray, who is that cute female there in the middle, the one with the sassy gait?" Starting to head her way, Ray said, "That is Jenny Lamp. You want to meet her?" I grabbed his arm and pulled him back.

What is this? I feel shy! I thought in amazement.

The next day I was at my desk and needed to ask the boss a question, so I jumped up and hurried over to turn down the hall toward his office. In my haste, I almost knocked over a woman leaning down to peek around the corner—in the direction of my desk! It turned out to be none other than Jenny Lamp. I stammered something and ducked into Rob's office. Jenny's version of the event is slightly different, but this is my story.

I had dated other girls and, as explained above, had been very serious about one of them, but somehow this was different. It was as if I knew from the very beginning that she was the one, but I was not considering settling down. I was enjoying the various ventures available to me at Kaiser. However, after the first evening of miniature golf, dinner, and movie *The Ten Commandments*, I came back to the apartment and tore up my score sheet. My friend Stan opined, "I see another declared bachelor has bitten the dust!"

Jenny and I waltzed through the summer and my "doubting heart" gave way to the bliss of being with a beautiful woman of impeccable character who beat me at miniature golf, and I loved it. We were together every waking minute that we were not working. I met her folks and she met mine. Stan believed from day one that Jenny was a perfect fit. I agreed, not realizing what was in store for us on a journey strewn with lovely gardens, dark valleys, and ambushes meant to cause serious harm. Real life is a challenge.

Dark Clouds

I reluctantly headed back to Morgantown to finish my degree. September 1957 to May 1958 was a very dark time. It was my fifth year in college. My classmates were all gone. I was taking courses I didn't like for the most part, and I had to be away from Jenny most of the time. As I approached completion of the engineering degree, I again became intensely plagued with the fear that God would soon punish me for my disobedience. The heart flutters returned. I had frequent headaches that I assumed were the beginnings of insanity or brain tumors.

Do You Know What You Are Asking?

On one of my weekends visiting Jenny, we spent a wonderful day visiting my parents and eating as much home cooking as possible. When we returned to Jenny's parents' house, she shared some painful times she had experienced as a child, causing tears to fill her otherwise lovely eyes. As I drove back to Morgantown, my love for Jenny swelled in my heart and my thoughts turned protective. I spoke to the windshield as I drove, "It hurts me to see her with tears in her eyes. Is there any way to protect her?"

My relationship with God was essentially one of fear and anger, yet for others God was merciful. Without thought for the consequences, I addressed God with, "I don't know what makes Jenny sad, but I am asking You to give to me whatever it is." The result was not dramatic, but I began to experience strange feelings, such as being detached. The changes really began to manifest themselves in the following days.

Whoa! What Is This?

A couple of weeks later I went home for the weekend to visit Jenny. Saturday was a beautiful autumn day so we went on an outing in the hills near Auburn. We walked for hours, eating apples from trees planted long ago, but now forgotten as the small farms were abandoned. We drank water retrieved from a dug well with an old bucket and a rope still hanging on the back porch of a large, empty house with doors hanging loose and making lonely sounds as the breeze moved the door. We wondered about the family that had once lived here and how many children had roamed these fields now overgrown with briars and brush. The scene brought to mind a prize-winning black and white picture my friend, Stan, painted of one such abandoned farmhouse. He captured the doors hanging by one hinge and the old rocker visible through the open door where once the mother had rocked her six or eight children to sleep. He called the painting "Once." A feeling of sadness overcomes me every time I look at the painting still hanging in Stan's house.

We selected an open hilltop for our picnic and from there we looked down over the green valley and the town of Auburn. The maple trees that lined the streets of the picturesque village where my parents lived were brilliantly dressed in their golden-yellow fall wardrobe illuminated by the fading autumn sun. This pastoral scene is indelibly printed in both our memories, and when we reminisce about our early days together, we always talk about that scene. Jenny and I stood there enchanted by the beauty of the trees and the warm waves of growing love between us.

As the sun dipped low and the maples faded into the dusk, Jenny broke the silence with, "I have never seen anything so beautiful. Now I am hungry." I got the hatchet out of the trunk to cut wood for building a fire. When I picked up the hatchet, there was a sudden sensation that ran up through my arm to my mind. The source of the sensation seemed to be external as if some force outside of me was trying to encourage some destructive action. The action was vague and not directed at anyone, but there was an alert that sounded within me that let me know the sensation I was feeling was not good, and in total opposition to my code of behavior. I had no idea what it was and was eager to lock the hatchet back in the trunk as soon as I had the fire going to roast the hotdogs. I said nothing to Jenny, and with the hatchet locked in the trunk, the sensation vanished and we enjoyed delicious hot dogs and a lovely evening by the fire as the gorgeous day yielded to the shades of night and the rays of a rising harvest moon.

My Mind Split in Half

I had always had a real love of hunting and fishing and spent many hours roaming the West Virginia hills hunting everything that was legal to hunt. Never once had I ever had a thought of shooting anything other than wild game. In the fall of 1957, soon after the wiener roast mentioned above, I went home with Eldon, my college roommate, to go to a football game on Friday night and squirrel hunting on Saturday morning. Jenny went with us to the ball game and on the way home she was between us in the front seat (that was before seatbelts). They were laughing and joking. I thought she was flirting with my roommate, and I endured the pangs of jealousy and rejection. But after we took her home, I forgot about these feelings and we began to plan the early morning hunt.

There was only one bed in Eldon's small bedroom and we had to share it, a very normal thing in those days. During the night, I woke up with a most unusual and painful feeling. I felt like my mind was split in half and I could not get it back together! I struggled alone in the dark, careful not to awaken Eldon, but it was a horrible battle. I was glad when four o'clock came and we could get up. Eldon's mother had prepared a sumptuous country breakfast, and we sat down to eat. As we ate, Eldon's father began to share with us an article in the newspaper about a man who had gone berserk and killed his family with a shotgun. I was stunned by the story!

As the family discussed the gory details in the story, I felt my face burning and my mind going numb. Never before had I thought of hurting anyone, but the prolonged fear that God was going to punish me with insanity for my disobedience came crashing in on me and I felt I was being invaded by the story. *So this is what happens when you go insane,* I thought.

As Eldon and I walked to the woods with our shotguns, I began to think about what would happen if I were to lose control. Would I shoot people like the man in the article? My mind spiraled, and I thought about the jealousy and rejection from the night before. The pain in my head and frustration in my mind got so bad, I unloaded my shotgun and hunted the entire day with an unloaded gun. I never hunted squirrels again.

Demons in the Dark

Jenny's dad worked in the oil fields in West Virginia, and he was often gone for several days at a time and home only on weekends. He had his own bedroom at the house to accommodate his late arrivals and late sleeping hours in the morning so he and the other family members wouldn't disturb each other. On one of those nights when he was gone, I stayed late and instead of driving back to my home in Auburn from Parkersburg at that hour, Jenny's mother invited me to stay in Mr. Lamp's room.

I woke up during the night and felt the room swarming with some kind of invisible but dark, sinister forces that were trying to attack me. Again it was a mental and emotional battle similar to the night with Eldon's family. The attack lasted for most of the night. I didn't mention it to Jenny or anyone else. Reflecting on this event, it is obvious there was evil intent on the part of whatever was in the room. It is also obvious they were actually being restrained by some force to prevent them from doing any harm except to cause mental and emotional stress.

Trapped in Space

I had long dreamed of being a pilot and was pursuing that dream by participating in the ROTC flight program during my senior year in college. Ground school and flight training were running simultaneously. I passed the initial training, soloed, and was doing quite well. However, the solo flights began to be unnerving and I noticed the fear becoming greater as the height above the ground increased.

One day during ground school, the instructor was showing a map of the universe on the wall of the classroom. Suddenly, my mind felt separated from my body as though it were suspended in outer space! It was an excruciating experience, a totally exhausting effort to rejoin mind and body. From that day forward, flying became a very painful chore with the ever-present fear that I would get up in the air and not be able to get back, at least not get my mind back. Even worse, I wondered if I would succumb to the urge to dive into the ground!

Sometimes You Push

The last solo flight to complete the ROTC flight program was a three-legged cross-country flight over the mountains from Morgantown northeast to Johnstown, Pennsylvania, then northwest to New Castle, Pennsylvania, for a fuel stop, then back to Morgantown. The plane was a Champion with a sixty-five horsepower engine that was started by manually pulling the propeller down and around, then stepping backward to get out of the way of the propeller. The plane had one radio to communicate with the towers at manned airfields. The fuel tank was mounted in front of the cockpit with a gas gauge like that in a Model A Ford. As long as the fuel was jostling in the small port with a floating gauge, there was fuel in the tank. When it stopped jostling, it was highly desirable to be on the ground.

The flight plan accounted for a light predicted headwind from the West. On the second leg of the flight, about halfway between Johnstown and New Castle, a computation of ground speed revealed a much greater headwind than predicted. I doubted I had enough fuel to make New Castle. To add to my dilemma, one glance at the ground revealed nothing but dense forest.

Slow flight gives the most economical fuel consumption rate, but the most difficult to maintain because of the natural tendency to want to hurry before the fuel runs out. I calculated the distance remaining, the amount of fuel on board, and the glide slope to New Castle. Just barely adequate, so I reduced to slow flight and began a very gradual decent, ever alert for any opening in the forest big enough for an emergency landing, just in case.

After several terrifying minutes with the fuel gauge no longer jostling, the New Castle airstrip came into view. It had to be a straight-in approach with no room for error. I called the tower and was granted clearance as requested. The wheels touched the first ten feet of the runway and rolled to a safe landing. As I pushed the throttle forward to taxi to the hanger, the engine sputtered and stopped. Totally embarrassed, yet grateful to be alive, I got out and pushed the plane to the hanger for fuel.

Before taking off again, I went to the pilot's lounge to calm my nerves. Lying down on a well-worn couch, I wondered, *What would the instructor say if I called and asked him to come get this low powered kite?* I wished I could share my fear with someone, but instead, a few minutes later, I strapped on the kite and took off headed southeast. The leg back to Morgantown was uneventful except for the two Air Force jets that swooped down out of nowhere from behind and dived down over the plane waving their wings, causing the Champ to bounce wildly in their wake. A quick look at the map revealed I was over a no-fly zone, and two fighters had been scrambled to intercept. A sharp right turn got a friendly wave from the fighters. That flight was just a precursor of flights in the future.

Breakup

Late in the spring semester I was scheduled to go see Jenny, but a week-end project at school changed my plans. I called Jenny, and she was not a happy camper. The discussion grew progressively louder and for the first time we were engaged in a full-fledged lovers' quarrel with the result being a mutual decision that it would be best if we just called the whole thing off.

Fine! So be it! I'm outta here!

CHAPTER 5

Welcome to the United States Army

What's under That Hood?

June 1958. Miraculously, I graduated with an Electrical Engineering degree and was designated a Distinguished Military Graduate that merited being commissioned as a Regular Army Officer in the Field Artillery, not in the Marine Corps. My first duty assignment was with the 9th Infantry Division Artillery at Fort Carson, Colorado.

My '52 Olds was burning almost as much oil as gasoline, so I decided I should upgrade before heading west. Stan Nuzum and I went to the Olds dealer in Spencer, and I test-drove every car I thought I could afford, but none felt right. Stan kept trying to get me to test-drive a sleek black one parked over in the corner, but I knew I could not afford it. When I had given up on the others, I finally relented, the salesman brought the mystery car to the front, and I slid behind the wheel. I dropped it into drive and touched the accelerator just like the other cars I had test-driven. Before I could get my foot off the accelerator I had peeled rubber for a hundred feet!

The salesman was grabbing for things that were not there and making funny noises. Stan was in the back seat yelling, "Turn 'er loose!" Reluctantly, I turned around at the top of the hill and headed back to the show room. The search was over, and the mystery car was mine. The salesman didn't know what kind of engine was in the car, but it ran best at 80 mph. Before I headed west, Stan and I decided to see what it would do. The speedometer had numbers up to 120 and the needle was past that point and still climbing when we ran out of straight road.

The next week I headed west in a beautiful black 1957 Oldsmobile 88 with red interior. I drove the entire distance from West Virginia to Ft. Carson, Colorado, without a stop except for fuel and coffee. Life was looking up!

I Really Tried, Honest

I went to church the first Sunday at Ft. Carson. No one spoke to me. The next Sunday I went to the post chapel. No one spoke to me. The next Friday after work some of the guys invited me to happy hour. They all spoke to me. I drank my first beer and had a great time with the new friends. I didn't go back to church or chapel. Therein began a life of reckless, inconsiderate living that was centered on satisfying my own desires.

Danger! Open Range

In the fall of 1958 I received orders to attend the Artillery Officers Basic Course at Ft. Sill, Oklahoma. The second half of the course was at Ft. Bliss, Texas, so having completed the first half, I packed the Olds with my duffle bag and headed west. The road through New Mexico had long stretches of nothing but sagebrush and antelope. I did notice signs along the way that said, "DANGER: Open Range," but I didn't have the slightest idea what that meant. There was no traffic on the road so I let go of the reins on the Olds and all the horses under the hood enjoyed the freedom. We floated down the highway. I was soon to find out what the Open Range sign meant.

The road began to have small rises and swales that were just high enough that an oncoming car may not be visible. Just as I topped one of the rises, the road in front of me was packed with cattle. So *that's* what "Open Range" meant! At more than 80 mph, there was no way I could even begin to slow down enough to avoid plowing into the herd. In a flash I thought, "This is it!" and closed my eyes, bracing for impact and certain death.

When the impact didn't happen, I opened my eyes and looked in the rear view mirror; the road was still crowded with cattle! Incredibly,

I was still on the highway. To this day I do not know what happened. Did I fly over the cattle or did the cattle part for an instant? I had no clue and all I could say was, "Well, it wasn't my time," and I turned the horses loose again.

Pam

We did have some down time during the course, even though there was lots of homework to do. Sensing the need for a break, three or four of us went scouting. I was back in my have-fun-and-date-'em-all mode, although I knew I was still struggling with my feelings for Jenny. Three of us went recruiting. My date was Pam, and we became quite involved. We spent lots of time together, and I became aware she was much more serious than I. However, I had other places to go, other adventures to live, and the Army was willing to help.

Flying High

In September 1959 I began flight training at Fort Rucker, Alabama. We all reported in on Friday before Labor Day to be told we were free until Tuesday. So, with nothing to do for three days, four of us headed to Florida, specifically to a sorority house. My date was not impressed with me. However, Mary, her roommate, was much more attractive to me. Consequently, I often found myself traveling to Florida on free weekends to enjoy the pleasure of her company.

But the real reason for being at Ft. Rucker was to learn to fly airplanes. I was at the front of the class because of prior training. Then things began to get really challenging. In four months I had eight close calls. One such event was a fire in the cockpit during takeoff. I pulled the lever on the fire extinguisher, but the fire did not go out. I radioed the control tower and was instructed to climb to 1,200 feet, jettison the left door of the L-19, and bail out. I made it to 1,200 feet, headed the plane out over vacant land, jettisoned the left door, grabbed the ring of my parachute, and prepared to roll out the door. As suddenly as it had started, the fire went out. It was breezy in the cockpit, but I brought the plane in for a safe landing.

Another day I was doing spins solo when the rudder pedal froze in the full left position, and I could not straighten the plane out. The plane went into a spiral, and I lost altitude fast! I wore western boots while flying because of the sloped heels that slid easily along the floor as I operated the rudder pedals. The boots had sharp toes and I managed to get the left toe wedged under the rudder pedal. I applied as much upward pressure on the toe as I could and began stomping on the right pedal with my right foot.

At about five hundred feet above the ground, the rudder had moved enough that I was able to gradually pull the plane out of the spiral just above the treetops. I could not steer to the right, but managed to nurse the plane down to a tail-first landing that freed the rudder when the tail wheel hit the runway. However, the momentum of the plane was to the left, and I took out half a dozen runway lights before stopping.

The next day the instructor thought it would be wise to ride with me to brush up on emergency landing procedures. With my recent history, maybe he thought I was going to need the practice. We climbed to altitude and the instructor told me to do a spin. As I was recovering from the spin, he grabbed the throttle and said, "Assume your engine just quit." From that point on I could not touch the throttle. I picked a peanut patch for landing and began the descent. It was perfect carburetor icing weather, and I wondered why the instructor was not clearing the engine as we descended.

Oh, well, I thought. *He knows what he's doing.*

As I flared out to set the plane down, he tapped me on the shoulder and motioned for me to pull up.

There was a tree line just ahead, and I opened the throttle rapidly. *SPUTTER, SPUTTER, SPUTTER.* "Carburetor ice!" I jammed the carburetor heat on and lowered the nose to gain airspeed. The engine finally stopped coughing and just as the first tree was about to come through my windshield, I pulled the stick back hard and jumped the plane over the trees.

The instructor grunted, "Good recovery."

When I landed back at the airfield, there were leaves clinging to the struts of the landing gear. I might mention that the instructor had served as a test pilot for the Air Force, so it was a minor deal to him.

On another day after practicing stalls, spins, and emergency procedures solo, I was returning to base when it felt as if the plane had stopped in midair. I looked at the altimeter—I was not falling. I looked at the airspeed indicator—I was still going forward. The discipline of trusting the instruments rather than feelings resulted in a safe landing, but this was the straw that broke the camel's back for me. I walked into the flight commander's office and resigned. I declined counseling with the Army psychiatrist and was reassigned to Ft. Bliss, Texas. My dream of being a pilot had been stolen by an enemy I could not identify.

Since I was ordered back to Ft. Bliss, I sent a note to Pam with my travel plans. In the meantime, Mary in Florida needed a ride home for Christmas. It worked with my travel plans, and she indicated she wanted me to meet her parents. I spent the night at their house and toured her town. She was a beautiful person inside and out, and her folks were really nice people.

I headed home the next morning wondering where this relationship would go, especially with such large landmass between Florida and Texas. I was burning both ends of the proverbial candle and still had periods of thinking about Jenny, but I always ended those thoughts with, "Give it up. It is over."

Across a Crowded Room

When I got home to West Virginia, I went to visit Stan, who was still working at Kaiser Aluminum in Ravenswood. He insisted I go see Jenny. "No way!" I exclaimed. "We're through."

But he convinced me I should at least go say hello. He said she would be at a wedding rehearsal that afternoon. I felt a hot poker go through my chest. *What is this?* I wondered. *Why do I care if she is getting married?*

Stan didn't say whose wedding rehearsal.

He persisted, so I went to the home where the rehearsal party was being held, saw her across the room, and was taken aback by how beautiful she was! Her face lit up when our eyes met, and she floated through the crowd to meet me. My heart seemed suspended.

"Whose rehearsal is this?" I blurted out.

She saw the look on my face and laughed, "It's my friend's. Whose did you think it was?"

I told her I was just curious, trying to regain a nonchalant expression instead of letting her know I wasn't sure and had been afraid to ask. We spoke only briefly because they were busy, but she invited me to come to dinner later in the week.

Life Gets Complicated

When I got back to my parents' home, they had received a call from Pam saying she was coming for a visit. Oh, boy! I picked her up at the airport, but I don't remember the trip back to my parent's house. They really liked her. She was a Baptist and hoped I would become a minister. (No way!) The day I was scheduled to have dinner with Jenny, I made some excuse to go alone and thought our guest would enjoy getting better acquainted with my parents.

German Chocolate

As soon as I entered Jenny's apartment, I knew she was the woman I wanted to live with for the rest of my life. Marriage had been a four-letter word up to this point, but I could feel all my reservations dropping away as the evening unfolded. After dinner, Jenny brought out a three-layered chocolate concoction she called "German chocolate cake." I'm a pie man myself, but one bite of that creation caused me to reconsider.

Dinner and dessert over, our discussion turned to the serious side of our relationship. I don't know how it happened, considering the state of my mind, but we did end the evening by renewing our commitment to each other and making plans for a wedding later that year. To this day, I tease her by declaring it was the German chocolate cake that won me over that night. Truth be told, it is still our favorite dessert although neither of us can afford the calories anymore.

Pam had been out of my thoughts throughout the entire evening, but as I sat in my car waving goodbye to Jenny, it hit me like a ton of bricks. In a few minutes, I would walk through my parents' door and there would be Pam waiting to greet me with a happy and expectant smile. What was I to do then? The drive back home was not a pleasant one for me that night. I felt guilty, but at that point in life, I was so mixed up I solved everything by avoidance.

Yes, I was not handling this well. Both Jenny and Pam deserved much more than I was giving either of them. Had I had my head on straight, I would have told Pam up front what my plans were when I went to Ravenswood that first day. Had I been thinking in a rational way, I would not have made contact with Jenny until I had come clean with Pam. Even now, as I write this, it overwhelmingly saddens me to admit that I blatantly ignored the emotions of these unsuspecting women while I made sure I was serving mine.

Show Down

Back at Ft. Bliss, I avoided Pam as much as possible. She finally called me and I knew I had to tell her about Jenny. I asked her if I could come see her. She invited me to her apartment, and I believe she sensed something was wrong. As I began to share with her about Jenny and our previous relationship and future plans, Pam began sobbing deeply and did so for a long time. She never uttered an accusatory word. I never heard from Pam again, although I was stationed at Ft. Bliss for a while after Jenny and I were married. I saw her once in the Post Exchange and we both turned abruptly and walked away.

It was years later that I realized how deeply I hurt her. She had truly loved me, and I had taken advantage of that love. On one occasion before I departed for flight school, I kidded her about being chubby. When she came off the plane in West Virginia I did not recognize her. She had a waist like a model! A friend of hers back at Ft. Bliss told me she had eaten nothing but salad for six weeks. I often have prayed that she was blessed with a husband who loved and appreciated her. I did try to locate Pam to ask her forgiveness and see how she was doing, but never made contact. Even as I write this, I consider my treatment of Pam as one of the most regretful actions in my life. It was years before I could tell Jenny this story, but, gracious lady that she is, forgiveness came with the passing of time.

MGA and Scenic Drive

The Army does not forgive so easy, even when it makes the mistake. While I was at Ft. Rucker, the Army decided to recover the uniform allowance they had erroneously paid me when I reported to Fort Carson. I could not afford the payment on the Olds 88 that had been my black beauty for just a few short months. I shared my dilemma with my flight instructor, who had an auto dealership in town. He paid off the loan on the Olds and gave me title to a '53 Cadillac in excellent shape. It made the trip to Florida, then to West Virginia, then to El Paso, Texas, just fine and I was resigned to live with this tank of a car for a long time.

Soon after my arrival at Ft. Bliss, my friend Jack and I were driving downtown El Paso. We saw a sleek, white sports car in a dealer's window. I wheeled my Caddy in and, before I could catch my breath, traded for a two-seated 1958 MGA convertible. It was fun to drive and much better on curves than Dad's '49 Ford had been.

At happy hour one Friday after work, I boasted of the agility of the MGA and my drinking friend dared to scoff. I bet him I could drive over Scenic Drive and never drop below 40. Scenic Drive is a crooked, narrow road cut into the side of a rocky, almost vertical mountain face. We bet a case of beer. By the time we were halfway over, he promised to buy me the brewery if I would let him live.

Inspiration of Cold Sweat

Jenny and I agreed on marriage in December, but I kept delaying the moment when we would set a date for the wedding. Was I really ready to settle down? One night in early May, I had a very vivid dream that she had decided to marry an old flame from high school days. I woke up in a cold sweat. Without thinking of the time, I called her, and we set the date: June 18, 1960.

Four days before the wedding, with a severe hangover from a bachelor party, I got into my MGA with one small suitcase and headed to Ravenswood in the blazing desert sun. That really hurt! I was headed for my wedding, and I was scared stiff. What a way to start a life. My dad did not want to conduct the ceremony because Jenny was not a member of his denomination, and it was a given that Jenny's dad would not even attend because I was not a member of his denomination. But it turned out my dad and the pastor of First Baptist Church in Ravenswood jointly performed the ceremony, and Jenny's dad finally agreed to give her away.

I knew I wanted to live the rest of my life with Jenny, but I was so emotionally unstable in relationships that I was numb throughout the entire ceremony. Our honeymoon was the trip back to Fort Bliss as the Army had given me only one week to return to duty. The MGA threw a bearing in Memphis, and Jenny had to pay the bill with her savings. Unbelievable that an Army officer could be so irresponsible. I was walking on unfamiliar ground, having assumed I would not live to enjoy life, much less be married to a beautiful woman. Life was surreal with ever-present fear of punishment from an angry God.

Gregory Hayward

Jenny and I hoped to wait at least two years before having children, and the Army was doing everything it could to help. Within two weeks after we reported back to Ft. Bliss I was ordered to the west coast for a highly classified school. We could see this being a common occurrence in my career choice, so we put aside our resolve, and on May 11, 1961, Gregory Hayward, a handsome, healthy, blonde-headed boy showed up at William Beaumont Army Hospital.

A boy! Our firstborn was a boy! That was the way I should have felt, but that was not the way it was. How could this be? I was not excited. In fact, I was very confused, and to this day I cannot clearly express my feelings on that day. Was it because I didn't deserve a healthy boy? It just did not seem real. But the Army has a way of introducing reality, and before I got used to the aroma of diapers, I was introduced to the aroma of honey wagons and a task that was to challenge my knowledge and stamina as never before.

South Korea

The Army decided I needed an overseas tour and the missile command at Camp Page, South Korea, needed a lieutenant with Honest John Rocket experience. The Honest John was a nuclear-capable, ballistic rocket that was launched from a mobile launching rail mounted on a five-ton truck. It was twenty-four feet long, thirty inches in diameter, and had a range of sixteen miles. I was part of the team that did the operational testing of the rocket at Ft. Bliss, Texas, so I got the assignment. The Army packed up our household goods and put them in storage, and Jenny, Greg, and I packed the car and headed to Parkersburg, West Virginia, where Jenny and Greg would live with her parents while I was in Korea. After about a month on leave, I boarded an airplane to San Francisco and from there a non-stop flight to Seoul, South Korea.

At the time, South Koreans used all organic substances to fertilize their crops, and in the hot, muggy month of July it was a challenge to inhale, but anything was better than flying in a turbojet for nineteen hours and resisting the urge to jump every time I walked by an emergency door on the way to the latrine. No, I was not suicidal. I now realize the urge to jump was coming from a source outside of my cognitive system, but somehow was able to inject these destructive impulses into my conscious mind, sometimes quite forcefully. At that time I did not have a clue about the source and was afraid to ask anyone. So I fought the battle alone.

The year in Korea was a good year professionally for me. I still marvel that I was able to perform that well with the battle going on in the background of my life. It was not until later that I understood how it was possible.

I shared a room with three other officers. One was a special agent, and we saw very little of him. The other two were infantry officers assigned to the infantry company whose mission was to provide security for the missile command. The curved ceiling of the Quonset hut was plastered with Playboy pinups. Scotch was my favorite drink and poker my favorite entertainment. My first night at poker was successful. I won enough to create a reserve, so I lived off my winnings and sent my paycheck home. I thought that was a commendable lifestyle.

Despite these distractions, I was privileged to play a key role in transforming an Honest John Rocket Battalion from a unit that had failed every inspection and operational test that year into a fully certified unit. Knowing about my Honest John experience, the battalion commander gave me, a lieutenant, the mission of preparing the battalion to pass all the failed tests that had to be retaken within one hundred twenty days. Sure, I knew the technical aspects of the rocket system, but this was not a one-man job. Fortunately, everyone chipped in, and we worked sacrificially during those next four months.

The testing team arrived unannounced from Hawaii, and the evaluation began about noon. We took a combined combat operational readiness test and a nuclear technical proficiency inspection under the most adverse conditions: a monsoon rain that turned to a blizzard as we prepared for a simulated nuclear rocket launch at first light.

As the officer in charge, my first responsibility was to operate the theodolite, a device used to orient the rocket launcher. The section chief operated the sight on the rocket platform, interacting with me as I gave directions to orient the rocket launcher on the correct azimuth. The task is normally simple, but in a blizzard it gets real tricky. The chief's response was slower than I thought it should be, and at one point I issued a loud verbal command and got a "Yes, sir!" in response.

When I was satisfied with the process, I charged over to the launcher to apologize to the chief for my verbiage. I shined my flashlight on his chest so I could see his face without blinding him. To my chagrin the "chief," was in fact the battalion commander.

"I guess I'm a little rusty on the launcher equipment," he said with a pleasant smile.

"Sir," I said. "You did great. Pardon my language."

The nuclear weapon was assembled and delivered and transferred to the truck-mounted launcher with flawless precision in spite of the bone-chilling wind. The test was completed with the simulated launch at first light. Soaked to the skin and weary from months of dedicated work followed by eighteen hours of intense concentration, we headed to base camp for showers and dry clothes before going to the briefing room to learn whether we would be praised or tarred and feathered.

Finally, the inspection team chief began: "I have never given a briefing like this before. I will cover the major deficiencies first."

I caught my breath and the battalion commander turned to look at me with an expression that said, "Miller, what went wrong out there?"

The team chief turned the page and said, "This is the first inspection of this type for which the page of major deficiencies is blank. We found zero major deficiencies."

The room erupted!

Artillery Punch and Mountain Climbing

After passing the roughest test the Army gives a nuclear-capable unit, we celebrated. The artillery punch, a concoction of various alcoholic beverages, flowed freely, and we closed the party with melancholy singing in one of the officer's rooms. This delighted the chaplain, who somehow got a commitment out of each of us to be in the chapel choir the next morning.

The delight of the victors was interrupted by the post commander, who was not delighted with the lack of sobriety among his officers. Suddenly the door burst open followed with, "We are a combat unit and there is not one of you that could walk straight—let alone fire a missile! All of you be in full field gear with backpack and be in formation in front of the headquarters in fifteen minutes. Maybe a trip to the top of the mountain and back will sober you up!"

As best we could, we headed to our rooms for our gear. My battalion commander met me in the hall and said, "Miller, you are sitting this one out. I'm taking your place up the mountain. You get some rest."

Never was an order easier to obey!

The Old Rugged Cross

True to our word, the Artillery Chorus was in the choir on Sunday morning. There were more than four hundred hymns in the book the chaplain could have selected. I wondered why he so delightfully announced, "The first hymn this morning will be 'The Old Rugged Cross!'"

I quickly learned that a severe hangover and "The Old Rugged Cross" are not compatible. I promised myself that in the future it would be one or the other. A seed was planted that morning in my heart, even though it lay dormant for a while with only an occasional incident to break up the baked soil.

Awesome Power of the Sea

The battalion at Camp Page had a history of going on a combination training exercise and R&R trip to the beaches on the Sea of Japan. We simulated an enemy attack, completed a tactical road march to the beaches, set up combat operations in the morning, and then enjoyed the pristine white beaches in the afternoon without a civilian in sight. On our first day at the beach, we were joined by a typhoon dancing around between Japan and Korea. It created some serious wave action near our location. Regardless, many of us took to the surf to challenge the forces of Nature.

After some time, another officer and I were standing in the pounding surf watching our unit clown. "Look at Williams. He's paddling forward and swimming backwards! How does he do that?" the officer asked.

I watched, intrigued for a moment until it became obvious Williams was not clowning—he was being taken out to sea by an undertow. I called for those close by to help and about a dozen of us quickly formed a human chain and moved toward Williams. A huge surge engulfed us and we were all caught in the grip of the receding surge. It was every man for himself.

The total helplessness of swimming against the raging ocean numbed my entire being. I was swimming as hard as I could and the beach was receding rapidly. The power of the sea left me absolutely helpless and I was being dragged to my ocean burial by an angry sea. I am not a great swimmer, and the exertion caused me to start gasping for breath while the surging waves filled my mouth and nostrils with sea water. When I could no longer muster the strength, I began to float face down, bouncing with the surges.

In the midst of that futility, a thought from years earlier surfaced. A friend who lived near the ocean had said, "If you every get caught in an undertow don't try to out swim it. Wait for a swale and drift to the side." Fortunately the beach was relatively flat, and the water shallow for some distance out. I waited for a swale. The first one was too deep, and I could not reach bottom. On the next try, my toes touched bottom, so I dropped down and jumped to the side. The beach curved outward and on the next try I was able to get a good foothold and was able to move several feet. The next time the wave carried me in toward shore and I was out of the undertow. I managed to get my feet on the floor and wade to shore.

I turned around to see the officer who had been standing beside me floating face down in the surf. It was like a bad dream. I knew I was too tired to swim to him, so I ran through the sand yelling at the top of my voice to a nearby group that had fully inflated air mattresses. I quickly borrowed one and headed in the direction of the limp form. I managed to get to him and pull him up by his hair. It appeared he was not breathing.

As I dragged him toward shore, others realized what was happening and jumped to the rescue. The battalion surgeon met the group on the shore and immediately began pumping the lieutenant's lungs and stomach. Miraculously, he coughed and a flood of water came gushing out his nose and mouth. He later told us his entire life had flashed before him before he lost consciousness.

To my utter amazement, we all survived, including Williams. Some recovered by themselves; others were rescued with air mattresses. I do not remember all the details, but this I remember: that night I tried to sleep, but when I closed my eyes, I felt myself helplessly dragged down into the limitless power of the ocean. It was an awful feeling. I had stashed a bottle of Scotch in my duffle bag and took a double shot to ward off the smothering, helpless drowning sensations.

Now, more than forty years later, there are still residual feelings when I recall the awesome power of the sea. It was another one of those incidents that flashed a warning across my screen, but the next week, life continued.

The Big Eye

Girlfriends at the Big Eye nightclub in the town of Chunchon were quiet common among the single soldiers stationed at Camp Page. I chose not to go there, normally. However, one Friday night after happy hour at the officers' club, my roommate Jim convinced me to go. We walked out the door of the club, and a big black staff car was parked there with a Korean driver standing by the vehicle.

Jim said, "Why don't we ride?" and headed for the back door of the sedan.

The driver opened the door and we got in.

"The Big Eye," Jim said, and away we went.

The driver took us to the Big Eye and headed back to the officers' club. Jim, a bachelor, rounded up two girls, and in our boozed state we agreed to go next door to play strip poker. One of the girls lost the first hand and began to undress. To my amazement, instead of seeing her, I saw a clear image of Jenny's face! I sobered up immediately, bolted for the door, and didn't stop until I was in my room. No more Big Eye for me.

There was a note taped to the door of our room from the battalion commander urging Jim and me to report to him first thing in the morning. I didn't sleep very well for more reasons than one.

Standing at attention in front of his desk the following morning, we were expecting dire consequences.

"Did you borrow the general's vehicle last night?" he asked.

Apparently the driver did not get back before the Commanding General of the First Republic of Korea (ROK) Army needed his staff car.

"Yes, sir," I stammered, my mind racing to figure out what the penalty would be for wrongful appropriation of a general's sedan.

"It was very embarrassing when the ROK Army Commander came to me and said, 'My vehicle is gone!' I immediately called the Military Police and they checked with the gate guard, who reported the vehicle with two lieutenants in the back seat had passed through the gate and returned with only the driver. I escorted the general to his vehicle and begged his forgiveness for the action of two of my officers. What in the name of heaven were you thinking? The ROK Army Commanding Officer of all people!" The colonel turned his back to us.

He is probably trying to recall the appropriate paragraph in the UCMJ to use to charge us, I thought.

After several minutes, the colonel turned around looking like the cat that caught the canary.

"I tell you what, Miller," the colonel said. "You got me out of a big hole with your work in getting us an outstanding on our inspection and training test. I'm going to return the favor and get you out of this hole."

I never heard about the incident again.

You Did What?!

Winter came to Korea and life settled down. That did not sit well with the operations officer, so he called me to his office.

"Miller, how would you like to expend one of those rockets stored in the ammo dump?"

The appropriate answer would have been an emphatic "No!" However, we scheduled the exercise with enough time to get all the requirements for clearance and safety.

On the morning of the exercise, the operations officer handed me the coordinates of the launch site. I looked on the tactical map, and to my surprise, the launch site was just a few hundred yards south of the Demilitarized Zone (DMZ).

"With snow covering the entire country side, that flaming rocket will light up half of Korea!" I protested.

The Honest John rocket has a solid propellant about eight feet long and twenty-two inches in diameter. It burns less than ten seconds, but develops 150,000 pounds of thrust, reaching a maximum altitude of

30,000 feet at maximum range of sixteen miles and 2.3 times the speed of sound.

"The light and sound from that blazing piece of steel will be seen and heard ten miles into North Korea!" My words fell on deaf ears.

We loaded up an Honest John rocket and road-marched to the firing site. The target area was more than twelve miles south. Everything was going as planned up to the final step of closing an access door through which the final arming process was completed. That was my responsibility, so I connected the electrical wires and closed the door only to realize the screws to secure the door were not to be found.

"I know I put those screws in my pocket, but which pocket?" I asked as I searched everywhere for them.

The section chief saw my dilemma and responded, "Not to worry Lieutenant, I always carry a spare set."

We got online with operations and the observers who were to document that the impact was in the target area.

10, 9, 8, 7, 6, 5, 4, 3, 2, 1, FIRE!

Honest John roared into the night sky, and indeed the entire valley looked like midday. We closed down, and I headed to the operations center where I was met by the battalion commander. He scowled at me.

"Miller, the observation team missed the impact," he said. "We don't know where that thing went!"

I was confident the rocket hit the target and casually removed my parka. As I stuck my hand into my fatigue jacket pocket, there were the missing screws. I held them in the palm of my hand and said, "Well, I'll be darned! There are the access door screws."

I should have been more discreet, but I couldn't resist the temptation.

"Lieutenant, don't tell me you fired that rocket with the door flapping in the breeze," he said. "It's no telling where that thing went!"

The veins in his neck were bulging. "Sir, I am sorry I was flippant. We always carry extra screws and I personally secured the door. I assure you that rocket hit in the designated impact area."

"Miller, you had better be right!" He turned to the operations officer and said, "Get a team out there and find out where that thing hit."

It was two tense hours until the report came in over the command radio: "We are in the impact area and the rocket hit within two hundred feet of the target coordinates. It ricocheted off the frozen ground and traveled another half mile, but remained in the safe zone."

The commander took a deep breath and exhaled loudly, then turned to me and looked like he wanted to kick my butt and kiss me at the same time. "Get outta here!"

"Yes, sir!"

Chapter 6

Surviving in Life's Crucible

Going Home

The remainder of the Korean tour was routine. I was approaching my three-year commitment to the Army and was within ninety days of rotation back to the States. I went to the personnel office to apply for release from the military to go back to Ravenswood and the job Kaiser was holding open for me.

The personnel officer greeted me with, "Lieutenant, you may want to think about resigning for a minute. I just received an alert notice this morning that you have been selected for the Artillery Advanced Course with an immediate departure date, meaning you will get to see your wife a lot earlier than planned. But, if you want to proceed with the resignation . . ."

I was already out the door to start packing! I came to Korea for a thirteen month tour. That was extended to sixteen months, and now I was going home after only ten months.

Debra Kay

Two days after President Kennedy was assassinated, Debra Kay blessed our life. This time I was excited. I vividly remember the night in Lawton, Oklahoma, when Jenny and I prayed for a little girl, and now at Ft. Bliss, Texas, on November 24, 1963, that prayer was answered in a beautiful, angelic girl. She was a delightful bundle of joy, and she stole my heart with her first smile. The picture of Jenny beaming with love for the delicate new life snuggled in her arms is a treasured memory. Another wonderful memory is that of Greg, just two years old, holding his little sister with a look on his face that said, "This is *my* sister and I am going to take care of her!" And so it would be.

Bottom of the Bottle

Before graduating from the Artillery Advanced Course in early 1963, I was offered the opportunity to get a master's degree in nuclear engineering. I declined because it had to be completed in one year, and I believed I would need more time than that. Sometime later the assignment officer came to Ft. Sill to distribute orders to all course graduates.

As he handed me my orders, he said, "We decided to honor your declination to get the nuclear engineering degree, so we selected you to be among the first to test a new master's level program in aerospace engineering to be taught at Ft. Bliss, Texas. It is a nine-month program beginning in March 1964. If it works, it will be incorporated into a master's degree awarded by the University of Texas—El Paso."

I think the one-year nuclear engineering degree would have been a piece of cake compared to what they crammed into our craniums in less than nine months. We studied hard during the week and played hard on weekends, yet all eighteen of us came through with flying colors. I graduated number eight in the class. Unfortunately, because our class was a test class, we didn't receive an official master's degree in aerospace engineering, but future classes did.

Lethal Graduation Party

We drove across the border to Juarez, Mexico, for our graduation party. With all the studying and cramming behind us, it was nice to lean back and just have fun. I stuck with rum and Coke for the entire evening and felt fully in control when the evening ended. Jenny was not as confident as I was in my ability to drive. She tried to convince me to let her drive home. I insisted that I could handle it and made it just fine, but I have no memory of one mile of that drive. I do remember that at home one of the other officers and I were balancing cups of hot coffee on our heads to convince everyone we were in control.

The next morning I could not get up—the hangover was excruciating. I tried to sleep it off, but the pain got worse. I don't remember how I got there, but I remember being in the dispensary talking with a doctor. They ran some tests and told me the alcohol content in my blood was still so high it could cause permanent damage or even death. At the very least, I would likely not have full control of my legs because the alcohol was oxidizing the motor part of my brain. I knew what that meant. The moonshiners in the mountains called it "Jake Leg" from drinking the high-octane moonshine. The doctor said he had no medical cure and suggested I go home and pray. I scoffed and hobbled out the door. I do remember that I had to put my hands behind my knees and pull each step to walk straight.

The next thing I remember I was in bed at home. I tried again to sleep it off, but every time I closed my eyes, I saw a tombstone with these words as if they were projected onto the bedroom wall: "Dick Miller Died a Drunk." I could feel my body sinking like I was being dragged down below the surface of the ocean. I felt helpless and knew I was in trouble. This was something I could no longer solve by ignoring it. Ironically, it was not so much a fear of dying, but the overwhelming sadness of my wasted life that became intolerable.

The Army had selected me as one of eighteen officers for the test program we had just completed. Years before, my sister told me that Dad sold the family farm, passed down from three generations, so she and I could finish college. These thoughts were unbearable. The doctor's words about praying kept echoing in my mind, but I surmised that if I gave in to prayer I would wind up being a preacher, and that was unacceptable. If I can just sleep this off . . .

I continued to sink, and the feeling that I was slipping below the surface of the ocean became more acute. The absolute powerlessness experienced in that raging Korean sea washed over me, and I felt it dragging me out to sea. I knew I couldn't handle this waste. So with no other options remaining, I resorted to the only thing left to do: I rolled out of bed, knelt down, and prayed another foxhole prayer.

"I don't even know if there is a God up there," I prayed. "But if there is, and you will heal these legs, I will spend the rest of my life searching for who you are and will never again touch rum."

Something like an electrical shock—without the pain—started at my head, went to my toes, and came back up through my body. As it did, it lifted me to my feet. I started dancing around the room free of pain. My legs worked like new! Most importantly, I felt pure love for the first time in my life, and my whole being seemed saturated with warm oil.

Did You Mean It?

I later found out that my "friend" had paid the bartender to give me a double shot of tequila with every rum and Coke. He found out it was me who set the trap for his attendance at his bachelor party, an event he did not want to attend. I led the team that orchestrated a very complex set of events that caught him totally off guard. The details are lost to the past, but suffice to say, it was so compelling it resulted in him almost missing his wedding, set for early the next morning. The doctored drinks were payback. What's that old saying? "With friends like you . . ." As near as we could figure, I had consumed over half a bottle of rum and a bottle of tequila in a four-hour period.

The next week of the course was a class trip to visit the defense companies on the West Coast. The first night there, we went to a lavish party with the most expensive whisky available, not by the drink, but by the bottle. My favorite was Haig & Haig Five Star Pinch Bottle. My drinking buddies got to the bar before me and ordered a bottle of Haig & Haig for me. They were stunned and thought I had surely flipped when I declined all of it and ordered a glass of milk. The search had begun.

Habit Breaker

After graduation in March 1965, I was assigned to a research and development organization (RDO) as an electrical engineer. We moved to the new location and joined a small church. Jenny and I were asked to be the youth advisors. I smoked and still had beer (no rum) in my refrigerator. One day some of the boys in the group reported to me that two of them had been kicked off the football team for smoking.

"I don't get it!" one of the boys protested. "You smoke and you out-run us all when we play flag football."

That night before going to bed, I talked with God about it. I reminded Him I had tried to quit several times unsuccessfully. "Now, if it would help these boys, I ask You to take the habit away."

The next morning I began my day with the usual ritual: sit on the edge of the bed, light up a Viceroy, inhale deeply, then head for the bathroom. This time, when I tried to inhale, I gagged. After three tries with the same reaction, I remembered my request the night before. To my amazement, the desire for a cigarette was completely gone. In fact, cigarette smoke became nauseating to me.

Walking on Thin Ice

The assignment at RDO was challenging and risky. My first job was to carry through on a project to modify a system originally designed for another purpose. The objective of the modification was to make it more effective in a secondary role. However, the characteristics of the two systems were very different.

The system was already in the final pre-production phase. After digesting the specifications and test results, I got this nagging thought: "Something is wrong here." The resolution of the nagging thought evaded me and I closed up the file and went home. At 0400 the next morning, I woke up and sat straight up in bed. "There is the answer!" So I dressed and went to the RDO Technical Library to search the records for data on the preponderance of use of the system in a previous engagement.

The data confirmed my suspicion. A computer analysis confirmed that the effectiveness of the modification was minimal. It became very clear that the increased capability was not cost effective.

The RDO staff agreed the cost effectiveness was questionable and sent me to the Pentagon to present a case for terminating the modification program. I was a captain who had never been to the Pentagon,

Headquarters of the US Military, and I was going to brief the high-level staff at a decision briefing with the objective of canceling the project.

A government civilian from another agency responsible for this modification's technical development was hostile and attempted to ridicule the proposal to terminate development as too late with too little evidence. After an hour of counter arguments, the thought came to me: *This man has a personal interest in this project that is overriding his professional interest.*

I questioned the thought, yet it persisted. I sat back, took a deep breath and said, "Mr. Jones, this equipment is for use by a specific segment of the Army and the user has determined the modification is not cost effective for their use. With all due respect for your diligent work so far, your personal interest in this project is secondary to the combat requirements of the user, and I wonder what is behind your interest."

Mr. Jones' face turned beet red and the veins in his neck looked as if they were going to explode. I thought for a minute he was going to come across the table.

The colonel in charge of the meeting said, "Mr. Jones, do you have a response to Captain Miller's comment?"

Mr. Jones just shook his head.

The colonel continued, "The using organization has determined the project is not cost-effective to them. It is canceled and the ten million dollars allocated for this project is withdrawn."

The colonel's backing was all the thanks I needed that day for my first major task at RDO. On top of that, we saved the Army ten million bucks!

An Officer but Not a Gentleman

The next project got even more interesting. I was to develop the requirements for a piece of equipment for rapid and airborne deployments. My boss came by my desk on Friday afternoon, handed me a packet, and said, "All the requirements for the system are in here. I'll be gone for two weeks. When I get back, I want a requirements document detailing the specifications on my desk, along with final coordination comments from the other organizations with whom we normally coordinate. Clear?"

I responded with, "Yes, sir."

I assumed the packet contained information that had already been informally agreed to, so I sat about finalizing the requirements document, a mammoth task to get done in two weeks. The major returned late Friday of the second week and came directly to my desk. I handed him the final draft and explained that I was still waiting on the final coordination document from one of the agencies. Without looking at the document, he threw it back in my face. It took me so much by surprise that I dodged and fell backwards, taking my chair down with me. Before I could get up he had stomped out.

What's eating him? I wondered.

Still puzzled by his reaction, I came to the office early Saturday morning to work on the project. The major was in his office talking on the phone and didn't hear me come in. Our offices were separated by partitions eight feet high, but open from there to the ceiling. I could not help but hear, and what I heard was disturbing. I began to write down his part of the conversation, and it became obvious he had been a guest for the past two weeks on a yacht owned by the company that had provided the packet he had given me before he left. He was expressing disgust that his project officer (that would be me) did not have the requirements ready when he got back.

I was dumbfounded. I had always believed the integrity of a military officer was above reproach. I slipped out of the office without him hearing me and went home with a big knot in the pit of my stomach. I discussed the situation with Jenny, and we agreed I had to confront the major regardless of the outcome, realizing it would be the word of a captain against that of a major—not good.

I made two copies of my notes, sealed one, and put the envelope in my safe at home. I went into the major's office Monday morning and without saying anything, handed him a copy of the notes. As he read, his face began to turn red, then purple. "Where did you get these?" he shouted.

"I was in my office Saturday and overheard your conversation," I said.

Interlaced with a few expletives, he proceeded to accuse me of a litany of infractions to include invading his privacy, and then ended with, "It's just your word against mine and I will see that your Army career is over! Now get out!"

I was shaken and went to my office to consider what my next action should be. Should I go to his boss or to the legal office? I called Jenny and told her what had happened and together we decided to let it settle for a few hours. Later that afternoon a very repentant major came into my office, apologized for his rant, and admitted that his action to try to influence the development of the system was totally wrong and assured me he had broken all ties with the company that had hosted him on their yacht.

"Captain Miller, I have made a gross error in judgment," he said. "I ask for your forgiveness and if you can see fit to keep this between you and me, I would be grateful for the opportunity to earn your trust again."

No one is perfect, I reasoned, and agreed to keep it between the two of us.

When the major departed the command a few months later, he showed me a copy of the efficiency report he had written on my performance. It was not sterling, but reasonable, and when I left the command and cleaned out my desk, I shredded the notes. I would live to regret that careless act.

Get off the Team

There was one more incident at RDO that challenged my integrity. I was on a team to locate targets for computer simulation of target damage analysis from an explosive device that was in the final development stage. The analysis found the system was ineffective against the targets our team located according to the higher headquarters' directive. The project manager (PM) of the system had his career on the line if this system failed now. Even so, I was astonished when he directed our team to locate only smaller targets.

I reread the directive and it was very specific: our targets were in accordance with the directive. I also called the headquarters that wrote the directive and the answer was an emphatic, "No, you may not change the criteria!"

I pointed this out to the PM, but he was not interested in discussing it. He said, "Miller, I am telling you to change the acquisition criteria. Either follow my guidance or get off the team!"

Amazed, I replied, "Sir, before I will change the criteria, someone has to amend the written directive from higher headquarters."

I was reassigned the next day and made no memorandum for record of the exchange. I would also regret that omission.

I want to make it very clear: I have served with and for numerous military officers from all the services. With the exception of these two incidents, I have great admiration for the integrity and professionalism of those officers with whom I have served. I mention these two incidents because of the impact upon my career.

The Black Hole

This tour of duty was a time of alternating between mountaintop experiences and treks through the swamps. One incident still causes agony in my gut. When our son Greg was six years old, we went through a nightly bedtime ritual of walking him to his room, tucking him in, turning off the light, and walking out again, only to have him back in the living room a few minutes later. We went through this routine for a period of several weeks, sometimes four or five times a night. The ritual continued even after a session with a counselor, who could find nothing to explain these nightly occurrences other than a rebellious nature in Greg.

The counselor recommended a spanking accompanied with the proper explanation of why it was being done. Although we were not opposed to this solution, we continued to hope it would stop. It didn't. Totally frustrated, and suffering from sleep deprivation ourselves, we took his advice and applied the hand of correction on his backside. We assumed that was the solution, because we had no further problems at bedtime with him.

Years later, Greg and I were talking about that house, and he shared with me that he'd been afraid of the hole in his closet floor, which was the access to the crawl space under the house. One day I had to go under the floor to inspect a water pipe. Greg wanted to go with me, so he and I went under the floor through the hole. While working on the problem, my flashlight failed and I headed back into the main house. I told Greg I would be right back and left him sitting in the dark. By the time I returned, he was in a state of sheer panic and I quickly moved him out of the "black hole" into the light of his bedroom. After all these years, it began to dawn on me that Greg was not being stubborn; he was afraid that a boogieman was going to come out of that hole and get him!

I was devastated to learn that our six-year-old son had been punished for experiencing the same fear that I had as a boy. Now forty-five years later, I still suffer remorse when I think about it. I loved Greg and would have done everything in my power to protect him from any threat. To subject him to such treatment is unfathomable to me! I would give my life for the opportunity to hold that six-year-old boy that I loved until he was not afraid. Then I would seal up that hole until he felt no more threat. This event was just one more example of how unprepared I was for the responsibility of providing a healthy environment for my children.

Twisted

When Jenny and I were married, neither of us had a personal relationship with Jesus. I was in rebellion and she had little interest in the spiritual dimension of life. The topic of being a preacher came up, and she emphatically stated she would not marry a preacher. Therein began a reinforcement of my disobedience because somewhere in a confused mind the thought was planted: *You have disobeyed Me and chosen Jenny over Me. You will be punished and so will she because she has influenced you to disobey.*

I assumed this was the voice of an angry God. The premise that punishment must be meted out against Jenny surfaced big time while we lived in that house.

I was struggling with not being a preacher and shifted the blame to Jenny. I thought I had the right to execute judgment on this source of opposition. That was like Old Testament justice, and I knew it was false. And yet I was unable to completely eliminate the recurring thought. It was difficult to decipher the truth from the lie. I was not yet aware of the shrewd counterfeit tactics of the enemy.

Last Chance

We attended church regularly, and I began to sing in the choir. One Sunday the preacher's sermon was about the prodigal son who finally quit running and returned home. I knew I had come to the end of my running, and it was now or never. I jumped out of the choir loft and "surrendered to preach." I figured Jenny would run out the door, but she came and stood beside me. The church granted me a license and for several months I filled in for preachers who were on vacation. I tried to resign from the Army, but received orders to Germany instead. I called my assignment officer and volunteered for Vietnam with plans to retire as soon as the tour was over.

My orders to Germany were amended, and I was to deploy to Vietnam with the 9th Infantry Division, the division to which I was assigned during my first tour of duty at Fort Carson, Colorado. We began preparing for the unaccompanied assignment in Vietnam. However, a few days later, the orders to Vietnam were rescinded and the orders for Germany reinstated. I was confused. I had finally stopped running, now I couldn't get out of the Army to go to seminary.

The pastor of the church we attended was a personal friend of a very powerful Oklahoma senator.

"One phone call and you will be out," the pastor said. I asked God what I should do. I was learning to listen for answers and the answer was very clear: "I do not need a senator to do My business."

"Yes, Sir!" I responded and told my pastor not to call the senator.

Beautiful Flowers and Strong Trees

God's nature is absolute, but operationally He is unpredictable. Case in point: During this tour at Ft. Sill, I was asked to give the graduation address for a class of thirty or forty enlisted men who had completed a course related to target acquisition. A few days before the graduation I began to write an outline for the speech—I drew a blank for five days! Finally, in desperation I asked God for help. The answer I received was *Get a copy of the roster of the class and spend your preparation time praying for them by name.* I was impressed because I normally received one- or two-word responses. I got a copy of the graduate roster the following day and spent the evening at home in my bedroom praying for each graduate by name.

On the way to work the following morning with no notes, I stopped for a traffic light and received the following instructions: *Tell them I love them and build your comments around this: The most beautiful flowers grow deep in the forest; the strongest trees grow out in the open.*

When I was introduced, I explained exactly what had happened, stepped down off the platform and shared what I had been given and expounded briefly, explaining that their personal character and personality is formed in solitude with their Creator. Their external strength would result from periods of adversity just as the tree is strengthened by the wind blowing against it.

I shall always remember the strong, warm blessing that flowed between us as I passed out their diplomas and shook each one of their hands. Each one made it a point to make positive eye contact that transmitted a heartfelt "Thank you!" I was amazed and blessed more than they.

Douglas Paul

The delay in orders gave us enough time to welcome Douglas Paul into our lives at the Fort Sill Army Hospital on June 3, 1966. I took Jenny to the hospital, left a phone number at the nurse's station, and went nearby to a friend's house to look at Model A Fords, assuming it would be the normal two- or three-hour wait. I had barely gotten there when my friend's phone rang and the nurse said, rather forcefully, "If you want to be here when your child is born, you better get here *now!*" I jumped in my car and hoped there were no MPs between the hospital and me. When I opened the door to the ward, the walls were vibrating.

I thought, *What a pair of lungs! I wonder whose kid that is.* Guess whose? It was my kid. Doug was not bashful about letting the world know of his displeasure at the disturbance to his cozy life. I was amazed at the difference in my acceptance of Doug versus the way I received Greg when he was born. I was confused about Greg, but I loved Doug from the first verbal protest.

The Dragon Speaks

A month after Doug was born, we cleared Ft. Sill and headed for Germany with a stop to visit families in West Virginia. The relationship between Jenny and me, instead of maturing, began to vacillate between bad and bitter with an occasional break for civility in public and at church. It was as if the proverbial immovable object had met the irresistible force and neither of us was able or willing to reach out to the other. We had tried counseling, but there was no evidence of any success. While on leave at my parents' house along the Kanawha River (just before it converges with the Ohio River), Jenny and I had a violent argument. I went upstairs to try to pray.

I said, "God, what am I to do about Jenny?"

Suddenly, from where I did not know, a vicious thought screamed at me, "Kill her!"

I jumped up, ran out of the house and headed for the river with one idea in mind: before I would hurt anyone I would give my life to the river! I had no idea what I was fighting. The "voice" had come from outside somewhere, yet it was not an audible voice that I heard with my ears. At the end of the headlong running and stumbling down to the river, I collapsed on the bank gasping for breath and shaking violently. I don't know how long I was there, but after some time a semblance of sanity returned and I began to feel remorse for my actions during the fight with Jenny. I walked back to the house and, after a much more civilized conversation, we made peace with each other and enjoyed a reprieve from our personal problems for the remainder of the visit.

Dad and I had a good visit. He gave me a copy of a book that had been given to him as an honorarium. The book was titled *Man's Ruin,* by Donald G. Barnhouse. The title seemed to fit my present condition, and I sensed the book had a message for me.

On the trip to the air terminal in New Jersey, I further proved myself a man in ruin. We drove our station wagon to the terminal. It was to be shipped to the port in Germany. It rained so hard we could barely drive. Jenny was frightened of flying and recovering from postpartum emotions and trying to take care of Doug, who was just six weeks old. Before we left my parents' house, her hands broke out in huge blisters from the emotional stress. I had no patience and yelled at the kids in the back seat. Only by the grace of God did we get through the next ten hours before I reported for duty in Kitzingen, West Germany.

I was assigned to the 3rd of the 76th Field Artillery Battalion as Commander of "A" Battery. The staffing was so low, there were no other officers and only one NCO above the grade of Corporal assigned to the battery. Everyone was in Vietnam.

Life was a dichotomy. I was performing every job to and beyond expectation, but my personal life was in turmoil. The search for God continued, but the news ahead was not what I was expecting.

Why Not

In the spring of 1967 our battalion was at the field-training center at Grafenwoehr, Germany, when I received word that the anticipated major's promotion list was in. Col. P. B. Welch, my battalion commander, came to see me in the field for what I assumed was good news. However, I was not on the list. My heart sank. How could this be? I completed the training exercise in a bit of a fog, dealing with many questions about the future.

When we returned to our base in Kitzingen, Col. Welch called me to his office to meet another battalion commander who was returning to the Pentagon for an assignment with military personnel. Col. Welch had already prepared a document for me to authorize the other officer to review my personnel file to determine the reason I had not been selected for promotion. Col. Welch received the results of the investigation within two weeks. The reason for non-selection was obvious and pointed directly to the two officer efficiency reports (OER) written while I was assigned to RDO. The first one was from the "yachting" major I had confronted about his illegal actions. It contained a single derogatory comment that was not in the OER he showed me when he left. I had trusted his word and had destroyed my notes about the event. I had no recourse.

The second OER was a special report written by the officer who directed me to locate targets in violation of the guidance document from higher headquarters. I never saw it. What hurt the most was that the report stated I was disloyal to the United States Army. There was no basis for appeal because I had not documented the incident. I was devastated, angry at the system, and angry with God. In both cases I believed I had acted correctly, and my conscience was clear. In both cases, my reward was an OER that cost me a promotion to major.

Col. Welch, without sharing with me the reason, began to assign me tasks in every staff function in the battalion and one at Division Artillery Headquarters. After five months of this extra duty that resulted in me working twelve to fourteen hours per day, he called me to his office. "Miller, do you have any idea why I assigned you all the extra duties?" he asked.

"Sir," I replied, "I didn't question why you gave me the extra assignments, but I did wonder why you kept all the other staff officers around."

He laughed and said, "I wanted to see what you were capable of. Now we get you promoted." He reassigned me three times within the battalion and wrote a special efficiency report each time specifically countering each negative comment in the two offending reports.

Pin On

Some months later I took an annual physical and as the doctor was examining my throat he said, "Uh, oh!"

That was not what I wanted to hear. He found nodules on my vocal cords. I was immediately referred to surgery with the warning to prepare for immediate transfer to a stateside hospital in the event the nodules were cancerous.

The surgery was performed, the nodules submitted for biopsy. I was sent home to recover. The next morning, while I was still in my robe, Col. Welch and Major Paul Slater, the battalion executive officer, came storming into the house and pinned major's oak leaves on my bathrobe. His persistence had paid off; the next major's promotion board selected me for promotion as a result of his extra effort. I think he was happier than I was.

It took a while, but I eventually forgave both the officers who submitted the unjust OERs.

The biopsy came back negative. However, the nodules kept growing back, requiring five subsequent surgeries to remove them.

Let me affirm that Col. P. B. Welch was one of the most conscientious commanders I served with. What he did for me was just one example of his interest in those in his command. His greatest gift was to cut through the fog to get the job done. His greatest frustration was with unimportant minutia. His favorite expression was, "Here I am up to my butt in alligators, and I'm being nibbled to death by ducks!"

Major Paul Slater was a brilliant artilleryman and a man of impeccable integrity. I was to meet him in another assignment.

You Want Me to Do What?

We attended a small American church in Kitzingen, West Germany, and I began to teach a Bible class. The pastor of the church rotated back to the United States. To my surprise, the congregation, by unanimous vote, asked me to be the interim pastor. Again to my surprise, I accepted. My track record was nothing to crow about, but perhaps taking on this responsibility would help me as I tried to minister to this church. I prepared every sermon using Barnhouse's book, *Man's Ruin*, and the book of Romans as the basis. I baptized some of those who responded to the messages, but every time I gave an invitation for people to respond to God's invitation to join His team, I felt a need to respond myself. Something was incomplete and the content in *Man's Ruin* began to have a profound effect on my appraisal of my spirituality.

Pleasant Surprise

One of the most pleasant surprises during the assignment with 3/76 Artillery Battalion was a call from the DivArty Commander to come to his office. "Captain Miller, I will get right to the point. I have a new West Point second lieutenant coming in next month. You are the senior captain in DivArty, and I am asking you to take Lieutenant Hicks under your wing and help him mature into an excellent soldier and officer."

That I was getting an officer was exciting. That I was selected to mentor a new West Point graduate was a double honor.

I wrote a letter of welcome, and Second Lieutenant Robert Hicks reported for duty in relaxed civilian attire needing a haircut. I heard the First Sergeant try to convince the lieutenant to wait until he was in uniform to report in for duty, but he insisted on coming into my office. To back up Top and to begin his training, I didn't even look up when he stepped in. I said something like, "If you are Lt. Hicks, come back when you look like a soldier."

In less than two hours, there was a crisp knock on my door, to which I responded, "Come in." There before me was a sharp soldier in a pressed uniform and a new military haircut. Standing outside the door was 1SGT Miller (not related) grinning from ear to ear with two thumbs in the air. Thus began one of the most enjoyable relationships of my career.

1SGT Miller and I teamed up to fulfill the DivArty commander's challenge. We made it rough on Lt. Hicks and he rose to the challenge every time. I had the honor of pinning on his first lieutenant bars and assigned him to the position of battery executive officer, a position he filled in a professional manner. I rated Lt. Hicks as the officer with the greatest potential of any young officer with whom I had served. When Col. Welch assigned me as the battalion operations officer, Lt. Hicks became the A battery commander, again performing in an outstanding manner. Then a short time later, he was promoted below the zone to Captain. He was on the way.

CHAPTER 7

Through the Valley of Shadows

Back to Reality

Boom! Boom! That was close! Charlie is letting us know he is still there. The two mortar rounds exploded near the barracks.

It took me a few seconds to return to the reality that I was still in Vietnam and the VC still had ammunition to throw at us. It was now dark and several hours had passed since I began staring at the ceiling, inviting the past to drift uninhibited through my mind. I grabbed a flashlight and ran out to see if anyone was wounded and to inspect for damage. The mortar rounds had exploded near one of the barracks, but the crew was on R&R and the shrapnel was absorbed by the revetment the crew had built earlier.

They Remembered

One day I was surprised to receive a letter from the church I visited in Tacoma, Washington, while on a pass at the completion of my training at Ft. Lewis. As I opened the letter, it was as if some warm, invisible power flowed from the letter into my hands, up my arms, and into all of my body. It was like being under a sun lamp, except the warm radiation was from the inside. I stood very still in wonderment as my mind drifted to El Paso, Texas, and the power that had healed me of alcoholic poison. When I finally opened the letter all the way, it contained the signatures of the prayer team members at the church who had covenanted to pray for me daily. I had passed it off, as often such promises are made superficially, but this group obviously was serious. I regret the letter was misplaced somewhere in all the moves. I did return to Tacoma years later hoping to locate the church but was not successful.

The Mayor of Chow Hiep

In life there are rare moments that imprint an indelible memory. One of those moments occurred to me in the tiny village of Chow Hiep, South Vietnam. When the VC came to power in North Vietnam, a Catholic priest in Hanoi led his entire parish on a road march to freedom. When they began walking, they were about one thousand strong. When I met them they were only two hundred strong, mostly children. The VC had continued to attack them and killed most of the adults. The priest built a makeshift schoolhouse and every child went to school every day. They had very little food, no clean water, and only rags for clothes.

We needed a radar location in that area and the priest, whom I named the Mayor of Chow Hiep, welcomed our team with open arms. After my first trip there, I wrote my dad, who was pastoring a parish in Wadestown, West Virginia, explaining the condition of the children. The parish quickly adopted the children and sent clothes and toys for all. They provided enough powdered milk each month for each child to have a glass of milk each morning and evening. Our detachment provided pure water and electricity for the village.

Each month when the boxes came in from Wadestown, I loaded up a trailer behind my Jeep and headed to Chow Hiep. As soon as someone in the village spotted the Jeep and trailer with boxes, school activities came to a screeching halt and the children lined each side of the road and cheered wildly, excited to see what new clothes, toys, and food had arrived from America!

One day I told the mayor about a duck that was always on the pond just outside his little house. He explained that they used to have many others, but this was the only one that had escaped the raids from the VC. He began feeding it and kept it for a pet.

When I received orders for rotation to the States, the mayor invited me to come the next week to be a guest for dinner. When I arrived, the children were all dressed up in their GI clothes and gave me a royal welcome. The mayor had set the finest table and opened a bottle of wine he had purchased twenty-five years earlier on his only voyage to Rome.

He was excited about sharing his precious gift with me, who represented those who had befriended his people, saying, "I have been saving it for a very special occasion. This is the most special of occasions," as he opened the bottle.

I think I know how David felt when his loyal soldiers brought him water from Jerusalem when they were hiding from King Saul. David was so astonished with their loyalty that he would not drink the water. Although I had not tasted alcohol in many years, with tears running down my face, I toasted the mayor and we sipped his only bottle of wine as we ate.

I never asked about the delicious roast duck, but I could not help notice his pet duck was not on the pond. I have never been so honored in this life and even now, as I write this account so many years later, my eyes fill with tears of respect for a fellow traveler who shared that which was precious to him. And it gives me great pain to suppose that when America withdrew our forces and the communist regime took over South Vietnam, the VC annihilated the mayor and his little village. But in my memory, I still hear very clearly the wild cheering of the children as they bid me farewell and waved until I was out of sight. I waved back and thought, *Perchance I will see them again*. Knowing it probably would never be, my sadness gave way to tears again as my driver and I headed back to Long Binh.

Chilled Out

Since the Army would not release me for seminary, I decided to take courses by correspondence, and then apply for release again when my Vietnam tour was over. The first course was Old Testament Survey. I completed the study through the book of Job and faithfully mailed the completed work back each week. The night after I mailed the last lesson on the book of Job, I was awakened and felt a sudden change in the room. It felt like the temperature dropped forty degrees. I was freezing and could not get warm, even with a blanket. I tried to pray, but could not speak. I tried to say "Jesus" and could not. I was sure I was finally going crazy. I was sitting in the middle of the bed at 0400 shivering and needing help, but had no one to go to. Then a thought from out of nowhere broke through the fog: *You shall know the truth and the truth shall set you free.* Where did that come from?

At first light, I dressed, somehow got through PT, and then called the Army chaplain for an emergency meeting. It helped to verbalize what was happening. He concluded it was a reaction to combat that all soldiers go through. We discussed that for a while and scheduled another session a week later.

I got through the week by working twice as hard and long. Trying to read the Bible gave me a severe headache, so I put it in the drawer and the headache stopped. 1SGT Tolson sensed something was wrong and respectfully inquired, but I said I was just tired and disappointed Jenny wasn't going to be able to come to Hawaii for R&R. Our refrigerator had crashed and the money for the ticket went to buy a new refrigerator. With three small children, what other choice does a mother have?

The next and final session with the chaplain was helpful, but neither of us understood what was happening. I determined that Christianity was a farce after all and since I had been searching for almost five years for the truth, I was looking in the wrong places. So I bought a book called the *Five Ways of Ancient Wisdom* to search the ancient religions for the truth. I enjoyed the book, and it didn't give me a headache to read. But I slept very little and drove the troops and myself harder.

Those Far Away Places

A few days later, 1SGT Tolson handed me an envelope and said, "You have thirty minutes to pack for R&R. There is a chopper waiting to take you to the airport." I protested, "Top, I'm not going anywhere! There is too much work to do here."

His reply was, "Oh, yes, sir, you are going if I have to have you tied and carried to the plane! You need a break and so do we!"

Top was very persuasive. On the way to the airport, I opened the envelope to see where I was going. Bangkok, Thailand? I knew I was on the right track, for Bangkok was a center of Buddhism, and I would have the opportunity to investigate this ancient religion I had been reading about.

When we were airborne, I relaxed for the first time in weeks. Thailand! Ancient Siam! That sounded good, as if I had been there before. Then my mind drifted back to the West Virginia hills and an event that happened when I was nine or ten. Dad brought home a portable Zenith radio (I can still smell it) with a hard, stripped plastic housing with two lids that hinged: one for the battery, the other for the dials. We got to listen to very few programs because the battery was too expensive to replace very often. One of my favorite programs was the Hit Parade that came on once a week with all the most popular songs. My favorite song of all times was "Far Away Places": ". . . going to China or maybe Siam . . ."

Of all the places I had dreamed of going, Siam was the most exciting. The summer the song was featured, it was my "privilege" to hoe corn down at the Duffield place by the paved road. The rows of corn seemed a mile long, and it was really hot with no wind blowing. I would watch the cars go by—three or four a day—and dream of visiting Siam.

I checked into the hotel, then went to my room to unpack. Within minutes there was a knock on the door. I opened it and a scantily dressed, young female stepped through the door, informing me she was there for my massage. I told her, "Thanks, but I didn't order a massage," and held the door open for her to leave.

Bay of Siam

On R&R in Thailand, you hire a taxi driver for the entire period you are there. My driver was a bright young man in his twenties, and I was completely at ease with him from the very start. The first day we toured the Buddhist temples. Then I told my driver I wanted to go to the Bay of Siam and invited him to bring his family. He wanted to know which one, his city family or his country family. He took his city family. We had a great time even though I felt like I was in a dream. I swam in the Bay of Siam!

On the way back to the hotel, I told my driver I wanted to spend the rest of the time studying Buddhism. He was excited and told me his uncle was a Buddhist priest and would be glad to help me. The next day

I was invited to a meeting with five priests gathered in a big room in one of the temples. The only furnishings were little stools to sit on and some kind of urn in the middle of the room. I was invited to sit on one of the stools away from their circle and observe.

I listened for a while, hoping to experience some pleasant confirmation. I was confused, but I realized this was not the place the power came from to heal me. I went outside and taught little children how to count in English while I waited for my driver.

As we drove by one of the big Buddha statues, I asked the driver to stop. I got out, walked up to the Buddha statue, and shook my fist at him. I dared him to do something besides sit there with his arms folded. He didn't do anything, so I got back in the cab and went to the hotel frustrated.

Still No Answer

I had searched for five years for the source of power that had healed me in El Paso. Now I was confused. The ancient religions, although containing many good precepts, contained no keys to unlocking the mystery of the truth.

I lay on my bed staring at the ceiling, wondering what I should do with the remainder of my R&R. I remembered that in the brochures I received in the R&R package, there was an announcement for an English-speaking Protestant church in Bangkok. It was Wednesday and the announcement indicated they had a Wednesday night service.

My driver found the church, but declined my invitation to go with me. I remember two things about the sermon. First, the hell's-fire-and-brimstone speaker convinced me I should feel guilty about shopping for emeralds instead of giving the money to the ministry. Second, after several minutes of loud condemnation, I decided I couldn't handle it anymore. I was so angry I jumped up and was ready to shout, "You don't know what you are talking about! We know how bad we are. Tell us what to do about it!"

I guess my military discipline took over as I jumped up, so instead of making a fool of myself, I bolted out the door, got in the cab, and told my driver to get me back to the hotel as fast as possible. I will *never* say those words again to a taxi driver. What the preacher started, the driver finished. It scared the you-know-what out me. I went immediately to my room, slammed the door, grabbed a piece of hotel stationary, and began to write furiously, telling Jenny there was no answer, and I was abandoning the search.

Who's There?

The desk I wrote at was against the wall opposite the door to the balcony with the bed between the balcony and me. I sensed movement on the balcony, but dismissed the thought as I was engrossed in getting my anger and frustration down. However, the feeling that I was not alone persisted, so I stopped writing and turned toward the balcony. As I turned, I heard myself saying, "Jesus, is that you?" The response was the same voice that I "heard" with the same internal ears in the helicopter several months earlier: *Yes. And I will forgive you of every rebellion and cleanse you of every sin you will confess to me.*

I fell across the bed toward the Presence I could not see and began pouring out my frustration, fear, and rebellion. I did a complete emotional and mental data dump. As I was confessing my rebellion, I noticed what appeared to be a large, clear plastic pipe going from just below my chest over to where the feet would be if a person were standing there. The pipe was filled with a brownish goop that looked like the stuff we used to take out of the grease traps in the mess hall when we pulled KP.

I had no sense of time. Presently, the pipe was crystal clear, the Presence was gone, and I felt clean and complete for the first time in my life. There was a wonderful sensation of total love, and I knew I had been cleansed by the same power that had healed me five years earlier and now I knew his name—Jesus! The search was over; a new journey was beginning!

Knowing, Not Feeling

I would like to describe what I was experiencing in the afterglow of His visitation, but I cannot. It was not emotional. I was not weeping, yet I was experiencing something that must've been joy. It was not "feeling;" it was "knowing." I lay there on the bed recalling the events leading to this day: my childhood dream of going to Siam, the broken refrigerator, the Buddha experience, and God's work through 1SGT Tolson to bring me to this place at this time. A journey culminated in this moment of surrender to the Jesus who had been pursuing me all along. Soon I became aware that I was hungry, not for food, but for more knowledge about the person of Jesus.

The next day I checked out of the hotel to head back to duty in Vietnam. The clerk, a young girl about eighteen, said in her broken English, "You Christian, yes?" I said, "I am now!" I asked her how she knew. She said she had seen the woman leave my room immediately that first day and had noticed I had no massages during the week. I was being watched by eyes searching for something.

The hunger for the Bible lasted for several weeks, and I read in the Jeep, in the chopper, before sleep, and immediately upon waking. I just couldn't get enough. It was amazing! I had read these books before, but now they came alive. The words were full of meaning—and I had no headache! To my utter delight, I also discovered the thought I had at 0400 a few weeks earlier when my room chilled out was actually John 8:32: "You shall know the truth and the truth shall make you free." Some would call this a "mountaintop experience." But then, for every mountain there is a valley.

Falling Down the Mountain—Different Voices

There is a physical law of gravity that whatever goes up will also come down unless held up by a force greater than gravity. I believe there are similar laws in the spiritual realm, but I was not prepared for the rapid descent that occurred soon after I returned to Vietnam from Bangkok. I was visiting one of the remote sites and went to the field urinal upon arrival. The urinal was a large funnel-shaped structure draining into a tank.

As I stepped up on the platform, I glanced down at the funnel, and to my utter amazement, there was what I perceived to be the face of

Jesus in the funnel and a "voice" screaming at me, "Do it in His face, in His face! In His face!"

I jumped off the platform and stood there trembling. I walked around the compound in shock. One of our crew found me and asked, "Major, are you okay? You look like you've seen a ghost!"

I assured him I was okay.

We completed the inspection and ate lunch. Then I excused myself to try the urinal again. The same face, the same demanding voice. After several hours, the pain was so great I considered going to the dispensary for medical assistance. Not able to figure out what I would say to the medic, I made one more attempt at the urinal. I closed my eyes and said, "Jesus, I will not desecrate your face, but I physically cannot go on like this. Help me." When I opened my eyes, the face and the voice were both gone.

Never have I enjoyed a visit to the urinal more!

Valley of Shadows

I remember two things about the last week in Vietnam. First, the pre-monition that I would be killed returned with a loud voice. There was a superstition about the last week in Vietnam: you know you have been fortunate enough to dodge the bullet the entire tour, but now that you are almost home free, you become acutely aware of the irony of being killed on the last mission.

I had moved about for about ten months with no fear, but I have to confess that during the flight to one of the support bases that last week, I experienced some apprehension. We did come under heavy fire from a .50 caliber machine gun as our Huey lifted out of the fire support base. I immediately thought my time had finally come. I heard sounds like a beaver slapping the water with its tail on a quiet night. I asked the pilot what that noise was, and he said it was .50 caliber bullets going very close to the plane.

Suddenly, the Huey was on its side circling the enemy location, and I was hanging in midair, facedown, toward the flashing machine gun, restrained only by my shoulder harness. The door gunner's machine gun, mounted in the rear door of the chopper, was also facing the enemy position. With two bursts of rapid fire, the gunner raked the enemy position with uncanny accuracy and destroyed it. It was incredible!

We were so close, and looking straight down I could see the impact of the door gunner's bullets as he walked the rain of steel right through the enemy position. The skill and daring of those nineteen- or twenty-year-old chopper pilots and door-gunners were amazing. They were truly "Daring young men in those flying machines!" With our mission accomplished and a target of opportunity taken out, we resumed the climb out and headed back to Long Binh. That was my last chopper flight.

The second thing I remember about that last week was learning that the Lord is an exacting God. Ten months earlier I had asked Him to remove the sinus headaches so I could do my job in Vietnam. He did. However, the day I turned over my military duties to my replacement, I acquired a very intense sinus headache. God's sense of humor, I guess.

Change of Command

By late 1969 the war effort in Vietnam began to deescalate. The 8th TAB was being deactivated, and I was given the choice of moving to another unit or rotating back to the States. Measure the decision time in nanoseconds. The change of command was esoteric for me. At the ceremony, I was awarded a Bronze Star and two Air Medals for aerial flight while engaged in combat. 1SGT Tolson was also awarded a Bronze Star. The 8th TAB was awarded two unit citations for superior performance. My job in Vietnam was finished.

Going Home, Again

I had a strange feeling walking out to the plane for the return home. I had come here to die. Now I was walking to board a plane that would be airborne in an hour on the way to San Francisco. The headache was so severe I had trouble thinking. After we were airborne, I moved to a seat away from the emergency door so I would not succumb to the urge to jump out. The long flight home was excruciating. I tried unsuccessfully to sleep. I didn't want to talk to anyone and avoided every opportunity to enter into a conversation. I was totally confused. How could I have gone through such exhilarating experiences with absolutely no fear of dying during most of the tour and now feel like my very soul was being stripped out of my body?

I finally opened my briefcase to find something to read. On top was a book 1SGT Tolson had handed me as I departed the Orderly Room. He said it was strange because it was a single copy and the book shipment normally contained two copies of each book. He thought it was meant for me. I picked it up, glanced at the title, *The Power of Positive Thinking,* and laid it aside, making a mental note to check it out when positive thinking returned to me. Reading my Bible only made my headache worse, and I felt like my mind was about to be detached from my body. I said, *Come on, Major, get a grip on your thoughts!*

The book in my briefcase again came to mind, so I took it out and read a few pages. Dr. Norman Vincent Peale claimed reading the book and putting it into practice would change one's life. I definitely needed some changes in mine. As I read, a faint glimmer of some internal light flickered for a moment. Reading the book off and on during the remainder of the flight somehow made it less stressful.

Home, Alive!

I wasn't sure what my homecoming would be like, since our parting left our future uncertain. Jenny, who dislikes writing, had written just about every day the entire tour to support her warrior. We also exchanged voice tapes so the children could listen and talk to me. It may sound strange, but I don't remember where Jenny picked me up, what our first minutes together were like, or the trip to Ravenswood. The headache was so excruciating I suppose the recording device in my brain malfunctioned. Life was unreal, and I was having trouble connecting the dots.

My first memory is of walking into the apartment where Jenny and the children lived. I got a wonderful reception. Greg, who was eight, stood at a distance trying to connect the person that left a year ago with the person who had just walked in the door. Doug, now three, began turning cartwheels all around the room, first in one direction then the other. Debbie, now six, reacted as she always did when I had been away for a day, a week, or a month: as soon as she saw me, she ran as hard as she could, blonde curls bobbing wildly, and then jumped! I caught her and swung her around while she hung on for dear life. When we crashed on the floor, Greg and Doug piled on, and the four of us had a marvelous time in the middle of the floor. It felt good to be alive.

A New Beginning

After getting reacquainted, we drove to Wadestown to visit my parents. Their house was situated on one side of a creek with the road and parking space on the other, so we had to walk across a footbridge to get to them. They saw us drive up and Dad walked down the path to greet us. He was ahead of Mom and stuck out his hand to welcome me.

"Dad," I said. "I don't want to shake your hand."

He jerked back like I had slapped him.

I added, "I want to hug your neck!" and proceeded to put a big bear hug on him.

He began to weep, and we hugged each other for a long time, both weeping. That was the first time my dad had ever hugged me. I hoped it was the beginning of healing for our relationship.

Mom's lovely face was full of joy and relief and thanksgiving that God had answered her continual prayers for her son in harm's way. We hugged for a long time. It felt really good. I glanced past her as we turned to walk to the house. Miracle of miracles, some of the beautiful dahlias in Mom's flower garden were still spectacular. Some of them were more than six feet tall with giant blooms. Beautiful!

My brother John had come to welcome us home, and while Mom prepared her usual feast for Thanksgiving, John and I went hunting for deer and ruffed grouse. John took the 30-06, and I took my favorite Iver Johnson single-shot 12-gauge with number six shot for the grouse and rifled slugs for the deer. The first field was good for grouse, so I loaded a number six and stepped over a big log, expecting to hear a grouse explode. Instead, to my amazement, I saw a big eight-point buck looking at me about thirty yards away. I didn't breathe, and my heart was pounding like crazy. I slowly retrieved a slug from my hunting jacket, and then carefully thumbed the barrel release lever that clicked when it released the breach. That click startled the buck, and it took one giant leap and disappeared over the hill. I didn't want to kill it anyway.

About that time, the grouse that had been drumming exploded out of the top of the fallen tree. I reacted naturally and cut off a sapling with the rifled slug I had just loaded. Grouse have an uncanny ability to put a tree between them and the hunter. We didn't get either a grouse or a deer, but we worked up quite an appetite, and it was great to carry a loaded gun without worrying about what I would do with it.

I shared with Dad my experience in Bangkok and mentioned that I would like to be water baptized. He felt strongly that once was enough and the baptism at age twelve was adequate. I didn't push. Restlessness soon set in, so we loaded up and headed for our next assignment at Ft. Sill, Oklahoma.

Metamorphosis

Our arrival at Ft. Sill was in some ways a homecoming. Being in the Field Artillery, we had spent a lot of time at Sill and had many friends in Lawton. We found a little house to rent because we were going to save lots of money so I could go to seminary as soon as I was able to resign.

The restlessness I had felt earlier turned into my old enemy—fear—and before long, it took all the courage I could muster just to leave the house in the morning. Nights were riddled with nightmares. I didn't know about the post-Vietnam syndrome so I thought I was losing it. Although counseling had never done much for me, I sought help from the pastor of a church we had visited. He agreed to come to my house, and at one point during the evening we wound up on the floor trying to "pray though" the storm.

Jenny watched for a while, but then, observing the agony I sank deeper and deeper into, virtually yelled at the pastor, "Leave him alone! Can't you see you're only making it worse?"

Startled, he sat up, looked at me for a long time, and then said, "She's right! You don't need to be saved, you need to be baptized."

Our son Greg and I were baptized together the next week by the same church that had licensed me to preach. Strange, how things happen, but then I've never been very conventional.

Thought Conditioners

End of story, right? Wrong! There were a few good days after the baptism, but the very familiar fear returned. One night I was up pacing the floor and remembered the book I had started reading on the plane. I quickly found it and began reading. Dr. Peale outlined a process of recovery from fear and talked of forty Thought Conditioners he had compiled in a little book that would be an effective tool in that recovery. I ordered the booklet and made a commitment to myself and to God that I would practice the process for forty days. Then if I didn't get relief . . . Well, I'd cross that proverbial bridge when I came to it.

The little book arrived quickly, and this claim caught my attention: "Whatever the condition of your mind, the Thought Conditioners which I am going to suggest are so powerful that they will displace unhealthy thoughts."[1] Sounded as if Dr. Peale had me in mind. The Thought Conditioners were positive Scripture promises from the Bible with Dr. Peale's comments about how to use the promise. I began memorizing one Thought Conditioner each day, beginning at first awakening and practicing throughout the day. I went to a quiet place during lunch and repeated the verse over and over.

Several events took place during the next few days that began to set me free. The first was a recurring nightmare in which I was encased in a concrete body cast like a mummy. I couldn't move and the trapped feeling was unbearable. During one of those nightmares, while in the dream, I understood that the cast was actually what I had erroneously perceived as the call to preach. Still in the dream, I spoke the name "Jesus" and immediately the body cast began to crumble and fall away. What a release! I no longer felt bound by the guilt I had carried for years by not becoming a preacher. Another hurdle conquered. How many were still in front of me?

The Screaming Woman

On another sleepless night, I went to the living room to exercise, hoping that would help me relax. I was doing sit-ups and got the impression that something was going to jab me in the head as I leaned back. I also "heard" a woman screaming at me, "Oh my God, Oh my God! My baby, you killed my baby!" The words sounded vaguely familiar to me, so I lay there on the floor, trying to remember if or when I had killed a baby.

A sudden urge to call my sister Lorena sent me quickly to the phone, even though it was the middle of the night. She answered immediately and I explained to her what was going on. She began to cry. "Don't you remember? When you were four, you and a little friend were chasing each other around a telephone pole. He fell on a sharp stick that pierced the back of his head and he died. His mother was hysterical and yelled at you." At that point, I began to weep from somewhere deep inside me, keenly aware that in some way this incident played a key role in my quest to be set free.

Subsequently, with skepticism of the entire profession, but at the urging of the Post Chaplain, who thought someone who understood children would be wise, I sought the counsel of a child psychologist, who helped me walk through the memory. During the exercise, I "saw" a little boy standing by a telephone pole, trembling. The others had gone and left him alone. The counselor advised me to go over, pick up the small boy, and tell him it was not his fault and hold him until he quit trembling. The little boy turned out to be me and we wept together. The screaming woman did not visit me again.

Twenty-One Days

My commitment to focus intensely on Thought Conditioners for forty days was beginning to bear fruit. I selected a new one every morning and focused on it all day, following Dr. Peale's suggested process of internalization of the verse. One morning, instead of being afraid to step out the door, I found myself eager to go to work. I glanced at my Thought Conditioner booklet. I was beginning that morning with day twenty-two. It had been twenty-one days since I made the forty-day commitment. The power of God's Word was obviously penetrating the false storage in my subconscious. I drove to work that day buoyed by the knowledge that He was shedding light on my path up the mountain. He has vowed, "So shall My word be that goes forth from My mouth; It shall **not return to Me void**, But it shall accomplish what I please, and it shall prosper in the thing for which I sent it" (Isaiah 55:11, my bold). I was excited and motivated to put His Word to work in my life.

Mums

My experiences resembled an onion. As soon as one layer was peeled back, another layer was there to take its place. For years I realized certain flowers caused me to have various emotions. For instance, mums caused me to feel melancholy, as if something bad was about to happen.

One day I was in a store where dozens of mums were for sale. That night as I was relaxing after turning off the light, I smelled mums and the image of a car turned upside down with women screaming and weeping flashed across my mind.

I called Lorena and she again provided the missing piece to this puzzle. She said that when I was six or seven, I was playing with some friends and apparently had done something to displease Dad and Mom, for they came by in the car and told me to get in the car with them. She explained that someone stopped them and gave Mom the news that her younger sister, Madge, had been killed in a terrible car wreck. Lorena said they drove on down to the place where the wreck was. The car Madge was riding in crashed into the back of a big truck and turned upside down, and Madge was killed instantly, decapitated by the truck. That would explain the nightmares of a car turned upside down. Lorena also said there were lots of mums at the funeral.

The child psychologist again walked with me through the event, concluding I had somehow assumed the blame for Madge's death.

Although I still don't know the twisted avenue such blame could have taken to land on me, I know that working through the event eliminated the negative reaction to mums, and I no longer associated them with upside down cars.

CHAPTER 8

Purging Begins

Pauper

For some reason I grew up with the idea that wealth was evil and nice things were inherently bad. I could not explain why I did not deserve to succeed and, therefore, would be denied the finer things in life. But I believed poverty was the next thing to righteousness.

I was a major in the Army, drawing a decent salary, and thanks to Jenny's financial acumen while I was in Vietnam, we were completely debt free. The fact that we were renting in a neighborhood where the average rental cost was half my housing allowance was commensurate with my level of righteousness.

We moved in, and I reported for duty in my new assignment as Chief of the Radar Maintenance Instruction Branch at Fort Sill. The cadre was predominantly senior warrant officers. By late spring, the world was rosy. I was out of the woods emotionally, and we were saving lots of money. And, as the scales of guilt of having been the cause of death of my playmate and Aunt Madge began to fall away, I began to sense that God was preparing me for a lesson about being grateful for the provisions He had planned for us. The more I considered the idea, the more I became convinced the Lord had another house planned for us. So, on Friday night before Easter 1970, I suggested to Jenny that we go house hunting the very next morning. Jenny loves to look at houses, so we called a real estate agent.

What Day Is It?

We met the agent early the next morning and looked all day without finding a house we liked. An ice storm, very common at that time of year in Lawton, was on the way, and we went back to our rented house to brace for the storm and plan another house search.

The agent sat on the couch looking through his listings, stopped at one house, and asked, "What day is today?" I looked at the calendar and gave him the date. He slammed the book shut, shouted, "Come on!" and headed for the door. We jumped in his car, drove to a nice subdivision, and stopped in front of a nice brick house with a For Sale sign in the yard.

As we stepped through the door, Jenny stopped and caught her breath: a beautiful sunken living room with a fireplace! She turned left to see a spacious kitchen. She was getting really excited.

"If it has a big master bedroom with separate bath and double closets, this is it!" she said.

Guess what!

We beat the ice storm back to the rental house, the agent called and made an offer, and we were the proud owners of our dream house with less than five hundred dollars down. The reason the date was critical was because the house had not been built to Veterans Administration (VA) specifications. In order to obtain a VA loan, the house had to be at least one year old. This house was one year old that day. God's provision and perfect timing astounded me. This was to be one of many lessons regarding His concept of an abundant life.

The Warfare at Home

We were excited about living in the new house, but there were still serious challenges in the relationship between Jenny and me. Even though we had been in and out of counseling for several years, victory always eluded us. I was an ideal husband while I was away from home, making frequent commitments to be a better mate only to walk through the door and get angry at some small infraction. Pouting was a plague to me. I would get miffed at Jenny and stay that way for days. I wanted to change, yet seemed powerless to break the pattern. I read books, attended seminars, and sought the help of counselors, all providing only temporary relief. I could not understand this totally inconsistent life.

To the world outside our home, I was a respected leader; at home I unleashed fits of anger at Jenny and the children, especially the boys.

Although guilt consumed me afterward, I returned to this behavior time and time again. My relationship with Debbie was more congenial and for reasons I can't explain, she escaped the rage I inflicted on the boys. But she had a ringside seat to most of my tirades, vicariously absorbing some of the abuse. Jenny was also responding negatively to the tension between us. She became impatient with the kids, lashing out at them when what she really wanted to do was lash out at me. The kids were caught in the middle, and it seemed there was no relief in sight.

The Upper Room

As inconsistent as it sounds, quiet time with the forty Thought Conditioners was a special time, and my day was not complete until I had shared Jesus with someone. I was always on the alert for such an opportunity. My job required me to coordinate staff papers with various offices at Ft. Sill. One particular staff action required me to hand-carry a staff action to four agencies. As I got in my car, I sensed the Lord say, "I want you to be very attentive today." I assumed I would be sharing my faith with someone during the day. However, the opposite turned out to be the case.

The first three people I visited invited me to the same church service the following Sunday afternoon. I thought they were a little too demonstrative for my conservative lifestyle, so I figured the meeting was a "holy roller" affair and didn't take the invitations too seriously.

The final coordination stop was at the post commander's office. There, the fourth person to invite me was the general's aide! He was a professional artillery officer, so I told him I would go if he would come pick me up. I was hoping he would decline.

"I'll be there Sunday afternoon at 1400," he said.

Maybe he won't show, I thought.

The meeting was in the country in a large upper room over someone's garage. I was greeted with a big bear hug from one of the women who invited me. She was glad I decided to come. She started dragging me to the center of the group, but I told her I was there only to observe. I didn't want anyone laying their hands on me! I pulled a chair to the back of the room, out of reach of everyone, and sat down to watch and criticize these emotional zealots.

Who, Me?

The leader of the group was a pastor from Texas who had been excommunicated from his denomination because he began to teach that fasting and the gifts of the Spirit were valid today. The service was very orderly, with the most beautiful singing I had ever heard. I would say it sounded angelic. Then various people began to share what they had learned during the past week. I was amazed at the connectivity of the various testimonies, as if orchestrated from a common source. The leader called for a time of quietly waiting before the Lord to see if He had a word for the group. After a time, the leader broke silence. "There is a man here in need of deliverance," he said. "If that man will come forward, the Lord will set him free."

I felt like a hot poker had hit me in my chest! I was the man, but I wasn't about to make a fool of myself in front of all those people! Some of them were soldiers who could possibly be under my authority at Fort Sill. No way! No one else spoke up, so after what seemed to be an eternity, the leader said something about the man having another opportunity later and moved on to the next activity. I don't remember much about the remainder of the service except that it could have been taken directly out of Paul's instruction in the New Testament.

I hung around after the service until I thought everyone had gone, and then I went to the leader and said, "I think I am the man."

He said, "I thought you were the one and waited for you to identify yourself, but I chose not to point you out."

Some of the others saw me talking to the leader and joined in our conversation. I was really apprehensive. The leader was gentle and understanding. He explained the nature of deliverance. The first step was to ask the Lord to identify any unclean spirits. He would be praying "in the Spirit," and I may not understand the words.

I wanted to know if this radical and untraditional style of ministry was true or of the devil as I had been taught. Silently I asked the Lord to give me the name of the spirit he was giving to the leader, if there was such a thing. The words "self-pity" came immediately to mind and I knew that was my validation word.

The leader did pray in a language I did not understand and after a few minutes he spoke to me. "Richard, the name of the first unclean spirit the Lord has identified is Self-Pity."

Okay, same name. I agreed to proceed. The leader said he would speak directly to the spirit and demand it to leave in the name of Jesus. He said I may feel like sneezing or coughing and should do it to release the spirit. When he ordered Self-Pity to depart, I began to whimper like a puppy being whipped, and I felt so sorry for myself. Again, the leader ordered the spirit to leave in the name of Jesus. This time I had a sudden sensation of riding a roller coaster and I felt something leave my body from the area of my solar plexus. I stopped whimpering immediately.

The leader identified two other spirits associated with the spirit of self-pity, a family of three. These were all removed, and the Lord said that was all for the day. I walked away from the session free of a heavy load and a good feeling of being in control of my emotions for the first time in months.

There were times I did regress and succumb to pouting, but the times were much shorter and less severe. The leader advised me to focus on a Scripture verse if it happened, and I did. The greatest help of all was the strength that was building as a result of internalizing the Thought Conditioners. Although I was making progress in my own spiritual walk, the relationship between Jenny and me still needed work. We would experience more conflict and travel a lot of rocky roads before we found our common ground, but there was improvement.

Jenny struggled with what I was going through with the deliverance. Her family background was rooted in a church that was adamantly opposed to the spiritual, or charismatic, work of the Holy Spirit. To add to the confusion, the denomination we then belonged to believed evil spirits could not dwell in the body of a Christian, so I was not able to discuss these things with the pastor or other members of the church. We did not understand what was going on and the process frightened her at times, but I was committed to being set free.

There were signs of progress from time to time. One of those occasions happened on a day I was alone in my office at noon practicing the Thought Conditioners. As I meditated on the Scripture for that day, dealing with peace promised by Christ recorded in John 14:27—"Peace I leave with you; My peace I give to you"—I felt totally at peace, similar to the events in Bangkok and El Paso. It was a wonderful experience! I remember thinking, *This peace is so powerful there must be a way for me to share this with other people.* I thought specifically about pastors who have so many challenges and so little time for themselves.

Over the next few weeks, I became intrigued with the possibility of a retreat center where pastors and others could go for true recreation. During this period, Jenny decided to seek help from a Christian counselor in Ponca City. We made the hour-and-a-half trip from Oklahoma City, where we lived, once a week, and while she was having the session, rather than sit in the waiting room with nothing to do, I located a local pastor and made an appointment to see him. When I shared the dream of a retreat center with him, he gave me a book that described precisely what I had been formulating in my own mind. Now I had a tool to help me plan my strategy. Jenny was not thrilled with the idea, but in those days, I believed I was to make the major decisions, so I began to look for land on which to build a retreat center. As I look back, I am amazed at the paradox of growth in some areas and abject failure in others.

Break's Over

There were two other deliverance sessions. Another family of three demons, all of which were associated with personality disorders, was identified and removed during the second session. Regretfully, I have lost the record of that session and the names of the unclean spirits.

The final deliverance session with the group in Lawton took place a few days later. The third family of demons was identified. It was a violent family. The strong man in that family was named Hate. The leader of the team warned me that I might have a severe reaction during this session. A wet towel was provided in the event I vomited. I became ill immediately when the team rebuked the Hate spirit and ordered it to leave. It resisted, and I remember being torn between releasing the spirit and retaining it. Eventually I became strongly compelled to speak to the spirit of Hate and said, "I no longer desire for you to stay and I order you to leave."

Immediately I began to wretch with the dry heaves. It was ugly. Finally, I vomited, and the spirit was gone.

The deliverance leader said he had seen this same reaction before, and it was always associated with a violent spirit. He believed that what I vomited up was the "nest" for the spirit of Hate. The other two spirits in this family were Destruction and Violence. They departed without argument.

In a subsequent session with the child psychologist, we traced the origin of this family of demons to the time when Dad had whipped me because I had not brought the milk buckets that were filled with black-berries. This incident was also connected to the night Dad was preach-ing and dragged me by my ear to the front of the church and made me sit there while he finished the sermon.

The psychologist concluded the combination of the guilt of think-ing I had killed my little friend and my aunt and now wanting my dad to die had created the emotional environment for the entry of the demonic spirits. And I found out they don't give up easy. There were days I was on an emotional roller coaster.

Jenny and I again tried marriage counselors, none of which pro-vided any help. One of the counselors informed me I was not "man enough for Jenny." That was a low blow that ricocheted around in my ego center for many years. The problem was he did not explain what he meant, and I didn't go back to find out. It is nothing short of miraculous that we stayed together during those days.

The church didn't help much either. I began to spend lots of time doing church activities and spent every Saturday evening with the pas-tor praying for the services on Sunday. We had three very active and energetic kids by this time, all less than ten years of age, and on weekends I routinely made myself available to help out at home; one, to give Jenny a break and, two, to reconnect and enjoy time with the kids. Jenny approached me about being gone every Saturday night and, in her mind anyway, neglecting time with the family. I explained my dilemma to the pastor and informed him I would be spending more time at home, especially on Saturday night. The next Sunday he took aim at Jenny from the pulpit for taking me away from spiritual activities. Of course, this didn't help our already strained relationship at all.

Strange Friends and an Infinite-Dimensional God

In 1971 the Army gave me one year, including a summer term, to complete a master's degree in the field of my choice. Once again, we were on the move, this time to Stillwater, Oklahoma, where I would be attending Oklahoma State University (OSU), seeking a master's degree in water quality management. I made this choice of study based on memories of my teenage years.

In the 1950s, my friend Don and I waded the beautiful West Virginia streams days at a time with split bamboo fly rods. Those streams flowed clean and clear, chattered in the riffles, sparkled in the sun, and teemed with small-mouth bass. But the last time I was home I visited my favorite stream and it was so polluted the bass population was near zero. My goal was to find out the causes and remediation of the pollution to help restore those once-healthy waters. OSU had a reputation for leading the charge in environmental engineering, and I was very grateful and excited when I learned I had been approved to pursue a master's in bioenvironmental engineering.

For the summer term, my advisor enrolled me in linear algebra and computer programming. It had been seven years since I had studied math, and the summer pace left me stranded in the maze of linear algebra. I was fine until we got into "n" dimensional space, meaning it could be any number of dimensions. I could visualize three-dimensional space, but beyond that? Nothing! Consequently, my mental gyroscope went into gimbal-lock and I froze up cognitively.

One afternoon I was lying on my bed, staring at the ceiling (I do this a lot) and thinking about what the Army would do to me if I flunked out. I said, "Lord, surely you didn't send me here to flunk out, but I don't understand this stuff they call linear algebra and 'n' dimensional space!"

There was no audible voice, but I heard, *Richard, you are here to learn, not flunk. You are limited to three-dimensional space, but I operate in infinite dimensional space, and all the mathematical laws function in any of those dimensions.* Amazing! That broke the mental logjam, and I thoroughly enjoyed the remainder of the course and made an easy B.

Jim Day

The first day of the fall semester, I began an organic chemistry class, and the professor divided us into lab groups. I felt an immediate dislike for one of the students in my group, and when the professor wasn't looking, I moved to the next group. To verify the even distribution of students, the professor counted again. "Okay, who moved? Miller, you are in this other group. Move back over there."

After the class, I walked back to my graduate cubbyhole. The student I was trying to avoid followed me. He accosted me with, "I'm Jim Day, and I was wondering if you can help me."

I asked, "What kind of help?"

Jim explained that since I was older, he felt I might be able to help him work through a personal problem. Personal problem? Me? Help? I invited him to have a seat in my cubbyhole.

Jim explained his problem. Then, he asked, "Can you help me?"

"Jim, I may not be much help," I said. "But I know the Person who can help you."

He wondered who that would be, and I introduced him to Jesus.

Jim and I became study partners and lifelong best friends. We often spent more time studying the Bible than we did studying organic chemistry, yet we both made good grades. To my amazement, I made As in every course except one. What a difference it made to be free of the guilt of not being a preacher and to be doing what I believed God had planned for me! It was a good year for all of my family.

At Thanksgiving, we invited Dan, a student who was not going home for the holidays, to spend Thanksgiving with us. Dan and our children became best buddies, and we saw a lot of him during the year. Jenny's home cooking added to the frequency of visits.

The God of Small Things

The year at OSU was one of the best of our military career. Life was slow paced, and God provided us an ideal house within walking distance of campus and the children's school. We looked at this house first, decided it was too expensive, and almost rented a cheaper, less desirable house. However, Jenny became very uncomfortable every time we visited the cheaper house, so we finally got the message and moved into the one He provided for us.

We made a monthly trip to Tinker Air Force Base (AFB) near Oklahoma City for groceries and supplies. On one trip to the Base Exchange, I was buying school supplies and thought I would get a packet of pencil lead just in case. The cost was fifteen cents. When I checked out, the lead was missing, so I got out of line and went back for another, assuming I had dropped it somewhere. After waiting in line again to check out, the lead was again missing from the cart.

The lead was not an immediate necessity, so we loaded up and headed back to OSU with Jenny driving. I often used her driving time to clean out the glove compartment. When I opened the door, lo and behold! There was a brand new box of lead I had bought on a previous trip! God takes care of sparrows and pencil lead.

Student Optimism Versus Experience

Since I was studying engineering, I decided to attend a Student Council on Pollution and the Environment (SCOPE) meeting and was elected president. Theta Pond was on my way to class and I noticed it bubbled on warm days and burped unfriendly odors. At the next SCOPE meeting, I presented the challenge to the group, and we all agreed to pitch in and clean it up. A committee of three students volunteered to organize the project and reported back to us at the next meeting. The plan included a student bucket brigade to get the bad stuff out of the pond. The committee members were sure they could enlist several hundred students and were adamant about the validity of their plan. We approved their plan and set a date.

The next day I made two phone calls. The first was to the local Army reserve unit that just happened to be an engineer company with dump trucks and dredging equipment.

"Captain, would you be interested in a community action project?" I asked.

He heartily said, "Yes," and we agreed on a backup plan just in case the student brigade turned out to be less than expected. The other call was to the new pastor of the church we attended. He had just purchased a house on a one-acre lot with soil so hard, grass would not grow. He was delighted at the offer for several loads of topsoil.

On the day set for the cleanup, two students and one dump truck showed up. The two students jumped into the murky sludge with buckets and stirred up the methane gas. One of the students was immediately sickened by the fumes. I called a halt to the efforts of the now one-person brigade and made the prearranged phone call to the engineer company. The captain had six dump trucks and the dredging equipment on site within the hour. We deposited over a hundred truckloads of very wet and aromatic organic matter, mostly leaves that had been decaying for many years, onto our pastor's yard.

Little did we know the pastor's neighbor had an outdoor wedding party planned that evening and the wind was blowing directly out of the south toward the neighbor's yard! The mother of the bride was very disturbed, to say the least. The pastor and I stood in the muck and explained our dilemma to our God of Small Things. Sure enough, within the hour the wind shifted to the north, and the wedding party had a delightful evening.

I visited the pastor a year later. "How's your lawn doing?" I asked. He laughed and responded, "That grass grows so fast, by the time I get it mowed in the back, the grass in front where I started needs to be mowed again!"

The Good, the Bad, and the Weird

My utilization tour for the master's degree was to Reserve Officer Training Corp (ROTC) duty at Panhandle State University in Goodwell, Oklahoma. Goodwell was a small prairie town of three hundred wonderful people. The closest house with a basement, an absolute requirement for Jenny because of tornadoes, was in Guymon, eleven miles away. We made a ridiculous offer that was accepted, mostly I think, because of the history and condition of the house. A young man known to use drugs and involved in an occult group had occupied the house. His room was painted psychedelic colors that we were never able to cover. That was Debbie's room initially, but she began to have nightmares, so we moved her upstairs and left the room unoccupied. We hauled truckloads of junk out of the garage and animal remains out of the attic. With some renovation, new carpet, and spiritual cleansing, the house became a comfortable home and profitable investment.

Because of my previous experience with flying, I inherited the ROTC flight program. My first challenge was to conquer my fear of flying and the compulsion to fly the plane into the ground. So I gritted my teeth and signed up for a commercial license program. My first solo was excruciating. My mind and emotions went wild. By the time I completed the flight, my flight suit was soaked with perspiration. But the way God put me together, I refused to live with this fear, so the next day I got back in the plane with my copy of *Thought Conditioners* and put the plane through power-on stalls and spins. In these maneuvers, the plane falls suddenly, and I hated the feeling. The next flight, I took a tape recorder and taped my reactions as I flew. That was very helpful, like running an experiment.

My confidence slowly returned and the compulsion to dive into the ground subsided, so I began taking our sons, Greg and Doug, on an occasional flight with me. I taught them to fly using the instruments because they were too short to see over the instrument panel. That proved to be a very timely activity. One of our friends needed a ride to Missouri and I needed to log some cross-country time, so I decided to fly him there with Greg as my copilot. The flight east was uneventful and dinner with my friend's family was enjoyable.

At dusk, Greg and I headed back west for what was predicted to be a quiet evening in the air under visual flight rules. However, Oklahoma weather is unpredictable, and about thirty minutes along the route, fog obscured the ground, and a layer of clouds obscured the horizon so I had no visual reference.

This is not good, I thought.

I was not instrument qualified and FAA regulations mandate a return to visual reference flying in such cases, so I began to set the navigation radios for a 180-degree turn. However, I noticed the needles on both radios began to fluctuate, making it impossible to know our actual direction of flight. I told Greg he was now the pilot.

"Just keep the artificial horizon level exactly as we have practiced," I said.

With Greg flying, I began to troubleshoot the radios and look for a probable course that would get us out of the haze.

Several minutes went by before one of the radios settled down, and I started the 180-degree turn. Just then lights appeared in the distance, and we again had visual reference. I was able to identify our location and discovered the wind had blown us about twenty miles off course, but Greg had kept the plane perfectly level. When I explained to him how important his excellent control was to our flight, he was very pleased that he had contributed to our safety. We completed the flight by dead reckoning, an easy task in the Oklahoma night because of the distinct identity of the small towns. The mechanic checked the navigation radios the next day and both operated perfectly. Really?

Turbulence!

Dr. Palmer, the president of Panhandle State University at that time, was a true patriot. When most universities were caving in to the anti-war and anti-military clamoring in the '70s and closing ROTC detachments,

Dr. Palmer stood against the tide and kept the ROTC program as originally mandated. To express our gratitude for his unflinching support of the ROTC program, I was available to fly Dr. Palmer anywhere it was appropriate to fly in a private plane.

On one of the trips to Stillwater, we were delayed on takeoff for the return flight by a fast moving thunderstorm. While Dr. Palmer rested in the lounge, I watched the storm. An Air Force reserve pilot who had just flown in through the storm informed me, "It is clear behind the storm all the way to the Rockies. As soon as you see the first star, you are good to go."

It was a beautiful night behind the storm, and the ride was unusually smooth for Oklahoma. Dr. Palmer released his shoulder harness and seatbelt and went to sleep.

Suddenly, out of what seemed like a cloudless sky, a flash of lightning started in the Texas panhandle and traveled horizontally in front of us for several miles along what appeared to be a narrow strip of clouds. There were no reports of turbulence, so I continued on course. As we approached the thin wisp of cloud, I noticed two wisps separated by several hundred feet vertically. Our approved altitude took us between the two wisps, and I suspected nothing as I entered the space between them.

Bad idea. The plane began to bounce so violently I could not control it! Dr. Palmer was thrown alternately against the ceiling and then down on the floor between the seat and the control panel. I attempted to reach the throttle to slow the plane down, but my right arm was flapping about like a sock in the wind! I felt certain the wings would be ripped off by the next violent bounce! In desperation, I yelled, "Lord, I can't control it! It is in your hands!"

I let go of the wheel and took my feet off the rudder pedals. Just as suddenly as it had started, it stopped. To my amazement, we were flying straight and level, and the plane responded to all the controls.

I helped Dr. Palmer back into his seat. He buckled up without a word and sat in silence the remainder of the flight. We landed without a hitch and taxied to the parking ramp. I offered to drive Dr. Palmer home, but he silently declined with a nod. I wondered if he would ever fly again. The next morning I went to his office and asked to be notified the minute he came in. As soon as the call came, I went to visit him. "How are you feeling, sir? I suppose you are through with flying for a while," I began.

"Oh, no. I've recovered just fine," he responded. And so it was. He was ready to go the next month and always wore his seatbelt very snug.

The Eye of the Storm

That was not to be the last violent storm I would experience while stationed at Panhandle State. Our detachment vehicles belonged to Ft. Sill, Oklahoma, and we took turns driving them there periodically for maintenance. In the spring, it was my turn to make the trip, so I loaded the station wagon and headed out on my own. On the return trip, a huge thunderstorm began to build in the Texas panhandle. I drove directly west toward the storm and watched the wall cloud build. I counted thirteen funnels that dipped from the wall cloud. Most of them spun out before reaching the ground, but the weather station was warning everyone to seek shelter. I stopped at a service station to inquire about the status of the storm. The TV station was tracking the storm and reporting that funnels were being spotted.

At that stage in my spiritual journey, the Lord was teaching me to trust Him and I sensed Jesus asking me, *Do you trust me to take you through the storm?*

Reluctantly, I said, "Yes."

The man at the station thought I was crazy, but with an elevated heart rate, I got in the station wagon and headed north. The storm got closer and blacker. As I drove into the storm, the wind was so strong I could hardly control the station wagon and the rain was so heavy I could barely see the road. I kept slowing down and was just crawling along, repeating, "Fear not, for I have redeemed you, I have called you by your name, you are mine" (Isaiah 43:1).

When I could no longer see the road or control the vehicle, I let go of the wheel, raised my hands in the air, and, just as in the plane earlier, shouted, "Lord, I can't control it! You've got it!"

A second later, I broke out of the storm and it was crystal clear with the terrain washed clean by the rain. A fresh and clean aroma filled the air. I can say at that moment I was filled with an inexpressible joy and heard myself praising God with words my mind did not know. I was at the crest of a rise, so I parked, climbed on a rock, and sat there for several minutes, inhaling the clean air and the beauty of the moment with a profound appreciation for being very much alive.

CHAPTER 9

Spiritual Warfare

A Goat on Sheep Mountain

Our family went on vacation during the summer of 1972 to Spring Canyon, Colorado, a retreat center nestled among the pine and aspen groves in the shadow of Sheep Mountain. The approach to Spring Canyon from Buena Vista parallels a sparkling mountain stream that cascades over spherical boulders worn smooth by the advancing glacier of a prehistoric ice age. In late September quaking aspen dressed in the most exquisite golden-orange autumn hues greet visitors.

Spring Canyon is more than a place. It is a beginning. It's at 9,000-feet elevation with two trout ponds fed by ice-cold spring water that is among the purest water found on planet Earth. Greg and Doug loved the excitement of pulling a fighting rainbow trout from the ice-cold water and delivering it to the kitchen, where it was transformed into delicious dinner fare. Debbie didn't care for the trout fishing but was so impressed with her first visit that years later she chose Spring Canyon as the place to begin her life with Tod, her mountain man from Montana.

Everyone helps with the chores at Spring Canyon. One evening after dinner I found myself doing dishes with Paul Pettijohn, the Executive Director of Officer's Christian Fellowship (OCF), who was also one of the speakers for the week (talk about double duty!). During the course of the conversation, we learned that both of our anniversaries were that day, and Paul suggested, "Let's get our brides and go celebrate!" So after washing the dishes and cleaning up the kitchen, the four of us went into Buena Vista looking for a memorable moment to top off our anniversaries. The only thing open in the small town was an ice cream parlor, so we celebrated with milkshakes and ice cream cones. That was the beginning of a strong, lasting friendship. I consider the Pettijohns among my closest friends, with Paul as my mentor.

That vacation was also the beginning of a relationship with Tok, a native-born Greek, small in stature, but a giant spiritually. Tok was also a guest speaker for the week and later played a key role in the life of our son Greg. While enjoying Tok's excellent teaching, I began to compare my life with Tok's, painfully aware of the joy radiating from every pore of this little giant's body. The stark differences took root, and I became frustrated and irritated at my own lack of spiritual maturity. One afternoon, I felt such internal turmoil I had to get out of camp and away from all those happy people!

Walking outside the retreat center, lost in the misery of self-condemnation, I turned my head upward and realized I was standing at the bottom of a steep, rocky crag known as Sheep Mountain, the backdrop for Spring Canyon. The barren, rocky precipice protrudes from the pine forest with only an occasional tenacious, stunted pine clinging by its roots anchored in a crevice of the stone face. The mountain is well named, for only mountain sheep are equipped with hooves and are agile enough to safely navigate its precipitous slopes.

I stood transfixed, gazing up at the ominous peak penetrating into an infinite blue sky. I was not a mountain climber, but the agonizing turmoil in my soul overrode any caution. An irresistible voice was calling to me, *Come on up!*

As I began the climb, my fear of dying from a heart attack as punishment from God resurfaced, and it occurred to me that what I was going to do might cause the dreaded heart attack. But that day I didn't care. The first part of the climb through the pungent, aromatic pines was tolerable. Then the boulders and loose rocks from the cliffs above made climbing treacherous and agonizing. I lived at 1,200-feet elevation; this climb began at 9,000 feet.

Soon my chest was pounding, I was dizzy from lack of oxygen, and my hands and legs were bruised and bleeding from frequent falls on the sharp rocks and sliding backwards through the loose shale. Yet I had no choice. I kept climbing straight up as if daring my pounding, aching heart to burst!

Now I was looking straight up at a sheer, insurmountable rock wall. I had no strength left, and I collapsed against the wall, slid down the first smooth rock surface, grabbed the stunted pine anchored in the rock to slow my rapid descent, and crashed against a boulder, facing down the mountain. Dazed, I looked down the mountain, then up at the sheer stone face above me. I exclaimed to the world below, "I only made it halfway and that's exactly how I feel! I feel like I'm halfway from Hell!"

I lay there gasping for breath from the thin air and wondering when my head would stop spinning. The pain in my bruised hands and legs brought me to reality, and I realized the pounding in my chest was becoming less violent. It appeared my ear drums were not going to explode after all. Using the tenacious pine, I pulled myself out of the crumpled position, braced my feet against the boulder, and lay back against the stone face of the mountain. I stared into the sky and watched a lone white cloud emerge from behind the peak and drift peacefully eastward. I inhaled deeply and exhaled slowly, releasing the tension in my soul to drift away with the cloud.

> *I also spoke to the cloud: "That actually felt good to say and not be afraid of retribution from God. Yet I have a vague premonition that the exclamation, 'I feel like I am halfway from Hell' has more significance than just a spontaneous interjection."*
>
> *The voice was not audible, yet I knew I was being given a mission. You are to keep a record of your journey and then publish the record.*
>
> *I have been back to Sheep Mountain many times, and each time amazed at how much I am like the mountain—neither of us has changed very much. I have kept a journal for forty years and am chagrined that recent entries are so much like those at the beginning. However, there is one significant difference: I finally stopped cringing from the assault of an unknown assailant and launched a journey of discovery realizing that I, the Prodigal,*

may travel a trail similar to John Bunyan's Pilgrim that may lead through leach-infested swamps and exposed to the scorching heat of the desert.

Introduction to Evil

It wasn't long before the first challenge presented itself. I had just returned to duty after the Spring Canyon vacation when one of the administrative assistants at Panhandle State came to my office and told me the Lord had told her to come see me about her son, Bill. Like many other young people in that area, he was involved with a gang that did drugs, drank beer to excess, and operated on the fringes of the local culture.

I made an appointment to visit Bill in his home. I asked him if he was aware of Satan and some of the practices going on around the area. He replied, "Sure, I know Satan. I made a deal with him, and now I have evil spirits living in me. Sometimes they tell me what to do that I don't remember doing—like robbing the post office."

Needless to say, Bill's parents were stunned. I asked Bill if he wanted to be free and he said he definitely was ready. I contacted a minister from Texas who was involved in a deliverance ministry, and he agreed to come and help. We gave Bill several Scriptures to memorize and meditate upon and all of us agreed to fast without food or water for three days before the set deliverance day.

That day came and the three of us went to a trailer adjacent to Bill's house. The first spirit identified was the spirit of infirmity. When the minister directed the spirit to leave, it refused and said in a high-pitched voice, "No, I will not leave! This is my home since four!"

Quite a struggle followed with Bill being mildly violent. Finally, the pastor said, "Richard, you speak to the demon." This was new to me, but I spoke to the spirit by name with bold authority, "Spirit of Infirmity, we have been fasting and praying as a testimony against you and according to the words of Jesus, you have to leave."

Bill gasped and coughed. I looked up and saw a flash of blue light disappear through the roof of the trailer. Bill collapsed on the sofa, exhausted. There were other spirits that left without argument.

When we went back to the house, Bill's mother was amazed at the rosy color of Bill's face and confirmed that when he was four years old he got sick, and the doctor could find no cause for the illness. She said he had been pale since then. We warned Bill of the danger of returning to drugs or association with the occult gang. He assured us he was going to church and joining with the young people there.

He remained true to his word and his life improved drastically. He became involved in a Bible study at the church and avoided the old gang completely. That is until he shared his experience with the class and one of the church leaders accused him of heresy and asked him not to come to the group again. Bill was devastated and embarrassed. He went for a drive and ran into one of his old buddies. They went to a beer party, and before any of us knew what was happening, Bill wound up in jail in worse condition than before. We were unable to help him and the last I heard he was still in jail.

I am not excusing Bill for what happened. He obviously was not strong enough in his new position to handle that first temptation. I also accept part of the blame for not mentoring Bill closely until he was stronger. But neither do I excuse the church leader who did not recognize the delicate tightrope this young man was walking. Instead of searching for biblical truth or seizing the opportunity to be used of the Lord to help Bill get back on his feet again, he reacted according to denominational doctrine.

One of the stories Bill related to me was about his involvement in the occult group that communicated with and received special powers from Satan. The leader of the group could levitate and travel outside his body. For instance, a poker game was cooking over in Guymon. The leader, Buck, told the group to go ahead, he would see them later. Bill claimed that Buck did not show up as promised, yet the next day he claimed he was there and told them who had won every hand, how much each player won or lost, the time he was there, and the door he entered through. Bill said he believed Buck because he was correct about every detail and, during the game, the back door of the house opened and closed. One of the players got up to see who came in, but found no one. The times matched as stated by Buck.

Bill also claimed the stretch of road from Guymon to Goodwell was called The Devil's Highway by many people living in that area. Superstition? Maybe. But there had been students killed along that stretch in auto accidents. One day I was driving to Goodwell along that stretch, minding my own business, rehearsing a speech I was to give that afternoon. With the stealth of a summer breeze, a thought drifted into my consciousness: *If you will follow me I will make you a great orator.* It was different from the vicious, demanding voice I had heard in Vietnam, but I perceived it was from an unhealthy source and rejected the offer. In retrospect, as I have learned more about the characteristics of evil, I suspect it was an offer from Satan or one of his minions whose area of operation was along The Devil's Highway.

Thus Saith the Lord

There was another group of young people in the Guymon area that were labeled zealots by the mainline church community. These folks invited me to meet with them for Bible study and worship, which I did for a while as part of my quest for the truth. From this group I gained insight into the motivation of martyrs in the early church and around the world presently. These people were courteous to others, yet very bold. If there was an issue they believed to be against the will of God, they would fast and pray until it was resolved or confronted.

For instance, the church we attended traditionally paid tribute to mothers on Mother's Day. They had flowers for the oldest, the youngest, the one with the most children, the one with the most grandchildren, and so on. I personally found no fault with the practice, but some in the zealot group believed it detracted from the real purpose of worship.

I didn't meet with the group for a couple of weeks before Mother's Day, so I was just as surprised as everyone else when one of the group walked into the front of the church during the tribute and proclaimed, "Thus saith the Lord: You are profaning my Holy Day with your traditions!" He itemized the traditions and challenged the church to repent. The man was gaunt and pale.

It took about five minutes for people to recover from the shock before two of the larger deacons picked the young man up and carried him to the sidewalk. I was really curious about his motivation, so I went out to confront him with the test of the spirits offered in 1 John 4:1–2: "Beloved, do not believe every spirit, but test the spirits, whether they are of God. . . . By this you know the Spirit of God: Every spirit that confesses that Jesus Christ has come in the flesh is of God . . . "

He told me he believed the Spirit told him to do this, but he initially passed it off as his own thoughts. When he received no peace about it, he committed to fasting to know the truth. Therefore he fasted for seven days and was thoroughly convinced the Spirit was telling him to confront the church. He professed that Jesus was the Christ, came in the flesh, was crucified, buried, and rose again the third day.

I was baffled by the whole incident, convicted by his boldness, yet questioning the appropriateness of such an encounter. I came to realize I had only scratched the surface in my quest for truth and began to be frustrated at my lack of growth and understanding.

Fort Riley, Kansas

Summer camp for Third ROTC Region cadets was conducted at Ft. Riley, and I was the Artillery Committee Chairman. Jenny and I drove to Ft. Riley in early May 1973 for a planning session. I had been putting in some very long hours recruiting cadets for the ROTC program at Panhandle State, so Jenny drove and I crawled in the back seat and went to sleep. Just before we arrived at Ft. Riley, I woke up and looked out the window at the most beautiful, peaceful countryside I had ever seen. The rolling Flint Hills as far as I could see were emerald green against a black background from the annual spring pasture burning. I remember thinking, *It's just like God waved His hand gently over these rolling hills and said, "Be peaceful."* My next thought was, *Maybe this is where we are supposed to build the retreat center.*

In early June, our family moved to an apartment in Manhattan, Kansas, for the summer. Jenny had the children most of the time by herself, but I did take time off from the ROTC training to celebrate our anniversary on June 18. I thought it would be romantic to go paddle boating at the Tuttle Cove State Park before dinner and a movie, so I made reservations for the boating and dinner. When we walked up to the boating concession stand, the man operating it was obviously in a bad mood. He looked at us, closed the door, and said, "I'm going home!" And he did. So much for our boating reservations.

We had a couple of hours before dinner, and Jenny suggested we look at a house she had seen in the paper. My assignment officer had verbally advised me to prepare to be assigned to Ft. Riley the next year, and Jenny loves to look at houses. We called the realtor, and she met us at the house. It was on the lake, interesting, but not our flavor.

That was our first encounter with Rosalie Thompson, and the beginning of a wonderful friendship that would last throughout our lives. She took us to an addition she was developing, and we subsequently purchased a lot with a nice view of the lake and the Flint Hills. We were visiting the lot just before going back to Guymon to finish out the ROTC tour when I commented to Rosalie, "It will be my luck for someone to buy that knoll in front of us and block our view with a big house."

Rosalie suggested that the way to prevent that was to buy it. "What? The whole thing? Who owns it? How many acres are there? What is the price?"

The Birth of Tuttle Cove North

Jim Day, my classmate and friend at OSU, now worked in Pratt, Kansas, not far from where we lived in Guymon. We visited frequently and talked about teaming up on a project. Both of us had just read the book titled *George Müller of Bristol* and were profoundly impressed by his faith-walk with an orphanage in England where he rescued thousands of orphans during the nineteenth century. We dared to entertain the thought that what God had accomplished through this great man of faith in England, He could do again in Kansas. Could we begin a work here and trust God to manifest Himself as He had with George Müller? In the fall of 1973 Jim came for a visit, and I shared with him my thoughts about the land in Kansas for a retreat center. We prayed about it and decided to investigate.

Although we hadn't seen him in a while, we continued to keep in touch with Dan, our Thanksgiving guest at OSU. During the time Jim and I were working on this new idea, Dan stopped by for a visit on his way to an assignment with the Air Force. At some point in our conversation, he shared with me that he had some money sitting idle in his financial cache and asked for advice on how to invest it. I skirted the question, but he kept insisting, so I told him about the land Jim Day and I were considering for a retreat center. He seemed interested and the three of us met in Manhattan.

The land was one hundred twenty-eight acres of beautiful lakefront, rolling hills. We stayed in a motel on the lake and spent all day walking every square foot of the one hundred twenty-eight acres. We sought the Lord by fasting for three days, drinking only water from a cool spring on the land. We agreed to an offer that was low enough to require God's intervention and at a price we could afford since we would each be making monthly contributions to the escrow account. Jim and Dan both had good jobs, and our cost of living was low enough to give us adequate discretionary income and that would not change when we moved to Ft. Riley the next year.

We made the offer. The owner laughed at the offer. We went home content that we had done our best, and it was not God's will.

Several weeks later, Rosalie called. The owner had decided to accept our offer if we would make semiannual payments instead of annual payments. We considered the counter offer and since the price was the same, we agreed and signed the contract in April 1974. One month later, I received orders, not for Ft. Riley, Kansas, as I had anticipated, but for Washington, DC! The higher cost of living totally absorbed my five hundred dollar per month contribution toward our contract. Then Jim Day's position was cut and he was without a job. What was happening? Dan was still solvent, but could not carry the entire load.

When the next payment came due, we could not make it and received a foreclosure notice from the owner's attorney. We had ten days to come up with ten thousand dollars!

"Do Not Give Up the Dream"

We had no resources for our part of the payment. Jenny stretched her budget as tight as possible and the children needed new clothes for school. With these problems pressing in on all sides, I went into the bedroom, knelt by the bed, and said, "God, it looks as if we made a big mistake. We haven't the money for the payment, so we'll just have to give it up."

Just then the phone rang. It was Hal, my prayer partner. He said he didn't know what it meant, but on the way home from work the Lord instructed him to call me and say, "Do not give up the dream I gave you!"

I hung up the phone and wept.

The next day Rosalie called and informed me that an Army colonel stationed near me in Northern Virginia wanted to buy twenty-five acres of land. I called him and told him we were under foreclosure and may not be able to sell the land. He said, "Just tell me how much you need and I will write a check today." I told him the amount and he sent a check to the escrow agent that day. I called the escrow agent and he said, "The check from the colonel cannot be used for the back interest. You will have to come up with the money to make the payment from other sources." What was going on? We now had eight days to come up with ten thousand dollars.

No! Not the Model A!

The next day I was having quiet time at the office and practicing Thought Conditioners to relax and trying to listen to the Lord. *Sell the Model A.*

What? I couldn't believe it! The boys and I had searched for years for a Model A Ford coupe! We had finally found one in Western Oklahoma and had brought it all the way to Virginia. It was in running condition, but required a lot of rebuilding. We rebuilt the mechanical parts and had begun to work on the body. Jenny resented the project because it not only consumed any extra money we had, but also a lot of late hours as well.

After arguing with the Lord for several hours, offering other alternatives that were not acceptable, I finally said, "Okay, Lord, if this is what is right, make me want to sell the Model A." By the time I got home that evening, I had no desire to work on the Model A that was in several pieces scattered on the floor of the garage. (That was another reason Jenny resented the A. We had to park our family car in the driveway, accessible only by walking outside in inclement weather.)

I called a friend who also had Model As and asked him what price I should ask. His estimate was less than I needed for the payment, but I noticed I began to feel good about parting with the car. I called the newspaper and put in an ad for the amount I needed. The ad came out the following day, and before I got home, I had three people begging me to hold the car for them. I gave the first caller two hours to drive down from Maryland. He was there with thirty minutes to spare. He gasped when he saw how many pieces the car was in. "Surely you will take less," he offered. I replied, "No less. It is this car or one hundred twenty-eight acres in Kansas." He wrote the check for the full amount. I delivered the Model A the next day and never looked back.

'65 Tang

At the same time, Jim Day, with no job, was struggling with the Lord about his part of the payment. He was instructed to, "Get in the 1965 Mustang ('65 Tang) you just finished rebuilding and go to the Ford dealer in Oklahoma City." Jim did not question the instruction. He immediately drove the two hours to the dealer and asked the salesman if someone there wanted to buy the '65 Tang. "I have no idea who it might be, but I will ask the other people." No one was interested.

While they were standing there on the lot, they heard tires squealing and turned to see a car racing into the lot. The driver jumped out and asked, "Who owns that Mustang?" The man wrote a check on the spot for the amount Jim asked. We made the payment with one day to spare. Did I say, "We" made the payment?

Eventually the colonel purchased thirty-eight acres, and that netted enough to pay the balance of the loan on Tuttle Cove North. We were puzzled at the direction the deal was taking. We had expected God to provide funds for the construction of the retreat center. Instead, we had to sell all but about fifty acres. The George Müller Factor was growing dimmer and, adding to our already strained resources, Dan lost interest in the deal, for which I don't blame him.

Meanwhile, I had a job to do for the Army that would impact weapons systems for years to come.

Magnetic Tape

My new assignment was to the Operational Test and Evaluation Agency (OTEA), an arm of the Secretary of the Army. The mission of OTEA was to make sure combat support systems met design requirements before production contracts were awarded. I was assigned as the electrical engineer. My job was to secure data acquisition systems to collect performance data under realistic combat conditions.

One of the weapon systems being tested was a laser-guided projectile designed to destroy enemy tanks. The projectile was fired from a howitzer. The challenge was threefold: a Remotely Controlled Target Vehicle (RCTV) system to control several unmanned tanks in combat formation in the test area; a system to detect and record the location of the laser spot that was marking the moving tank; and a system to detect and record the point of impact of the projectile.

A brilliant physicist from Harry Diamond Laboratory solved the latter two challenges. This was ten years before satellite guidance systems were available, and the ability to remotely control several tanks in combat formation was a different story. I searched every military agency that had any remote control technology and found none to meet the requirements of our test. The experts in the field said it could not be done with existing technology.

However, I had another Source. One noon I was having quiet time in my office, practicing Thought Conditioners. "Lord, You have given me a job to do. I believe You support the military of the United States and I need Your help to locate a remote control system for the laser guided projectile test." I immediately received two words: *Magnetic tape*.

"Is that all?"

Silence.

When my supervisor returned from lunch, I informed him of the conversation with the Lord, and we brainstormed the meaning of it with no solution. The following week I was at Ft. Carson, Colorado, making preliminary plans for the test, examining the proposed target area, and setting up logistical support for field-testing the data acquisition system developed by Harry Diamond Lab. My supervisor called me and began with, "Does your God only operate at night?" He had awakened in the middle of the night thinking about an article he had read several months earlier about a company that was controlling cars for crash testing. He thought the company was in Colorado and the name was some military term.

I called the telephone operator in Colorado Springs and told her my dilemma. She was very helpful, and we started through the yellow pages. She asked if the name could be a military command.

I said it could be.

"Well, here is one that may fit. It's Kaman Science in Colorado Springs."

"OK, please give me their number," I said.

I dialed the number and a very courteous voice said, "Kaman Science, how may I direct your call?"

I said, "I would like to speak to the person in charge of remote vehicle control."

"One minute, sir, while I connect you."

My pulse began to race!

"This is Dr. Bryce. What can I do for you?"

I explained what I was looking for and he said, "How soon can you get here?"

Within the hour I was examining the Kaman system, and by the end of the next day, I had negotiated a multimillion-dollar contract. Kaman was so confident they could develop the system we needed that they were willing to fund the project up front with one million dollars. The next day, I was on the way to the office of the Assistant Secretary of the Army to get approval to spend ten million dollars to develop the system. After an extensive query, the request for funds was approved and Kaman began refining their system to control at least six unmanned tanks in simulated combat formation.

The commanding general of OTEA visited Kaman for the prototype demonstration. We did a complete dry run the day before and everything worked fine. The next morning the general got in the golf cart used for the demonstration, pushed the start button, and nothing happened. The cart was dead!

The president of Kaman invited the general for a cup of coffee while the technicians searched for the problem. During the coffee break, the president asked the general to permanently assign me to the RCTV project until it was fully tested and accepted. They were fully aware that I was due to rotate in a few months so they obviously wanted to maintain continuity of personnel on this exciting project. The general did request an extension for me, but the Army would only grant a one-year extension.

The technicians rapidly found and resolved the failure, and the golf cart sprang back to life. In a matter of months, we field-tested the system and signed a contract for modifying twenty-eight tanks to receive the control system, the heart of which was a computer in the belly of each tank recording on and reading from a magnetic tape!

Recounting this story confirms the promise from God in Psalm 91:14–15: "Because he has set his love upon Me, therefore . . . he shall call upon Me and I will answer him."

God is not only faithful; He has a great sense of humor. Solomon wrote about this trait of God in Proverbs 25:2: "It is the glory of God to conceal a matter, but the honor of kings is to search out a matter." I am no king, but I believed God would provide an answer. He hid the answer with a two-word clue; it was up to us to search for the answer. We were all delighted with the result.

CHAPTER 10

Gregory Hayward

Germany—Blessing or Curse?

Our family had several serious discussions about the extension with OTEA. Greg was a sophomore and to take the one-year extension would mean moving him between his junior and senior year in high school. I was offered an assignment in Grafenwoehr, Germany, as the Facilities Engineer for the Seventh Army Training Command. This assignment was offered as a precursor to a career path to colonel or general. I felt Greg's welfare was the most important issue, and the decision was left up to him. He wanted a few days to think about it. After a week, Greg was ready to give us his decision. He appreciated us all thinking of his welfare, but he felt our family would benefit more if my career progression was permitted to take the programmed course.

Before we made a final decision, we called the school Greg would be attending. It was a boarding school in Nurnberg, more than an hour away. The counselor assured us the school was excellent and discipline at the school was strictly enforced. Although we were not thrilled with the boarding idea, Greg assured us he could handle being at the school during the week and returning home each Friday for the weekend. We turned down the extension at OTEA and headed to Germany during the summer of 1977. The project at Kaman Science was doing exceptionally well, so I felt I had fulfilled my mission there.

The Home War Continues

It is important that I digress for a moment and talk about the condition of our family life. I think it is best described as incongruous. There were periods of near-perfect interaction and joyful harmony, but also periods of anguish and deep turmoil, times when Jenny and I found ourselves disagreeing about the most trivial things. The tension was high, and I am not proud of the way I handled my role as a husband and father at that time. I could not control my anger. I would react badly, regret it for days, ask for forgiveness, and swear I would never act that way again. But I did, again and again.

One such incident involved Greg and Doug. They were playing in their room, making lots of noise. I asked them to quiet down or I was coming up. Vague threat! The next time the noise level rose, I dashed upstairs and tried the door, only to discover it was locked. That produced more anger, so I kicked the door open, grabbed the boys, dragged them to the front room, and spanked them with a belt.

Later I was filled with remorse; I begged God for forgiveness, but was so ashamed I could not face the boys. What was happening to me? The fear of going berserk and doing even worse harm to my family hung like a black cloud over my head. This was a replay of my hunting trip with Eldon many years ago in West Virginia.

I asked God frequently to take my life before I hurt anyone else. Probably the incident I regret most of all happened near the White House. The five of us were on a tour of the Capitol area. Greg was misbehaving and at one point I flew off the handle and kicked him in the butt with the broad side of my foot! I tried to stop the kick before it hit him, so it didn't hurt him physically, but I will carry the image on his face to my grave.

Then there were good times. To give Jenny a break, after Sunday dinner the children and I did the dishes, then went for an exploring trip to some of the surrounding parks and forest. I loved our kids and thoroughly enjoyed these outings. They also enjoyed them because I never got angry with them no matter what they did. For instance, one of them threw the other's shoes in the river. I broke two ribs getting the shoes out, and we all thought it was hilarious. I have an indelible image of Debbie running along the path with blonde curls bouncing, her face beaming with delight. Greg, an avid skier on the slopes, appeared as liquid motion to anyone who took the time to watch him, which I did frequently. Doug was mischievous with perfect coordination, and a joy to watch at any sport.

Germany Again, Only Better Until

Our arrival in Germany this time was pleasant. Our sponsor had rented a beautiful house for us in the country until quarters became available on post. They had the refrigerator stocked and all the beds made when we arrived. The German people in that area were very pro-American, and we were treated as very important people. Our landlord brought us fresh-baked bread occasionally and seemed proud to have us living next to his farm.

Just around the hill was a wonderful gasthaus, the Obersee, which served delicious food. Their specialty was chicken cordon bleu. Doug never forgot the place because every time he was there, they were out of the cordon bleu.

Greg's experience with the boarding school was not very satisfying. Just imagine a bunch of fourteen- to seventeen-year-old kids in a dorm in a foreign country, and you may have some idea of the challenges. But when all the kids were at home in Graf, we had great times. Jenny and I volunteered to be the youth directors for the chapel. We had an active group, and because we were stationed close to many ski slopes, we often took them skiing on winter weekends. They earned money by washing cars to pay for their equipment rental and lift tickets. The Post Commander even granted us permission to meet in the historic Grafenwoehr Water Tower. The young people had a blast washing cars and each other and made lots of money because there was no commercial carwash anywhere near. Greg was definitely in his element on these trips, Doug showed his daring streak, and Debbie hated ski lessons.

Greg was a perfectionist in some ways. His dream was to be a photographer for *National Geographic*. He got all the books and magazines on cameras he could find and finally decided on the one he wanted. He passed up many great buys until he could afford the exact one. He was the same with skiing. He studied all the ski areas and settled on Val d'Isere, France.

In early 1979, Greg, Doug, and I loaded up the camper and headed for France while Jenny and Debbie went to Rome. We purchased a book called *Europe on $5 a Day* and found a campground adjacent to a ski area containing twenty-eight ski slopes. When we got there, the campground was under six feet of snow! Duh!

The local mayor had a hostel for skiers and was gracious to extend to us free parking against the snow bank and the use of his showers and meals. We were one-hundred yards from the first of the twenty-eight ski lifts, so we put on skis at the camper in the morning and returned the same way at the end of the day.

The first day we started at the beginner's slope to get me in shape. Doug met another boy his age, and they built a jumping ramp and dared me to try it. I finally gave in and came swooping down on the ramp with a flare. There was one problem: the ramp was steep and their skis short and stiff. My skis were long and limber. You guessed it. I heard the binding release on both skis as I lifted off. I looked down to see my skis dangling by their retainers and was paying no attention to the position of my ski poles. *Crrruuunch!* One end of the right ski pole jammed into the snow, the other end into my ribs.

I landed in an agonizing *frrumpp*, gasping for breath. I rolled over to breathe and saw Doug and his friend doubled up laughing. I tried to laugh, but it was too painful. It was one of those instances where it "only hurts when you breathe." I refused to let a few sore ribs dampen our time together and managed to stay up with them. I was younger then.

Above the Clouds

One morning we got up to rain and clouds so heavy we could not see thirty feet in front of us. This trip was very important to Greg, so I asked God to lift the clouds. We played a tape as we ate breakfast. The first song had the phrase, "God sent a mighty wind and blew the clouds away!" Greg said, "Dad, if we can get to the big gondola, we can get above the clouds!" The lifts were running, but we could not see to ski. We were determined to make the best of it, so we locked arms and scooted down some of the slopes on our behinds. At one point we nearly went over a cliff that was—we found out later—several hundred feet straight down!

We did get to the gondola and climbed out through the clouds and into the most spectacularly beautiful world I had ever seen! The view was breathtaking! The snow-covered mountain peaks of the majestic Alps appeared to be floating atop the white glistening clouds that divided the world below and heaven above.

Greg was in paradise! The snow was perfect powder and the slopes not crowded. I shall always have a vivid picture of Greg flowing down the slopes, oblivious to all else, living his dream.

Denominational Doctrine Versus Loving Dialogue

That perfect day, I regret to say, did not end with a perfect evening. At dinner that night, Greg wanted to discuss his thoughts about spiritual things and some of his thoughts deviated from my own beliefs. He was a near genius and a deep thinker who was having trouble accepting what we believed. I became very angry and came down on him hard for questioning our beliefs. He hung his head and went into a world of confusion. Even now, I am weeping inside because of my mishandling of that golden opportunity. Only a merciful God in heaven could forgive me for this inexcusable failure.

The next day Greg wanted to fulfill his dream of skiing all twenty-eight slopes in one day. With some concern, I encouraged him, "Go for it!" That he did. Doug and I skied all day and met Greg as he was on the slope leading to our "campground." He had skied all twenty-eight slopes!

When we returned to our duty station in Grafenwoehr, Greg and I did have several good times doing dishes. We walked back through many of the bad times and I asked and received his forgiveness for my misbehavior. A healing process began for both of us and my love for Greg took on fresh meaning. He was reluctant to talk about spiritual things, but when he did I listened.

Greg graduated in May 1979, turned eighteen, got a good job with the military, and began saving his money. His first purchase was the camera he had selected earlier. That was a happy day. Next, he began to save for a Euro rail pass to tour Europe as a photographer before returning to the States for college. Speaking of returning to the States, we had another major decision regarding Debbie.

Mom, I'm Lost!

Because of the boarding school situation, we were determined not to send her to Nurnberg High School. Jenny's sister Edie had a daughter the same age as Debbie, and they were delighted to have her come live with them until we got back to the States the following year. Jenny and I took Debbie to the airport in Frankfort with reservations to Columbus, Ohio, where Edie would pick her up. She had a connection in New York City at the same terminal and the airlines assured us a hostess would meet her and escort her to the next flight. After the plane pulled away from the gate, Jenny and I headed back to Grafenwoehr to wait for Debbie's call that she had made it.

At 0500 the next morning, the phone rang by Jenny's head, and all she heard was, "Mom, help me, I am lost!" Jenny jumped straight up in bed and began yelling at the operator, *"Do not hang up!"*

The operator was threatening to disconnect because Debbie did not have enough change to pay for the call. Jenny's frantic explosion convinced the operator it was an emergency and agreed to reverse the charges. I was yelling, "What is going on?!"

Debbie was in a dark corner of the airport in New York; all the attendants had gone and the only person in the area was a man sweeping the floors and watching her. She was frantic with fear for her life. I got Jenny down to a sitting position on the bed and took the receiver from her clutched hand. Frantic as I was, I knew I had to think this thing through very carefully. Debbie finally settled down enough to tell me the number of the pay phone she was calling from and I told her to stay in the phone booth and we would call her back if we lost the connection. Jenny talked to her and we prayed for help: "Lord, only You know the solution to our plight. Please help us!"

I sat quietly for a moment to wait for an answer. I sensed I was to go to the duty officer's desk. I sprinted to his location and told him that Debbie was stranded in New York. "I don't know what you can do, but I believe the Lord told me to come see you," I said breathlessly.

"This is amazing," he replied. "I just got off the phone with Chaplain Pete Sharber. He was checking in to let us know he had arrived safely."

Pete, who had been at Grafenwoehr for most of our tour, was now stationed at the Chaplain's school in New York City.

The duty officer got Chaplain Pete on the phone and I explained to him our dilemma. I then gave him the phone number where Debbie was standing by.

"You give Debbie my phone number and tell her to stay in that phone booth until I get there!"

I ran back home, told Debbie to hang up the phone and wait for Chaplain Sharber's call. Within the hour Pete had picked up Debbie and she was safe at his house. We all wept with joy! Again Psalm 91:15 was confirmed: "He will call me and I will answer him; I will be with him in trouble; I will deliver him and honor him."

All rejoiced except Edie—who was waiting at the Columbus airport. We had no way to contact her. That was before we had cell phones. Edie's husband was ill, so she asked at her church for someone to ride with her. The only person available was one of the men. Since it was a short trip up and back, he agreed to go with her. Edie and her friend waited for several hours after dark and then gave up and got separate motel rooms for the night. We finally tracked Edie down and gave her the new arrival time. Later that day she, Debbie, and her male friend arrived in Ravenswood, somewhat embarrassed, waiting for rumors to fly.

We found out that Debbie's plane in Frankfort had taxied to the end of the runway out of our sight and sat on the runway for three hours because of inclement weather in the area. The late flight caused her to miss her flight from New York to Columbus, and she spent all her cash riding around on buses between two airports in New York City trying to find another flight to Columbus. This was a nightmare I never want to live again.

Visit from Tok

I had been praying with and for Greg to reconcile his struggle with what he believed about God. We needed someone outside our family circle to reach that place in Greg we could not get to. A short time later, we were thrilled to learn that Tok was visiting OCF groups in Germany. I contacted him, and he agreed to come to Grafenwoehr to speak to our chapel group and spend some time with Greg. After the meeting with the group, Tok needed to go back to Nurnberg, and he invited Greg to go along with us. It was beautiful to observe how gently and effectively Tok involved Greg in a deep discussion about his relationship with the Lord. By the time we got to Nurnberg, Greg was at ease talking with Tok, and they had a great time. Tok recommended a book for Greg to read, and he agreed to read it right away.

We exchanged hugs with Tok and headed back to Grafenwoehr. The ride was much too short for me. Greg and I were able to share man-to-man, and we enjoyed discussing where he was on his spiritual journey. It was amazing how God had again come to our rescue.

Seven Days of Agony

Near the end of October 1979 on a Friday night, Greg asked if he could use the car to go say goodbye to a friend who was rotating back to the States.

"Sure," I said. "Just remember how crooked those back roads are."

I gave him the keys, and he walked toward the door, turned, and waved with a warm expression on his face that showed how much he loved me.

I waved back and said, "I love you too."

Greg was not home when we went to bed. Jenny was worried, but I assured her that he had decided to stay over with his friend. I was awakened before daylight with an apprehensive feeling. I got in the other vehicle and drove to the friend's house. It was extremely foggy. There was no one up at the friend's house, and Greg's car was not there. I drove to his girlfriend's house, but he was not there either. I drove back to post very slowly, searching both sides of the road for the car, but did not see it or any indication of an accident.

We were to have breakfast and go volksmarching that morning with Herman and Peggy Kincaid, our new chaplain and his wife. Volksmarching is a German tradition of families getting together and walking along prescribed routes. It is festive, with booths of various German sausages along the way and a decorative souvenir at the end of the march. Jenny and I went on over to the Kincaids' house and shared our concern with them. We decided to call the Military Police (MP). The desk sergeant said they did have a report of an American car in an accident with no serious injuries, although a young man had been taken to the German hospital. The license tag number was ours! As the realization set in, dread encompassed me. I felt as if the Sea of Japan were again dragging me out to sea. I was helpless.

I tried to drive away the feeling by repeating, "They said no serious injuries, no serious injuries, no serious injuries . . ."

Herman, Peggy, Jenny, and I rushed to the German hospital that specialized in automobile crash victims. The doctor met us in the lobby. After we confirmed our identity, the doctor told us Greg was in extremely critical condition, and it would be a miracle if he lived. I felt like I was falling through space with no bottom. I thought, *This can't be real! It must be a bad dream and I will wake up.* I barely heard what the doctor was saying.

When a German civilian found Greg about daylight, he was lying beside the road where his car had crashed into a bridge abutment. When the Good Samaritan delivered Greg to the nearest hospital, the staff saw no visible sign of injury. Greg was talking, so they set him aside to perform emergency surgery on another crash victim. By the time they got back to Greg and examined him closely, they realized his lungs had been severely damaged, and he was bleeding internally. He was too weak for surgery, yet without it he would not survive. Peggy Kincaid called the prayer chain at the chapel and they began a prayer vigil. Within an hour, the doctor came out and said Greg was suddenly gaining strength and surgery was possible.

The surgery was successful. The doctor was so pleased with the results that he decided to leave for a ski trip he had put on hold pending the outcome of surgery. He had removed a portion of one lung, but he expected a full recovery with only minor limitation on extremely heavy activity. I was so grateful and prayed silently, "Lord, thank You! I will carry him for the rest of his life if necessary; just let him live."

However, there were complications not visible to the doctor, and the next seven days were a wild roller coaster ride. Greg was on life support and heavily sedated. The hospital had no provisions for anyone except the patient and asked us to be there only during visiting hours, so they would be unencumbered in caring for Greg. We would go home only to get a call to come to the hospital as Greg was ebbing away. The prayer chain would be activated, and by the time we arrived at the hospital, Greg would be much improved. The next day was the same pattern. It got to the point Jenny and I could not handle the phone ringing, so Chaplain Kincaid called the hospital and had all calls come to him.

Peggy Kincaid never left Jenny's side as long as she was awake. Herman Kincaid never left my side except when I was at the office. I could not handle just waiting, so I tried to work. The engineering staff was exceptionally helpful.

We consulted with the Army doctor about the possibility of having Greg transferred to Walter Reed or another military hospital. The doctor's opinion was that the hospital Greg was in was the very best for crash victims, so we agreed to trust him to the hospital and to the Lord.

On the fifth day, the doctor came in during our visit and explained that physically it appeared that Greg should be able to breathe on his own, but when they reduced the sedation medication he went into mild convulsions. The doctor was puzzled. "It's as if he is opposed to regaining consciousness," he said. Greg was lying with his face toward the wall with his body tense.

The next day we visited during the afternoon visiting hours. The doctor met us and told us, "Your son must soon begin breathing on his own because the pure oxygen being used cannot be continued much longer. However, there is something strange going on with your son that I have not experienced and do not understand."

He escorted us to Greg's room and pointed out that Greg was now laying face toward us with a peaceful expression on his face and his body totally relaxed. The room was hushed. One of the nurses whispered, "There is another presence in this room."

Whatever battle Greg had been fighting was over, and he had won!

We visited again on day seven. The room was still hushed and Greg was peaceful, but another attempt to permit him to regain consciousness met with the same resistance. Doug had wanted to visit Greg again, so we went home to bring him to the hospital. It was Halloween night, and he was with some friends when I found him. As we returned to the house, Chaplain Kincaid met me with the dreaded news: "Richard, Greg has gone home." There is no way to prepare for the death of a child. I was numb.

I remember the house was full of people and the command executive officer, a tall, matter-of-fact colonel, met me at the door, didn't say a word, just gave me a bear hug, and held me until I stopped shaking. Jenny, Doug, and I held each other for a long time. Everyone tried to be helpful. The greatest comfort came from a neighbor who took my face in her hands and said, "Richard, just remember: this was no surprise to God." That statement and the concern in her eyes were a stabilizing remembrance in the days that followed.

Why Are You Beating Me?

I don't remember anything more about the evening until after everyone had gone, and Jenny had taken the medicine from the doctor so she would rest. I finally convinced Herman to go home for some rest, and I started upstairs to the bedroom. I stumbled and collapsed on the bottom step. I thought someone was standing over me beating me with a club. I cried out, "God, why are You beating me? Is Greg's death not punishment enough?"

Greg had been questioning his relationship with the Lord, and he and his mother had a disagreement before he left the house that fateful evening. The guilt and pain associated with not having the opportunity to resolve the disagreement and say goodbye to Greg was excruciating for Jenny in those first days after his death. She required a doctor's care and medication.

We called Debbie the next day. We had not told her about Greg's accident—a mistake for sure—but we kept hoping to have good news for her. She was really shaken and wept for a long time. She later told us that when she sat on her bed that night, Greg came and sat beside her and said, "I am okay. Do not worry."

She said the bed actually moved beside her and she felt him there.

He Isn't There!

I also called my brother Donal, a retired colonel, who had served in the personnel branch of the Army. Between Donal and the local folks, they took care of all the details. The Army gave us the choice of returning to Grafenwoehr after an extended leave or being reassigned to a stateside post of our choice. We chose the stateside option because Debbie was already in the States, and we needed to be together. It was then that we noticed a most amazing change taking place. It was as if a protective bubble encompassed us, and God was holding each one of us. We walked around like we were almost weightless. It was incredible!

One of the sergeants on the engineer staff volunteered to escort Greg's body back to Ravenswood, where Debbie was living, and where Jenny and I met and began our life together. It was comforting to know that a close friend was with him on the way home. As soon as they got there, we arranged for a viewing at the funeral home for family and friends. I didn't know what to expect when Jenny saw Greg's body in the casket, so I was prepared for a difficult experience. To my amazement, when she saw his body she stood as if transfixed for several moments. Then she turned to me with her face glowing and said, "He is not in there! I am so glad!"

Chaplain Pete Sharber, who had rescued Debbie in New York, came to officiate at the funeral. We commended Greg's body to the earth in West Virginia, on a hillside plot donated by my best friend, Don

Cornell—the same friend who first met me in Auburn with, "Hey, you wanna play football?"

Bones on Fire

True to its promise, the Army gave me the choice of assignments. We still owned a house in Dale City, Virginia, and eventually I accepted a position at Cameron Station, Virginia, as the facilities engineer. The staff there was great and I began the long walk back. As God began to let us walk on our own again, I trekked through a very dark and painful valley. We stayed with my brother, Donal, for a month while the people who'd rented our house in Dale City found another place to live. When we moved in, it was difficult to walk past Greg's room. But sometimes I would go in and stay as long as I could.

The guilt stemming from the way I had treated Greg overwhelmed me. The nights were the worst. There were times it felt as if my bones were on fire, and I trembled uncontrollably. To attempt to mitigate the unrelenting guilt, I began to write Greg letters listing the events where I had hurt him. At first I could not ask him for forgiveness because I considered my actions unforgivable. I just told him how very sorry I was that I had hurt him so many times.

I knew I needed help and was eventually led to a Jewish counselor in Northern Virginia. His being Jewish comforted me. On one of the early trips to see him, the pain in my mind was so horrific, I only functioned mechanically to drive the car. The session resulted in some relief of the pain in my mind, but on the way home, I felt as if a giant vacuum was attached to my head trying to suck my mind out of my body. Again it was the citing of Thought Conditioners that eased the pain until I was able to function.

Another stabilizing force was reading the ten-volume set of Donald Barnhouse's commentary on the book of Romans while riding in the carpool to and from work. Then came Barnhouse's book, *The Invisible War*. This scholarly discourse on the details of spiritual warfare began to shed light on the events in my life. I began to see a pattern of directed influence meant for evil in my life. Barnhouse wrote, "There is no truce in the invisible war. There is no armistice in the invisible war. . . . The field of each battle is the heart of man."[2]

Greg's Choice

In time I was able to go back over the events surrounding Greg's accident and his time in the hospital. One of the haunting images was of him lying along the road in the freezing fog, alone and unable to breathe correctly because of his injured lung. At one point I asked the hospital to take part of my lung and transplant it for Greg, but was told that would not be possible. Gradually I began to understand what was going on in the hospital room that had fascinated the medical personnel.

With all the evidence provided by records of what is called "near death" or "out of body" experiences, it is obvious a body can be sedated or comatose and the person have perfect recall of events during that time. Conversations while out of the body, called Near Death Experiences (NDE), have been confirmed in recent books such as *90 Minutes in Heaven* by Don Piper, who described the accident: "About 11:45 A.M., just before I cleared the east end of the bridge, an eighteen-wheeler . . . weaved across the centerline and hit my car head-on. . . . I remember parts of the accident, but most of my information came from the accident report and people at the scene."[3]

Piper was pronounced dead at the scene. For the next ninety minutes, he claims he experienced heaven where he was greeted by those who had influenced him spiritually. He heard beautiful music and felt true peace. Mr. Piper kept his heavenly experience to himself until friends and family convinced him to share his remarkable story that has been made into a movie by the same title.

Don Piper also wrote the Foreword to *Imagine Heaven,* a book John Burke recently published that contains more than one hundred stories of people who experienced NDEs. These reports, collected from thirty years of research, contain many similarities. Burke wrote, "I've concluded that the core common elements of near-death experiences (NDEs) are a gift from God to color in the picture revealed by the prophets and Jesus."[4] The common elements indicate that all cognitive and sensual functions were not only operational but were enhanced. One such report from a woman who experienced a NDE confirms this enhancement:

> Unlike on Earth, where I was plagued by doubts and fears, in heaven there was nothing but absolute certainty about who I was. This was a far more complete representation of my spirit and my heart and my being than was ever possible on Earth, a far deeper self-awareness than the collection of hopes and fears and dreams and scars that defined me during my life, I was flooded with self-knowledge . . . revealing for the first time ever, the real me.[5]

My sister Irene also reported a similar experience. She clinically died on the operating table and went through a tunnel toward a bright light. She was in the presence of a spiritual Being who conversed with her through thoughts. He asked, "Irene, is there any reason for you to go back?"

Irene responded, "Yes, there is. My husband is not a believer. If I go back I will dedicate myself to leading him to You." Instantly she was back in her body, to the utter amazement of the medical team. Irene recovered, kept her promise, and saw her husband born again before he died an untimely death soon after retiring from the Air Force.

In all of these accounts, there were discussions and decisions made on the other side of life. Therefore I am convinced that Greg's spirit was engaged in a battle to decide whether to go or stay. I believe he was able to see into the Beyond and compared life there versus what he was experiencing here. Armed with a clear vision of the difference, I believe he chose to go where love was pure. Therefore on the sixth day, having made the decision to go, he was totally at peace, and his Escort was present in the room—so real that the hospital staff sensed that presence even though they didn't understand what was happening. In any case, our son's last hours were peaceful, and God had another surprise for us later on.

CHAPTER 11

Rays of Hope, Clouds of Fear

Unequivocal Love

During the recovery time, someone gave me M. Scott Peck's book, *The Road Less Traveled*. Peck's commitment to truth and to the discipline of unequivocal love presented a refreshing approach to life that was foreign to me. Mr. Peck claimed there are four tools that comprise discipline: " . . . delaying gratification, acceptance of responsibility, dedication to truth and balancing. . . . Therefore, after analyzing each of these tools, we shall in the next section examine the will to use them, which is love."[6]

My paradigm was that relationships were determined by performance: If you do well, I will love you. As I reflected upon the arguments presented by this renowned psychiatrist, I eventually dared to compare them with my own lifestyle. A definite conflict existed between what he proposed and my life, but a seed of love began to emerge amidst the tares of painful experiences and chauvinistic practices. Sometimes I visualized myself similar to the warped and twisted pine sapling struggling for nutrients in the crevice of a rock near the upper tree line on Sheep Mountain near Spring Canyon, Colorado.

It is interesting to note that even as rays of hope from reading Mr. Peck's discourse shone through my foggy window, a strange thought began to surface and became persistent: "Scott Peck knows about God, but does not know Him in a personal relationship." I tried to discard the thought by reasoning that I was of no status to counsel a noted psychiatrist and author. However, the thought grew more persistent, and I reluctantly wrote a letter to Mr. Peck explaining my great appreciation for his book and humbly suggesting that he examine whether he had a personal relationship with the Lord or just a scholarly knowledge of Him.

To my great surprise, I received a gracious letter from Mr. Peck! He thanked me for my letter and acknowledged that it had pinpointed his condition. Then he affirmed that his relationship with Christ was now a personal one. The next paragraph floored me. He invited me to participate in a seminar with him in Washington, DC.

I considered his invitation briefly, but a cloud of doubt cast a long shadow, and I declined with the excuse that we were moving. But the fact is that I was afraid Scott Peck would discover that I was much less than he perceived me to be. The enemy had won another scrimmage, and I missed an opportunity I believe God provided. I treasure his letter. Even after more than three decades, my stomach still cringes with regret when I read his invitation and my declination.

Unpolished Brass

The assignment at Cameron Station was a good assignment. I received many accolades for performance and an efficiency report from the commanding general that recommended me for immediate promotion to colonel and below-the-zone promotion to general officer. But it was not enough. I was not selected for promotion to colonel because of the two negative reports still in my personnel records. I didn't care very much. Something in me had died with Greg, and I was not recovering very well.

Early in my career, I made a vow that if I ever went to work without shining my brass and shoes, I would retire. One day after I arrived at the office, I realized I had not polished my brass or shined my shoes. I called my branch assignments officer and requested a retirement package. He tried to convince me to stay and offered me another choice assignment with OTEA, the job I would have wanted if I stayed in.

That evening we had a family conference. We developed a list of three options and began a process of prayerful exploration and elimination. The decision to retire was not a knee-jerk reaction to the brass that was not shined. Always in the back of my mind was the thought that sooner or later something would happen to trigger the development of the retreat center in Kansas. We as a family began to prayerfully consider three options:

1. Stay where we are.
2. Accept the assignment to OTEA.
3. Move to Kansas to develop Tuttle Cove North (TCN).

Option 3

Option 3 was to move to Kansas and start working on a plan for Tuttle Cove North (TCN). After Greg's death, we decided to enroll Debbie and Doug in a Christian school in Virginia. Debbie was graduating that spring and would be going to college, so Doug and I headed for Kansas to begin the investigation of Option 3. We had a great trip and found a Christian school that Doug could attend. When we visited the school, Darren, one of the students, and Doug hit it off immediately and Doug was excited about attending the school. There was one more stop before heading home with our report.

For some time before this trip, Jim Day and I had begun researching the feasibility of doing passive solar energy research on TCN. I had been working with the Department of Energy (DOE) to put together a project to collect empirical data on passive solar, earth-sheltered houses. The land we owned in Kansas was ideal since all sites had south facing exposures. DOE had five hundred thousand dollars to fund a research project to collect the data. I had submitted a proposal to DOE that was accepted, and I was instructed to find a university to host the project. While in Kansas, I visited the Engineering Department at Kansas State University. The idea seemed viable, and I was requested to prepare a draft proposal to be used by the university to prepare the official proposal for DOE. Option 3 looked good. We returned home to evaluate as a family.

You Again

Jim Day and I prepared the draft proposal, and I flew back to Manhattan to deliver it and coordinate the agreement with the university. The plane from Kansas City to Manhattan circled over Tuttle Creek Lake on final approach. As I was looking down at the area around our property, I "heard" the same voice that had yelled at me at the urinal in Vietnam. This time it said, "If you set foot on that property, I will kill you!"

The threat was so real I did not go to the property for two days. The third day I said, "Lord, I will not be controlled by fear, so I am going. I ask for your protection."

I still feel the apprehension I experienced as I drove to the property. There was an electric fence around the property near the road. I stood by the fence and felt like I was going into a battle zone. In a desperate move, I dove over the fence and landed in a rolling heap. I jumped up and ran around the property declaring, "He who is in [me] is greater than he who is in the world" (1 John 4:4). I began to laugh, not because I was alive, but at the ridiculous notion that Satan had any power to touch me without Jesus' permission.

The Fleece

It looked as if God had finally given the nod for us to develop TCN. The family vote was unanimous for the Kansas option, although Doug was not looking forward to leaving his friends in Virginia. As a final confirmation, I put out a fleece: "Lord, there is no way, short of your intervention, that the Army transportation personnel can respond quickly in the middle of peak season for military moves, so I ask you to remove this obstacle in our path by having the transportation office schedule a furniture pickup within fourteen days."

I called the transportation officer to explain my situation. He looked at his schedule and said, "I could schedule a furniture pickup ten days from today." Okay, then! God really worked fast on that one.

I called Rosalie. We bought a house sight unseen based upon her recommendation. It was a good decision. Our house in Dale City sold immediately at a nice profit and all that remained was the retirement formality. Two weeks later, I was standing on the parade field at Fort Myers, Virginia, participating in my retirement ceremony. I was fine until the band began to play the Washington Post March and the soldier in me was shouting, "No! No! No!" But it was too late.

A Hand Soft as Heaven

After our house in Dale City sold to the first couple who looked at it, we moved temporarily into a house our church used to house missionaries on leave. On Sunday an invitation went out for an escort for a speaker from Pakistan. I volunteered. I found out her name was Madam Sheikh, the author of the book, *I Dared to Call Him Father,* one I had recently read. I was moved by her story of conversion to Christianity and her escape from Pakistan before the death sentence could be carried out by her relatives.

I picked Madam Sheikh up at her hotel, and we began the drive to the place she was to speak. After introductions and a short time getting acquainted, she began to talk freely about her mission. "God has sent me to America to tell the churches to wake up before it is too late."

Then she reached over and cradled my right hand in both her hands. I cannot adequately describe those hands. They were soft as a cloud, yet I felt a warm flow of peaceful energy flowing from her hands into mine. I glanced at her, and she was looking at me with a glowing, heavenly smile.

"Richard," she said, "You are concerned about your son."

"Well, I think about Doug's welfare," I said. "But I didn't think I was concerned about him."

"I'm not speaking about Doug," she responded with a twinkle in her voice, "I am speaking of the son that is not with you. The Lord has instructed me to tell you that you need not be concerned; your son is with Him."

I was speechless. Warm assurance continued to flow from her hands to mine. I could feel my arm getting warm, then my face, and then my whole body responded with a gentle shudder. We had not discussed Greg at all, so how would she know? Yet, I knew it was true and from that day I never questioned her affirmation that Greg is in the presence of the Lord. A thousand times since I have wondered, "Lord, why would You bless a wandering, earthly pilgrim with such a heavenly confirmation?"

From experience I knew mountaintop ecstasies fade in the valley, but for the next few days the warm glow from Madam Sheikh's soft hands caressed this prodigal's soul with surpassing peace.

God, Have You Forsaken Us?

The next week we headed to Kansas and settled in to the new house on Drake Avenue in Manhattan. We had no debt and a nice nest egg set aside for this exciting adventure, or so I thought. My next task was to enroll in a doctoral program and get approval for the solar research project. To make a long story short, neither happened. The program I desired was not available, and delays in the project approval process resulted in the expiration of the time-sensitive funds. I did work as a research assistant, enrolled in other courses, and wrote other proposals. None of these resulted in funding for the project. *Well then, I will just do the research on my own!*

The Price of Helping God

A pastor visited TCN and expressed a strong desire to build a house on a seven-acre plot that was separated from the remainder of the property. Over a period of weeks an agreement was reached and I designed a passive solar, earth-integrated house and formed Mastercraft Construction to proceed with the construction. The project incorporated the latest in passive solar theory and earth-integrated technology. Several hundred sensors were imbedded in the foundation, walls, and ceiling to collect the data to compare theoretical characteristics and actual results. Things were really looking good, and I interpreted the happenings as God's plan for the use of the land.

I was on the roof completing the sheathing when the pastor came by and asked me to come down for a chat. "Dick, I am not able to complete this house." I was stunned! But after recovering, I decided I would help God by helping one of His servants and agreed to take over the house, finish it out, and try to sell it. By now three years had gone by since we had moved to Kansas. I owned two houses and my stipend at the university was due to end.

In the meantime, the government laboratory that had agreed to provide the instrumentation to collect the empirical data called to inform me they would not be providing the equipment because an organization in Manhattan had objected to my research. Really?

Friday the Thirteenth

We put both houses on the market and, at the suggestion of Jim Day, who was then working at Ft. Riley, I went to visit the Director of Public Works at Ft. Riley. The following Friday, August 13, our house in town sold, and I was offered a position at Ft. Riley. The buyer of our house in town, a vice president of one of the local banks, needed immediate occupancy. Against Jenny's wishes and good judgment, we moved into the house at the lake before the sheetrock was finished. Jenny's nose began to bleed from the sheetrock dust and our relationship once more began to deteriorate rapidly.

Jenny had never agreed with the whole concept of TCN, although she wholeheartedly agreed to the move to Kansas. In those days, my paradigm was that I made the major decisions. I did not realize what a wedge I had driven between us by not accepting her input. Her reasons for moving to Kansas were far different from mine. Looking back now I see how offensive and degrading that was to her, but the desire to make my dream a reality won out over all other thoughts. I became blind to the position of each of us in Christ. We again went to counseling, but the results were no better than before.

Then to confirm what I thought was God's direction and blessing, a prominent couple in town heard about the type of construction we had used on the house at the lake. They came by for a visit and asked me for a proposal to build them a house. I looked at their lot, recommended a style to fit their lot, and presented them with a model made out of Styrofoam. They accepted the model without changes. I recommended a commercial contractor as the only one capable of building the house, but they insisted on another contractor.

Red Flags

Red flags on a firing range mean to cease firing because there is some danger present. A red flag went up about the house, and I discussed my concern with the preferred contractor. After several hours of discussion and visiting other houses the company had built, I reluctantly signed a contract with them as the primary subcontractor. It wasn't long before it became obvious this was a very serious and costly error.

The construction was a disaster from the beginning. I was working at Ft. Riley and could not be on site all the time. The fireplace did not draw, the roof leaked, and I got calls at all hours of the night and day, in church, at work, or while traveling. There was no place Janet, the home-owner, could not find me. Every subcontractor was going over budget, one went bankrupt, and I had to pick up the tab for the unfinished work, so it became necessary for me to look for additional income.

The position at Ft. Riley as a civilian was interesting for a while, and I was able to help with some strategic planning and revamping the system for getting projects expedited. However, as a regular Army retiree, I had to forfeit about half of my retired pay to work as a civil-ian employee. Very timely for me, Kansas State University (KSU) announced an opening for an electrical engineer. I applied and was offered the job immediately. Although the salary was about the same as the position at Ft. Riley, my retired pay was restored in full, providing the additional income I needed. We agreed on a reporting date, and I gave the appropriate notice to Ft. Riley.

Oops

The Saturday before I was to report to my new position at KSU was a cold, rainy October day. I decided to go to Janet's house to try to find the leak while it was raining. I set the long extension ladder with rubber grips on the wet concrete patio floor and climbed about fifteen feet up to look for the leak. When I leaned over the stub wall at the top of the ladder, the rubber feet on the ladder slipped, and I went crashing down. Instinctively I crouched as a parachute jumper does to break the fall by rolling, but my left foot came down on a rung of the ladder that beat me to the concrete patio, and my buttocks hit the concrete between two rungs. I lay there in the rain, totally numb, thinking, *This is it. I can't move, no one is home, and in this chilling rain, hypothermia will set in soon.*

After several minutes, feeling began to come into my legs, then my arms. I tried to get up, but my left leg gave way with a crunch. "This is not good," I thought. I managed to drag myself to the patio door, which was locked. I banged on it anyway. Much to my surprise and relief, their son was home, heard the racket, and came running to the door. I asked him to call my wife. It seemed like an eternity before she arrived. Why we didn't call 911, I have no idea. It never crossed my mind. I was military and wanted to go to the Ft. Riley hospital, which turned out to be a Godsend.

What Happened to Him?

By the time we were on the way to Ft. Riley, the pain was becoming more severe, especially in my back at shoulder level. Jenny was driving eighty miles per hour and started to slow down for a small town that was notorious for speeding tickets.

"Forget the police," I shouted. "Let's go!"

Just then a siren screamed, and Jenny stopped. The policeman came to the window, took one look at me, and said, "What happened to him?"

All Jenny got out was, "He fell off a ladder and—"

The policeman jumped in his car, turned on his siren and flashing red lights, and escorted us to the gate. He obviously notified the hospital that we were on the way, because two medics with a gurney were ready for action when we got to the emergency room door. By now the pain was excruciating.

X-rays revealed a crushed left heel and two crushed vertebras. The doctor on call that day just happened to be a renowned pediatric surgeon. He alerted me that there was so little bone remaining in my left heel that he may have to freeze the ankle, making it rigid. I said, "Doc, I have a high pain tolerance, but this is over the top. Just do what you have to do!"

Never have I appreciated anesthesiology more.

Six hours later I woke up in the recovery room with excruciating pain in my left hip. "Did I break a hip also?" I asked.

"No," the doctor replied, "I sorted through the mangled pieces of your left ankle that was mostly powder and found a small piece of heel bone big enough to hold a pin. I borrowed a piece of bone from your left hip and fastened the two pieces together with metal pins, then connected them to the anklebone stub with other pins. We'll see what happens, but don't be surprised if you have to have the ankle frozen rigid within ten years."

The scraped hipbone, the foot-to-knee rigid cast, and the waist-to-neck body brace made every movement painful. I tried to be tough and refuse the pain medicine. I was glad when the nurse talked me out of being so tough.

The Big Squeeze

After the nurse turned off the light and left the room, I closed my eyes and quietly waited for the medicine to mitigate the pain. Whether awake or dreaming, I'm not sure, but I saw myself between two giant boulders so big I could not see the top or bottom of them. The top one began to very slowly come down as if to crush me between them. I was helpless to move and remember thinking, *Lord, are you going to crush me?*

Amazingly, I was neither afraid nor claustrophobic. The mammoth boulder stopped just as it came in contact with my body. I lay there very quiet for a long time as a warm sense of confidence permeated my soul and mind. Then it was gone. I do not understand the full significance of the experience. I just remember a complete trust in the Lord's ability to stop the boulder.

Boss, I'm Gonna be Late for Work

I was due to begin the new job on Monday after my fall on Saturday. Instead of reporting to work on Monday, I called my supervisor-to-be from the hospital and said, "I'll be a little late for work. The doctor says I may be able to walk in two weeks."

He made some remark about that being a fine kettle of fish and wished me rapid healing.

I stayed a week in the hospital and spent a week at home. Although we were not on the best of terms, Jenny was an ideal caregiver, and I wrote a poem in honor of her commitment, called "The One Who

Stayed." When I reported to KSU two weeks late, they had a cot set up in my office, and a handicap permit to allow me to park close to the building. I could sit or stand for two hours before the pain in my back became unbearable, and I hobbled back to the cot with careful haste. Everyone was helpful, and I was able to do the job I was hired to do. I learned to climb around the catwalks on crutches in the back brace.

Enough of This

The job was very rewarding, and I was able to implement modifications that resulted in significant savings in electrical power. After a few months, my boss, Mr. Albertson, decided to retire. The day he departed, he called me to his office. "I want to share a thought with you. It is this: 'You can judge the decadence of a society by the extent the society goes to protect those who would harm it most.'"

I didn't understand it then, but over the past three decades I have observed the truth of the statement in our own society.

I was one of more than thirty who applied for the vacancy my supervisor left. I made the top four, but was not selected.

So Long, Kansas, Again

I had seen a very small ad in one of the trade magazines for a facilities engineer at the Mike Monroney Aeronautical Center (MMAC) in Oklahoma City. It sounded interesting, and Jim Day had moved to Oklahoma City, so I thought it would be a good excuse to visit him, especially if someone else was paying the bill. I had one resume remaining from the KSU application on special blue-gray resume paper, so I sent it to a company named FKW Inc. They had the maintenance contract at MMAC.

There were two other reasons to pursue the Oklahoma City position. First, the relationship between Jenny and me seemed to be over, and I was just waiting for a good excuse to get out of the way without hurting the children. Deb had graduated from college and was living in Colorado. I had made up my mind—as soon as Doug was out on his own, I would declare our marriage a hopeless case. I believed Jenny felt the same way. Secondly, I was broke and in debt because of the two disastrous construction projects.

Down to Egypt

I was invited by FKW for an interview on a Saturday. Dean Wadley, the owner, and his brother, Greg, showed up for the interview in tennis clothes, having just competed in a tennis tournament. The position was intriguing, but was I really ready to give up my dream for TCN? I told them I didn't think I was ready to leave our retirement home we had built in Kansas. Two weeks later I received an invitation to come for a second interview. I walked up on the TCN property to my favorite quiet place to think it through.

We had completed the house the pastor started, but at a great personal expense. The constant battle over the Janet house had drained all of us and left me with a racing heart every time the phone rang. Our savings were depleted. I had sold my truck and boat and was several thousand dollars in debt. The salary in Oklahoma City was thirty percent higher than what I was making at KSU.

I went for the second interview and eventually accepted the position. Jenny and Doug stayed in the house in Kansas. It was a Godsend in many ways. It gave Jenny and me a separation without anyone knowing about the pending breakup. In Oklahoma City, I felt great relief from all the stress. I was making enough to pay back the debt without declaring bankruptcy, the phone didn't ring with an irate homeowner on the other end, and I was given a challenge that comes only once in a lifetime. Dean Wadley offered me the opportunity to help him expand his company and afforded me great latitude in choosing the avenues of expansion.

I also began a dangerous journey into other relationships. Mentally, I had already severed the relationship with Jenny and was beginning to find opportunities to get to know some very attractive females. Around the world there had been other opportunities for other relationships, and although tempted a couple of times, I had never considered it an option and had remained faithful to our vows.

I recall thinking, *I am tired of being protected. It would be nice to be pursued.*

I got my wish. The first night I was in Oklahoma City, I went shopping for some things for my apartment. An attractive woman sought my help about an item on the aisle close to where I was standing. The item required some assembly and soon she said, "I'm not much good putting things together, but I am good in other areas. Would you consider helping me put it together in my apartment?"

Even for a naïve country boy, there was no doubt about the offer. I was caught off guard and had to think about how to get out of this situation. I was ready, but not *that* ready. I thanked her for her confidence in my construction ability, but informed her I was already running late for another appointment.

Another opportunity began as a friendship with a woman separated from her husband, and it progressed to the point of being serious, but not physical. One night as I lay on the floor, I began pounding it with my fists and begging God to let me out of the relationship with Jenny. I believed she had never loved me as she had so stated recently. I believed I had done irreparable damage to her emotionally. The event lasted until about 0400 in the morning. Then I heard in my spirit God say, "You have the choice to end the marriage, but that is not my will."

Jeannie, our friend from years past, lived near Oklahoma City, so I went to see her. I told her what I was struggling with. She encouraged me go see Jenny. She had heard that Jenny was under a doctor's care and not well at all. I should not have been surprised when she told me Jenny was looking at other relationships as well, but I was. I had been gone nearly six months. That night I challenged God as I had with the Model A: "God, if this is what you want, make me want to go back."

The next day I told the other woman our relationship had to stop before we regretted our actions. That night I called Jenny and together we decided it was time to talk, so I made plans to go home for Christmas. To my amazement, on the way home, God gave me a real desire to reconcile our relationship. Jenny and I spent the next four days forgiving and being forgiven. She came to Oklahoma City the next month. We renewed our vows and started over.

Recovering, Somewhat

When I began the position of manager in Oklahoma City, my self-worth was at the bottom of the barrel, yet the opportunity afforded by FKW sparked some latent strength. Work has always been therapy for me, and I certainly needed some now. In addition to the owner, there were three people on board when I arrived whom God used to help me recover. Travis Brown was my assistant project manager, and I selected him to replace me when I moved to corporate headquarters. Travis was loyal, and of great value in interacting with the government counterpart. His loyalty and reinforcement helped me personally and gave me space to begin to regain confidence.

Ken Siekman lifted my spirits. Ken was vice president of business development. We began to have opportunities to expand the company at other locations based upon our excellent reputation. We performed everything the Federal Aviation Administration (FAA) asked us to do and did it flawlessly. During one of our periodical reviews, the FAA director asked, "Is there anything you folks can't do?"

Dean Wadley responded, "We don't deliver babies."

Because of our expansion, I was moved to corporate headquarters to help write proposals and act as the Vice President of Operations. Ken and I had great times. I taught him the military construction process, and he taught me how to be comfortable with the important people in the business world.

Then there was Carol Hooper. She was the administrative assistant to the executive crew, and a true professional and quick learner with absolute dedication to the FKW mission. Ken, Carol, and I, along with other support staff, like David Tolman, an electronics guru, spent many long hours in the trenches writing proposals and keeping track of numerous projects. It was hard work, but we had an excellent team that not only bonded but also would do anything for the team and perform any task. The day a proposal had to be mailed out, vice presidents and clerks worked side by side editing, reproducing copies, filling note-books, and then making the final dash to the FedEx box just as the truck was pulling up.

Within five years we grew about ten-fold, with contracts at twenty different locations around the nation, ranging from facility maintenance to digital telephone systems to automated warehouse construction and maintenance.

Investment in Excellence

Having Jenny with me was a great boost personally and also financially. She took a position at the FAA as a government employee, and we set our sights on getting out of debt and into a better way of life. The FAA was in the process of sending all employees to a one-week seminar called *Investment in Excellence.* As her spouse, I was invited to attend the seminar. Dr. Louis (Lou) Tice had developed a model of the human mind and techniques for replacing false information stored in one's subconscious with the truth. I saw connectivity between Tice's process using "Affirmations" and Norman Vincent Peale's "Thought Conditioners." I began to add the Tice process to my learning and realized significant personal benefit.

The combination of the reinforcement from Jenny, the three friends mentioned above, and the affirmation process began to produce positive changes in my life. I found that the false information stored in my sub-conscious, some as early as age four, could be replaced with true infor-mation. I went through the Lou Tice seminar twice and then became a certified facilitator.

I approached Dean Wadley about presenting the seminar to the FKW corporate staff. He was receptive to the idea, and we sched-uled alternating sessions so offices could continue to function. Carol Hooper also took the facilitator training, and assisted with the train-ing. It was well-received by everyone, and I was especially happy with the results. During his closing remarks on the last day of the seminar, Dean said, "This is the best thing that has happened to our company."

Later on, I was invited to attend a worldwide conference at Lou Tice's headquarters in Seattle, which I readily accepted. During the conference, I had the opportunity to share with Dr. Tice and his staff how great I considered their seminar and my desire to delve further into the process they had developed. We were all treated to a feast of fire-baked salmon. In one of the group sessions, we discussed ways to improve the seminar by adding a more definitive spiritual dimension.

Members of the group were offered the opportunity to help develop the concept. When I returned home, knowing this would take a lot of research, I decided to counsel with my pastor to get his take on my possible involvement with the Tice team. His advice was to look at developing a similar program based upon biblical truth, but staying independent. I decided that was the thing to do and enrolled in Oklahoma State University (OSU) as a PhD student to begin research that would support such a seminar.

Eternal Building Blocks

Meanwhile, I still had contracts that needed attention. I boarded a plane for an early flight to one of our project locations. It was my routine each morning to have a quiet time with the Lord before starting my day, but because of the early takeoff time, I planned to use the travel time on the flight to have an unhurried time of prayer and reading my Bible. As we approached cruising altitude, I took out the travel Bible Doug had given me for Christmas and began to read. I had been asking the Lord to show me the spiritual construction components of our eternal being. I sensed I should look up the passage pertaining to heart, soul, and mind.

I found it in Matthew 22:37. The Pharisee had asked Jesus what the greatest commandment was. Jesus replied: "You shall love the Lord your God with all your heart and with all your soul and with all your mind."

I believe the Spirit quickened my understanding to know that when Jesus answered the question regarding the greatest commandment, He described the construction blocks He had used to create the eternal components of the human being: the heart, the soul, and the mind. I was elated and began a study of those building blocks and how they are related. A synopsis of the results of this study and my proposed definitions of the heart, soul, and mind are at Appendix A, Module 3: Definition and Functions of the Heart, Soul, and Mind.

A literature search to support the study of the definitions revealed a sparse field of documentation dedicated to these definitions and that which was available was often ambiguous in the definitions, sometimes intermingling definitions of heart, soul, mind, and spirit. Since Jesus is the Creator, I believe His response was all-inclusive, and there are no other components with which one may love God and, further, each of the components is unique and definable.

I approached the study as an engineer, beginning with the hypothesis that heart, soul, and mind were distinct, with each having a distinct definition and a distinct purpose. Then using best-fit procedures from engineering experiments, I listed every reference to heart, soul, and mind in the Bible and the associated use in each case to derive a probable definition. From this list, the dominant use suggested that the heart is the center of value, the soul is the center of identity, relationships, and emotions, while the mind is the center of cognition and logic.

Regent University

The study at OSU did not fit the exact criteria I was looking for, so I began to consider other options. During that summer, Jenny and I visited our dear friends Paul and Lorraine Pettijohn in Yorktown, Virginia. One of the many sights we toured was the Regent University campus at Virginia Beach. As we passed through one of the buildings, my attention was drawn to a rack with brochures. When I picked up the brochure, I sensed a quickening in my spirit similar to the reaction I had when I opened the letter in Vietnam from the church in Tacoma. The brochure was an advertisement for a new program at Regent University, a PhD program in Leadership Studies. I knew this was the answer. I enrolled and was accepted in the doctoral program.

The first year was very challenging. Although Mr. Wadley generously allowed me time to work on the doctorate, I still had a full time job to concentrate on as well. The most difficult task in my study was learning the new language in a field distant from the rigid language of engineering. Even with all this stressful and fast-paced life I was engaged in, there were moments when I was reminded that there was a humorous side to it also. Such a moment occurred early on in the program between my advisor and me.

When I began the doctoral program at Regent University in 1997, one of the first assignments was to read a certain article and post our comments online using the electronic bulletin board to which all students had access. I read the article half a dozen times. It made absolutely no sense to me as a practitioner in leading an organization. Already exhausted from a full day of challenges in the corporate world, I posted the following comment: "This article makes absolutely no practical sense. If I were to use the language contained in this article in a presentation to the personnel in my organization, they would laugh me off the stage!"

The professor was up late also and came back with, "You are in a doctorate level program and need to learn to write and speak at that level. If you made a presentation to a group of academicians in the language of your comment, they would not only laugh you off the stage, they would tear up your paper!"

Now I have never been one to back off from a challenge, so I posted: "Professor, in the corporate world where I work and intend to stay, the academicians are outnumbered at least one hundred to one by working people who speak plain English."

The professor responded, "I shall do a bit of research and get back to you."

Two days later the professor posted his findings on the bulletin board. He wrote: "The percentage of the population with doctorate level degrees is presently less than you opine. It is, in fact, less than one half of one percent."

The exchange was never mentioned again.

Wandering in the Desert

When I accepted the job with FKW, I agreed to stay for five years. However, I enjoyed the job and could find no reason to terminate. The hard work of helping to build the company was successful and consuming. Unfortunately, with my almost total absorption in the work, it became evident that Jenny and I still had unresolved issues. We had been in and out of counseling during that time. During one of the sessions the counselor asked me, "Is there another woman involved?"

I truthfully responded that there was not, but I realized I had emotionally and romantically drawn away from Jenny. She asked for an explanation, but I told her I could not explain it. I am amazed that she stayed. Also, in the morass of wandering since Greg's death, I realized I no longer trusted God but had been afraid to admit it.

The next six years were not exciting. We began to bid against companies five to ten times our size, and we spent more than we were making and began to decline along with the camaraderie of the once close FKW family. The time for departure was at hand.

Debt Free, Fancy Free

It had been eleven years since I came to FKW. It took the first seven years to pay the debt we had incurred in Kansas from the houses that were disasters. During the last four years we were blessed with the ability to save enough for a down payment on our next house. A significant chunk of our nest egg resulted from Jenny's negotiating skills in buying and selling two houses for a significant, tax-free profit because we lived in each more than two years.

In the spring of 1998, Dean Wadley, the owner of FKW, decided to close the company, so we began to make plans to move on. Jenny and I had dreamed of owning an RV and touring America. We went to a dealer in Oklahoma City to look at pop-ups we could pull behind our Jeep Grand Cherokee. We didn't find one that caught our fancy, so we thanked the representative and headed for our car. As we were leaving the lot, just out of curiosity, we took a look inside a large fifth wheel parked at the exit. A fifth wheel trailer connects into the bed of the truck instead of a bumper hitch and is more stable on the highway. Jenny stepped inside and exclaimed, "This is it!"

My response was, "Whoa, this will not pull behind our Jeep!"

We purchased a Ford One Ton dually, thanked Dean Wadley for eleven productive years, said goodbye to lots of good friends and closed the chapter on our wanderings in "Egypt." On July 3, 1998, we picked up our forty-foot Travel Supreme fifth wheel RV in Indiana and headed west.

CHAPTER 12

Family on the American Highways

From Country Club to Septic Systems

By 1998 our son Doug had married Connie and they had their first son, Luke. Doug was now a KC-135 pilot stationed at a base near Spokane, Washington. They were preparing to move to Okinawa, so we chose to go to Spokane to help with the move and spend some time with them before they departed. They were getting their house ready to sell, and I volunteered to help. Be careful volunteering! My primary task for the move was digging out the septic tank under the deck. We didn't want to tear out the deck, so I spent several days under the deck with a camping shovel in a space that did not permit a sitting position.

Eventually, I located the lid to the tank so it could be pumped before the contract on their house could be closed. It was a humbling experience: from vice president with a country club membership and any American car of my choice, to being hunkered down under a deck digging out a septic tank! Anything for our children, right? I won't attempt to describe what I saw and smelled when I pried the lid open, but while holding my nose, I said, "I wonder if this is what my rebellion has smelled like to my Creator."

Grandsons and Black Cherries

Our grandson Luke was three years old at that time and his brother Logan was one. I had a great time playing with Luke, giving Connie more time to take care of the baby and perhaps grab a minute of rest once in a while. Luke called me "Opa," the German equivalent to grandpa. We often played hide-and-seek with each other. One time, when we visited them at Christmas, Luke, then just one-and-a-half years old, was just beginning to connect words and had learned to navigate the stairs.

On that day, he was coming down the stairs when I jumped out of hiding and scared him. It took him a few seconds to catch his breath, then he lit into me. He planted both feet, pointed his finger at me, and let me have it: "Yoooblitseryaddablattinzfissingn rounlyfrr!" he said in perfect gibberish.

He caught his breath and turned to proceed down the stairs, but decided he was not through: "Duckishshooomredishyfisschmooo and *opabladdishful*."

He stamped his foot and stomped down stairs. We were all gasping for breath from laughing so hard.

I guess Luke forgave me and on this trip I made it up to him when we went to the self-pick cherry farm. The black cherries were ripe. Doug and I carried Luke and Logan astraddle our necks, and they ate more cherries than they put in the bucket. When we got back to the house, Connie put them in their high chairs while she prepared dinner. I was eating cherries and got the hand signal from both boys that they also were ready for more cherries. They devoured the cherries as fast as I could halve the cherries and remove the pit.

Connie did not notice how many cherries they were gulping down, but the next morning, after she changed Logan's diapers, she educated me on cherry limits. Lesson learned, and I was about to learn some other lessons the hard way.

Tools for Transformation

I do listen to counsel from time to time and listening to my pastor was one of those times. Acting on his suggestion, I began to develop a program of personal transformation based upon Romans 12:2: "And do not be conformed to this world, but be transformed by the renewing of your mind." I reasoned if my heart was "desperately wicked," as posited by Jeremiah 17:9, it would be logical to begin there. Yet I had no desire to have my heart changed. After all, I had been making great strides in the spiritual realm, or so I thought. (Hmmm. I think another Scripture verse applies here; something about pride coming before a fall . . .) In any case, I decided to begin the experiment. I searched the Scriptures for verses regarding the condition of the heart and found Psalm 51:10: "Create in me a pure heart, O God, and renew a right spirit within me." I began to repeat the verse at least twenty-one times as I went for my morning walk behind the RV park at Fairchild Air Force Base. As I walked, I began to realize the heart referred to in the Scripture was not the heart that pumps blood, but the heart that is the center of value.

Then I learned to write a Personal Transform that helped me affirm the content of the verse as my own so that I would internalize and absorb the energy contained in the Scripture verse. Based upon previous research, I concluded that a Personal Transform must be personal, present tense, positive, specific, and contain words that express excitement. My initial Personal Transform for Psalm 51:10 was: "I am delighted that the Lord is purifying my heart!" As I repeated the Scripture verse (or Scripture Transform, as I started calling it) and then the Personal Transform, I visualized it as a capsule of energy drifting down into my heart at the center of my being. Then I watched as the capsule opened up like a time-lapse video of a flower to release its power to cleanse my heart. I repeated this exercise at least twenty-one times during my morning walks.

Initially, it was merely an act of will, but after several days, I actually began to desire a pure heart. I had committed Psalm 51:10 to memory years ago, but real change suggested by Romans 12:2 did not happen until I ingested the Scripture and my spiritual and cognitive networks absorbed its energy. I then began experimenting with other verses and developing other Personal Transforms with positive results.

Ready to Relax

Since I chose not to attend the residence session at Regent University in the summer of 1998, I could not enroll in the fall semester. Oregon seemed like a good place to explore, and we had a grandson on the way in Redmond. We parked our fifth-wheel camper in daughter Deb's front yard and set about to get ready for winter. I constructed a storage building and moved the stuff out of the garage so mother and new baby would have some protection from the elements when getting in and out of the car. I also purchased about seventy bales of wheat straw and built a wind barrier around the RV. With all essential tasks completed, I planned to relax and enjoy the break with nothing to do that required any mental energy. God had other plans.

Start Writing

One morning about 0400, I woke up and heard, *Get on the computer and begin to write.*

Does God work only at night? Anyway, I got up and turned on the computer, and God did a data dump in my head. The information came faster than I could write, and in less than two months, a seminar titled *Tools for Transformation©* (TFT) was in its final draft.

Did I Hear Correctly

Anson was born December 21, 1998. In a few months it was spring, and time to move on. Jenny and I spent two wonderful years touring America in our fifth wheel, visiting family and friends with me working on the doctorate whenever we could find a telephone hookup for the computer. The real challenge was finding libraries to conduct research. I had the privilege of using university and public libraries in Oklahoma, North Carolina, Virginia, Kansas, Oregon, and online.

As I neared the end of the coursework, the prospect of comprehensive exams, covering the entire six years of coursework, loomed ahead like a gorilla. I disliked exams and the fear from my dark, early college days began to haunt me. I intensified the practice of Scripture and Personal Transforms and was comforted somewhat by the remembrance that God had led me here and would see me through.

We were in West Virginia for an extended stay with my sister Norma in the small town of Jane Lew. She had a trailer park conveniently located by her restaurant and graciously allowed us to park our RV in it for as long as we wanted to stay. I shared many wonderful times with her as she prepared scrumptious meals and desserts for the next day's menu. I also enjoyed being her taster for new recipes.

One day while having quiet time in the RV, praying for help with the comprehensive exams, I somehow sensed that comp exams would not be necessary. The Lord must have planted that thought in my mind, because all apprehension dissipated and a strong sense of peace surrounded me. The next day when I went online to submit a lesson to Regent, there was an email from the professor with whom I had the electronic bulletin exchange during my first year in the program. He was announcing a new doctoral program for students whose interest was primarily practical application of leadership in the marketplace. It was called "Doctor of Strategic Leadership." A comprehensive interactive paper was required in lieu of comp exams. Yes! I had heard correctly. I transferred to the new program within the hour. God had answered my prayer.

The integrative paper required evaluation of all leadership theories and concepts presented in all the coursework. It took several months to complete, but it was worth it. I learned much more doing research for the paper than memorizing for comps. The professor confirmed this when he declared the comprehensive integrative paper to be excellent and the completion of all requirements for graduation.

Dun Rovin'

Jenny and I traversed the United States three times, always looking for the place we were to settle, always with the thought in the back of our minds: What is the best spot in this country to build a retreat center if not Kansas? After three years, we finally settled on Manhattan, Kansas, for many reasons, but the most obvious was that we already had title to a beautiful piece of property. We parked the RV on our land and proceeded to build our dream house on a beautiful spot facing Tuttle Creek Lake. Although I wasn't abandoning the dream of building a retreat center, I also wanted to test the waters for marketing TFT seminars. We moved into the house in May 2001 expecting to spend the remainder of our days there.

We fully expected to be marketing TFT seminars immediately upon graduation from Regent University and built the house with a full walk-out first floor to be used for the training area. The construction process turned out to be extremely stressful with delays and cost overruns by subcontractors. It took fourteen months instead of the planned nine months. Cost of construction went up twenty percent and we lost thirty percent of our investment savings when the stock market plummeted.

Rainbows

Three times over the past twenty years, I have stood in awe of a beautiful rainbow arching over the TCN property. The first instance was just after we moved into the house originally intended for a pastor. One freezing morning, about daybreak, I walked to the lake to watch the sun come up. I felt as if I were being beckoned to walk across a small frozen cove so I could see the sun better.

The air was sparkling! It was so cold the moisture in the air was freezing into minute crystals. I was facing east, enthralled by the beauty of the moment, but sensed I should turn around. There, arched directly over the TCN property, was the most brilliant rainbow I have ever seen. This phenomenon of God's creation held me spellbound in utter amazement for several minutes. I was filled with a peace about our future here, although uncertain about how it would happen.

The second rainbow appeared when the contractor was roofing our dream home in 2000. We were coming upon two weeks of perfect construction weather, ample time to complete the roof, but the framing subcontractor walked off the job with the new floor exposed. He didn't call and would not return my call. At the end of the two weeks, we had a thunderstorm that drenched the subflooring. I drove out to the house on Friday to see what the damage was, and as I topped the rise and turned toward the house, a beautiful rainbow stood perfectly arched over the house. I got out of the car and stood there in amazement, again receiving God's peace and assurance that things would work out. And they did.

The following Monday, the subcontractor showed up with a new determination to finish the job. It turned out he had come to a place in the roof structure that he could not figure out and became so frustrated he decided to quit. Over the weekend he pinpointed a mistake in the blueprint, so now he brought his findings to me and together we figured out how to make it work.

The Serpent

The third rainbow came several months later. Gerald Deaton, a long-time friend and an expert in flooring, agreed to come to our house in Manhattan to lay the carpet and help with the tile in the new house. Jenny and I had to take a trip, so Gerald decided to stay in the RV by himself and continue to work. He is a real prayer warrior and has been involved in spiritual warfare for several years.

Then the Lord led him to fast and pray over the house, which he did for five or six days. On the last day, as he was praying, he saw an image of the house and a giant serpent wrapped around the foundation. He got out of the RV and walked around the house, literally slaying the giant snake. Soon after that, the subcontractor hired another team to complete the roof and siding. This team was superior in craftsman-ship and even came up with a sunburst over the porch to highlight the house. It was then that the third rainbow appeared, as if to celebrate the cleansing of the air surrounding our house.

Cleansing the Land

There were other occurrences that now fit into the puzzle. One day I was walking in the small cove below the house and began to have an uneasy feeling that seemed to come from the other side of the cove. It made my skin crawl around my ears and neck. I walked around the cove and found an altar set up out of huge stones. A closer look around the altar revealed remains of small animals. A few yards away there was an area with stone benches and another altar in front of the benches. It was creepy. I tore down the altars and dislocated the benches, then walked home with a very uncomfortable feeling in my spirit. I began to try to find out if any resident in the area had any knowledge of a Satanist group. There were unconfirmed reports that such a group existed.

Later we learned the high knoll on TCN was likely a ceremonial site used for worship that may have been other than biblical. I shared this with other prayer warriors who had experience with "cleansing the land." Two of those warriors came to the land and confirmed there was an unfriendly spirit hovering about. They read Scripture and spoke specific prayers used in similar cleansings. We experienced no more unfriendly activity and, in fact, erected a cross near the spot and held Easter sunrise services there with wonderful results.

In retrospect, the threat to me from the enemy in 1981 as I flew over the area, "If you set foot on that ground, I will kill you!" was two-fold. It was not only an attempt to prevent me from building a retreat center on TCN, but also to prevent me from being a vessel through which the land would be cleansed of Satan's evil control. Various sources support the claim that satanic activity is geographical. This claim was affirmed by the incident when Jesus ordered the legion of demons out of the Gadarene as recorded in Mark 5:10: "Also he begged Him earnestly that He would not send them out of the country."

Dr. David Jeremiah collaborates Barnhouse's claim that Satanic forces are geographically assigned. In his book, *Agents of Babylon,* Jeremiah argues,

> This record [Daniel 10] makes it apparent that Satan assigns his demons geographically. It's probable that he assigns one demon prince to head the satanic activity of each principality or government on the face of the earth . . . it's against this army of evil princes that we are in daily conflict.[7]

Worst Case

Before we started building the house in 2000, we did a financial analysis that included a worst-case scenario. The worst case was that we could barely make it if I would have no income other than my retired pay, the RV would not sell, and the house exceeded our maximum loan amount. All three of these possibilities became a reality. I explored every avenue for work in the local area to use my doctorate, to no avail.

One day, on the Regent University alumni website, there appeared an ad for a position for an associate professor in the new Department of Leadership at a nearby university. The ad contained the description of the degree I had been awarded a few months earlier. Finally, here was the ideal position. I prepared the requisite application. Several weeks later I received a letter informing me another candidate had been selected. What was going on? There was nothing but brick walls every way I turned.

Well "Yes," but "No"

The RV went on the market as soon as we moved into the house, and two years later it was still on the market. The monthly payment and the increased construction costs depleted our savings and the stress was onerous. We were now among that illustrious group of people known as "retired," but I had no intention of sitting down while the world passed me by. My enthusiasm for putting the hard-earned doctorate degree to work through TFT was very high.

One church group agreed to beta-test the seminar. I presented it to the group of twelve people one night a week for six months. An analysis of the before and after data showed positive results. A synopsis of the TFT and the beta-test results are presented at Appendix A.

I presented these results to several pastors. There were no immediate takers, so I got busy with life and set the TFT on the shelf.

The Three-Thirty Visitor

The stress from the bombardment of apparent failure from every effort degenerated into a morass of despair. I was not suicidal, but I became keenly aware of the reason people reach the point where death is more palatable that the depressing fog of living. By this time, I was experiencing the helpless feeling I went through when we lost all our savings and vehicles on our previous stay in Kansas. I came to the conclusion that Satan could not kill me directly, but could accomplish the same result if I permitted the stress to wreck my health. I frequently woke up after three or four hours of sleep with a strong feeling of impending doom.

This cycle became so consistent that regardless of what time I went to sleep, I was awakened at 0330 by what I began to call the Three-Thirty Visitor.

Where once I had a very close relationship with my Lord, it seemed He had now abandoned me. Without the assurance of His presence, I returned to the fear of insanity and the resulting chaos. I was amazed I was able to function at all. I also found that Job of the Old Testament and I had one thing in common. We both declared that, "Though He slay me yet will I trust Him" (Job 13:15). I meant it some of the time. I have no way of knowing for sure, but there has been a pattern of unexplainable incidents that could have had a very negative impact on my longevity.

Fleece for TCN

The only stabilizing force during those days came from the Scripture Transforms I focused on during a one-hour walk every morning. During one of those walks I voiced my frustration to the Lord and laid the whole thing about TCN before Him. If there was to be a retreat center here, send someone to donate as much as ten dollars for that purpose. If we are to sell and go somewhere else, send a buyer.

Three days later on my walk to the lake, a neighbor met me on the road and asked if I had any lots for sale. I took them on a tour of the property and they asked for a price for a twenty-acre tract that was separate from the main TCN property and a price for the entire fifty acres that remained of TCN. We negotiated a price for the twenty-acre tract and proceeded to close the deal.

I became totally exhausted from hard labor on a road required by the contract and from lack of sleep. I developed an irregular heartbeat from the fatigue and stress and concluded I would soon die from a heart attack and Satan's prediction would come true. "For the thing I greatly feared has come upon me, and what I dreaded has happened to me" (Job 3:25).

The RV finally sold, but we had to come up with thirteen thousand dollars to pay off the loan. We cashed in another IRA and charged the remainder to our credit card, due in two months. The stress was ter-rific and energized a new metamorphic phase that wrought numerous attempts by unknown forces to destroy the forming butterfly. I needed a change of scenery! I was soon to learn that God has a very distinct method of changing one's internal as well as external scenery.

PART TWO

OUT OF THE ASHES, NEW LIFE

CHAPTER 13

On the Trail with the Master Trainer

Encounter with a Burned-Out Stump

The change of scenery was a trip to Sisters, Oregon, on Easter weekend 2002. We were spending the holiday with our daughter, Deb, and her family. Prior to our arrival, Deb had made arrangements for me to present the TFT seminar proposal to the pastor of her church and another pastor in a nearby community. Both presentations were courteously received, but no invitation was extended to present the seminar. I knew that TFT was worth the time and effort I had put into it and believed Christians would benefit if they put it into practice. Why wasn't I able to convey this to anyone else? Doubt crept in.

The night held no sleep, only darkness. Finally, before daybreak, I got up and went for a walk, meandering while I tried to think through all these recent happenings. The sun was just creeping over the horizon as I arrived at an area on the edge of a national forest that had been largely destroyed by fire several years earlier. As the sun came up, it illuminated the remains of a giant ponderosa that had been stripped of its branches, and its life, by the fire. But it stood in defiance of the forces that had robbed it of its ability to breathe.

I have learned many lessons from God's nature, and my senses became alert to the possibility I might learn one here. I wondered if this tree and I had something in common. The thought drew me closer to the goliath silhouetted against the early dawn as if it was saying, "Come closer!"

As I began walking toward the giant wooden monolith, excitement stirred within me. I arrived at the base of the giant, stood looking upward along its charred height and spoke to it: "OK, I am here. Now what?"

Have you ever talked with a tree? Well this one said, *Look where your feet are*. Near the base of the giant were the remains of another large tree that had almost totally burned. The stump was charred and hollowed out by decay, as shown in the picture preceding Part 2. Out of the decayed ashes a new ponderosa pine sapling was growing. As I stood there looking at the new life coming out of the ashes of the dead tree stump, I understood this was a picture of my life. I was being promised a renewed life. I was overwhelmed by the Presence of Joy! I began to laugh and could not stop. I danced around like Scrooge after the visit from the ghost of Christmas Future. It was delightfully incredible.

When I came down off the mountain, so to speak, I wound my way back to Deb's house, where everyone was already dressed for Easter Sunday services. When I walked through the door, Deb asked, "What happened to you?"

I began telling them about the little tree, and the joy welled up in me and I began laughing all over again. By the expression on their faces, I knew they wondered if I had truly lost it. I assured them all my gears were still aligned and we began to rejoice together. But they were still reluctant to take me out in public.

Not One, but Two

There were moments that I found it difficult to control my joy, but we made it through the day. However, I noticed Jenny and Deb were watching me out of the corner of their eyes. I went back to the remains of the stump the next morning with a camera. Lo and behold! To my surprise there was not one, but two saplings growing close together out of the ashes—one just slightly taller than the other. "That is Jenny and me!" I exclaimed to all the creatures in the forest and began laughing and dancing all over again. "God is bringing new life for both of us out of the ashes of our past!" And so it has been.

For my next birthday, Deb presented me with an enlargement made of the picture of the old stump cradling the two new lives emerging out of the ashes. It sits in a very prominent place, and it always brings a smile to my heart and joy to my soul. When the clouds cast shadows in my life, I mentally go back to the forest and the stump and receive strength to face the challenges that come into our world.

Political Aspirations

When we first retired and hit the road in our Travel Supreme RV, we visited our son-in-law's parents, Michael (Mick) and Dot Ann Ricker, in Whitefish, Montana. Aside from the fact that Mick had to cut some trees for us to make the turn into his driveway—and the wheels of the RV crushed a clay drain pipe—it was a wonderful visit. One day I was walking around their property with my grandson Anson astraddle my neck. There was a huge bull in a pen nearby. Anson saw it and, in the language of an eighteen-month-old, let me know he wanted to get closer. I have no idea what the bull had to do with the recollection. But a thought jolted me: if America continues on its present path, this little boy will have no life as we know it and, in fact, may be persecuted. I made an unspoken promise to that boy right there that I was dedicating the remainder of my life to do everything I could to help restore America.

Early in 2002, our retirement dream house on Tuttle Creek Lake was essentially completed, so we sought avenues to get involved with the local and state government. Politically, my father was a Southern Democrat who supported Harry Truman. When I registered to vote I did so as a Democrat. However, Jenny and I agreed party affiliation should be set aside until we discovered our own First Principles. As we studied the history of America, we became Originalists, believing the Declaration of Independence and our Constitution are still our guiding principles. Since there was no Originalist political party in Kansas, Jenny and I agreed the platform of the Republican Party was the closer of political parties to our beliefs, so we registered in Kansas as Republicans.

We attended a Meet-and-Greet gathering at the park and met the leaders in the local party leadership and began to get involved. In the 2004 election cycle, Jenny and I supported the Republican House of

Representatives candidate for our district. He lost by just a few votes. Even more important, Paul Barkey, a retired Army chaplain, and other conservatives joined forces to support a Marriage Amendment for Kansas, defining marriage as between one man and one woman. The amendment passed with an overwhelming majority. We also teamed up to defeat a proposal to modify the city ordnance to provide special privileges for a certain class of citizens. Paul also ran for state representative for his district and asked me to be his campaign manager. We fought a good fight yet did not win. My greatest admiration for Paul and Jan came from their total devotion to their son, who was confined to a wheel chair. He was in every parade, at every candidate forum, and Paul's greatest supporter.

Then in 2006, I was drafted to run against a man who was now an incumbent and very popular. Paul Barkey agreed to be my campaign manager and we had a great time. Jenny and I walked the district and one of us knocked on every Republican's door in the district. We had rallies that were supported by numerous Republicans from the Kansas House and Senate. We came close, but as they say, "Close only counts in horse shoes."

In the 2008 election cycle, I was again drafted after all other potential candidates had turned down the invitation. The party president came to our house at 2200 on the last night before the filling deadline asking me to run again. "We have to have someone to carry the conservative message!" I agreed to carry the message knowing the odds of my winning were not good.

Again, Jenny and I went door-to-door in the sweltering Kansas summer and on into the autumn season. Again, we ran a vigorous campaign but did not win. We made many new friends and enjoyed the entire process. The greatest enjoyment for me was interceding on behalf of each family as I approached their house singing, "Bless this house, O Lord, I pray . . ." In the end even our opposition commended us for running a good campaign.

Jenny, the Mentor

Beginning with her first encounter with the party leaders, Jenny was a stalwart supporter of conservative values and restoration of the founding principles of America. She eventually became President of Riley County Republican Women. By the end of her first year, she had doubled the number of women actively involved.

Because of the combined efforts of many like-minded conservatives, by 2011, the officers in the Riley County Republican Party and the Riley County Republican Women were predominantly conservative. A conservative woman won the House seat in our district defeating the man who was my opponent.

I claim the pivotal event resulting in this great turnaround was Jenny's staunch activism, which sparked a cooperative relationship among the party members. Her active support of my campaigns and her tenacious work among the women of our county earned for her my utmost respect, as well as the respect of the community at large. The woman who succeeded Jenny as President of Riley County Republican Women was Jenny's close friend and protégé. To Jenny I say, "Well done!"

House Church

We passed through Denver, Colorado, on one of our trips across this great land and heard of a House Church conference going on there with John Eldridge as guest speaker. Deb and Doug had introduced us to Eldridge's book, *Wild at Heart*, and his writings had become favorites with our family. Jenny and I attended the conference and were so impressed with the House Church movement that we decided to consider the possibility of a house church in our home. We talked with the folks in our small group when we returned home and the idea was enthusiastically received. In 2005, The Harbour Church was formed. The group asked me to serve as pastor, and I was ordained under the auspices of an international church chartered for the purpose of supporting small churches worldwide.

We met in our house on Sunday morning, beginning with a country-style breakfast, then singing the glorious old hymns, normally a cappella, followed by a Bible lesson, which I facilitated. On Tuesday night we met at Bob and Alma Buchanan's house for a simple dinner and mutually agreed upon a discussion topic. Jenny and I enjoyed this close fellowship and Tuesday night became our favorite night of the week.

The group remained small with five or six families involved. We had wonderful sharing times with absolute trust among the members. Since that time, I have conducted funerals for two of our charter members, Clark and Vida Blockcolsky; Clark first, after a ten-year battle with various strains of cancer. He was a real fighter and continued to work as proprietor of the Blue Valley Electric in Olsburg, Kansas, until a month before he said, "OK, that's enough. I am ready to go home!" Vida, his only sweetheart of six decades, followed a few months later.

I am still amazed that the Lord gave me a mission while I was still struggling with the Three-Thirty Visitor and mental input that oscillated like a radio at the edge of its reception area. It was warfare, and my stubborn makeup was a plus in this case. Sometimes, when the input was oppressive, I would get up, go over onto the property, and confront the enemy head-on, preparing to return to him the action he demanded of me at the urinal in Vietnam.

The weekly preparation time for the Bible lesson was probably more beneficial to me than to the group, but they kept coming back. Maybe it was for the breakfast Jenny prepared every Sunday, but it baffled me that anything productive could come from a spiritually and mentally vacillating pilgrim. In retrospect, I see in my life the protective hand of a loving Father who sees the future and operates as the great I Am such that He sees the final outcome in the present tense.

Toward Home

With the turning point in my journey being the encounter at the burned out stump, I began to view the pain of my past to be surpassed by a journey toward home. The Lord had tried me and exposed the sludge in my life. For several months He allowed me to travel without any awareness of His presence. I suppose He is bringing me out so that He can bring me in, to expose what is in my heart just as He did the children of Israel in bringing them out of Egypt.

As I am writing this portion of the record, by world standards, Jenny and I are near the top of the ladder. We live in a 4,200 square foot house on forty acres on a lake with a million-dollar view. We drive a nice car and a Ford pickup. We spend our summers in the cool Northwest in a house we share with Deb and family. But these pale in the light of having our names written in Heaven, to live in America, to be healthy and to have wonderful, healthy children and grandchildren. We have good friends all over the world. Best of all, Jenny and I are becoming best friends.

I have kept personal journals since 1972 and have referenced these in the writing of this book. I have also included excerpts at appropriate places in the book. The font for the journal entries will be different to distinguish it from the text of the story. The following excerpt from one of my journals describes the conditions where Jenny and I grew up:

It is two degrees Fahrenheit (2°F) outside this morning and I sit in a comfortable chair at 68F watching a beautiful sunrise over the lake. So what have I to complain or be concerned about? It is a humbling experience to consider where we came from in the hills of Appalachia; living in a house so poorly insulated that the snow blew through the cracks in the winter; where we walked a mile to the nearest store, had a hand pump for water and a two-holer for an outhouse. We used to say we were so poor the church mice brought us care packages.

Why is my life not beaming with joy? I have attended myriad wonderful inspirational seminars that have been somewhat helpful, but not healing. The processes these folks build their seminars on are helpful to millions, but do not ferret out the false-truths buried deep in the subconscious of some people, such as me, who have been injured emotionally from the beginning of their lives.

The term "false-truth" appears on the surface to be ambiguous. However, Jesus used the same "ambiguity" in Matthew 6:23, saying, "If therefore the light in you is darkness, how great is that darkness." The term false-truth may be new, but the concept that false information may be stored as truth in a person's subconscious mind is not new and is a valid concept in psycho-cybernetics. The *Tools for Transformation* seminar contains a detailed discussion of this concept in Appendix A.

No Thanks

Looking back, I recall hearing God challenge me to get involved in the battle against Satan and his minions in some form of deliverance advocacy. I became acutely aware there were areas in my life that I had not surrendered to the Lord and was still not willing to do so. Reasoning that I would be ineffective in the spiritual battle, I turned down the assignment. However, in God's own plan, I have been seriously involved in the battle.

I am totally convinced that my only source of strength in this battle is the Word of God, which I have been assimilating for the past thirty years. Although I understand that the battle is not over, I cling to the promise that eventually He will bring me "forth as gold" (Job 23:10). I feel vulnerable, having believed for thirty years that I knew what His plans were for me, but I am ready to roll up my tent and go as soon as He says, "Move out!" The exciting aspect of the waiting now is that I am facing toward Home. And it appeared I would not have to wait long.

Rwanda, the Dream

In the spring of 2010, Paul Pettijohn walked into our house in Kansas, hardly said hello, put both hands on my shoulders, and exclaimed, "You and I are going to Rwanda!"

We were going to teach godly entrepreneurship to thirty officials in the Rwanda government. After Paul departed, I walked out into the Kansas night and looked into the majestic heavens that spread out like giant wings and enclosed me as part of the cosmos. With arms stretching toward the stars, I exclaimed, "Lord, You and I make a perfect team. You are perfectly strong; I am perfectly weak!"

Then I began to laugh joyously and could not stop. The laughing and dancing lasted for several minutes. It was a wonderful repeat of the encounter with a burned-out stump in Oregon several years earlier. We developed the material and made reservations for a Sunday departure. On the Friday before we were to depart, Paul stepped out of the shower and said to Lorraine, "I have a severe headache." Before she could respond, he collapsed and was dead before he hit the floor.

I was devastated! Paul was not only one of three best friends, he was my mentor. I agreed to proceed with the training, but the folks in Rwanda who had scheduled the training were so devastated they canceled the program entirely. I assumed that trip was another false start for me and forgot about Rwanda.

Kansas in the Rearview Mirror, Again

That year, Jenny and I began to get the impression that our sojourn in the beautiful Flint Hills was once again coming to an end. Leaving would mean selling our dream house. We consulted real estate agents we knew and the news was not very promising. Although Manhattan had not been hit as hard as other places, the housing market was still very slow. We were advised that we should expect at least a year for the house to sell. We shared our thoughts with our House Church group for prayer. Some were initially angry with us for abandoning them, but in due time they all reluctantly agreed it was in our best interest to be closer to our children and grandchildren.

Therefore in August 2010 we solicited proposals from three real estate firms. The appraised value from each of them was lower that we were willing to sell the house for. However, we selected an agent and began to negotiate the listing price and conditions. My lowest price was well above the agent's appraisal, but we didn't have to sell and considered the location premium and the quality of construction well above average. The agent finally agreed to list the house at the higher price and told us to prepare for a long wait. So what? I like it here!

Two days later, as we were having dinner at a local restaurant with our friends, Jenny's cell phone rang. She answered and just about jumped on the table. Everyone in the restaurant looked our way to see what was going on. When she quit stammering, she said, "That was the agent! We have an offer that is almost full price! She wants us to come to her office as soon as possible to accept the offer!"

We quickly ate the remainder of our meals then made our way to her office. During the paperwork bonanza, I panicked for a minute when she said the couple insisted we leave my beautiful old cast iron potbelly stove.

"No way!" I exclaimed.

"You can't be serious!" the agent said.

I was serious, but the look on Jenny's face caused me to rethink how serious I was.

"OK," I said. "Give me the pen!"

It turned out the couple "just happened" to be passing through Manhattan with no serious plans to move to Manhattan, at least not right away. Just to look the housing market over while there, they "just happened" to contact our agent, who took them on a tour of our house. They actually left for home Thursday morning, but were so impressed with the house they turned around and came back to make the offer. They were the first couple to look at the house. Coincidence? Or Divine intervention?

Then came the test. By the first of December the couple's house in Northern Virginia had not sold and the sale finalization was on hold. We decided to take a step of faith and flew to Sisters, Oregon, to spend Christmas with Deb and investigate the housing market there. It would be nice to live near our daughter and her family during our retirement years. Little did we know what we would discover when we arrived.

Walton's Mountain

Our grandchildren, Anson and Tate, really enjoyed the replay of the TV series *The Waltons*. When we came in December to examine the possibility of moving to Sisters, Anson and Tate asked for an audience with us.

"Opa and Oma, we want to do like the Waltons did on Walton's Mountain. So can we look for a house that we can all live in?"

After long discussions of the pros and cons of such an arrangement, we began to look for a house that would accommodate all six of us.

Although we were excited about all these new possibilities, I was dragging my feet because I was still dealing with all the dreams that had gone unfulfilled: the retreat at Tuttle Cove North, the *Tools for Transformation* seminar, and the doctorate degree at Regent University. How had I so completely misunderstood the Lord's plan for all of these undertakings? At the same time, I could not deny the circumstances surrounding the sale of our house that were so amazing. I could only believe the Lord was orchestrating the events, so I reluctantly went along with the search for a house.

We eventually made an offer on a three-story house near Sisters that was big enough for our two families. I did not like the house and really didn't look very close as we toured it. Tod and I wanted to make a ridiculously low offer on the house, but were shamed into raising our offer by our wives and the agent. With the offer made and Christmas over, Jenny and I began the flight home.

As we picked up our car at the airport, Jenny's cell phone rang again: the financing came through for our Manhattan buyers, and our offer on the three-story house was accepted. We were well on our way to living the Walton lifestyle, with a few slightly updated modifications—and the challenge to get our furniture out of the Manhattan house in two weeks in the middle of a terrific snow storm.

House on the Prairie

Danny and Teresa Dodge, good friends of ours, owned a car hauler that they insisted we use to take enough furniture to Oregon to last until we could get settled. Because the weather over the Rockies was not passable in a truck and trailer at that time, they also invited us to stay in Danny's parents' farmhouse, standing vacant at that time. We spent two months with the Dodges, secluded in the country, helping with the cattle and farm animals and just resting. It was a good time for the two of us to stop and sort out our lives.

We did have one three-day period that was tenuous. Danny must have electrical power to operate breathing apparatuses. With a blizzard on the way, Teresa and I decided to get the emergency generator operational. It would not even growl!

With snow stinging our faces and piling up anywhere it hit an obstacle, our attention level went from urgent to panic. My four-wheel-drive truck was fifteen miles away, hooked to the loaded car hauler. My front-wheel-drive Buick made it halfway. After several attempts, we were able to get Teresa's van close enough to get jumper cables to the generator. *Growl, growl, growl.* Nothing. *Growl, growl, sputter, sputter* and then off with a *roar*! That was scary! With numb hands we gave each other a high five and rushed to the house for some hot tea.

The wind howled all night and the lights flickered as we prayed. Fortunately, the power stayed on and our first task the next day was to replace the battery on the generator.

It's a Done Deal

By the middle of March the weather had cleared in Kansas and we closed on the house in Sisters at a title company in Manhattan. All that remained was for the weather in the Rockies to clear. On March 20, it looked as if we had a short window, so we said goodbye to our good friends, cranked up the F-150, and headed west! The first day out, all went well—the roads were clear and traffic was light—but it got really interesting in Wyoming. As we departed Laramie, the winds from the northwest began to pick up with gusts of fifty miles per hour. We began to see signs: "No Light Trailers Beyond This Point." We reasoned that did not apply to us because our trailer was fully loaded. I offered to drive, but Jenny said, "Nope, I can handle it!" And she did, like a pro.

Five days and a small fortune in fuel costs later, we guided the superb-performing F-150 into the Miller/Ricker driveway in Sisters. We were greeted by Tod, Deb, Anson, and Tate with a big WELCOME HOME banner across the entrance to our new home.

Much to my surprise, the newly painted interior and new carpet on the ground-level floor we were to occupy—compliments of the bank when we closed—made the place look decent. *Okay*, I thought. *I can handle this.*

In July we returned to Manhattan for the remainder of our furniture. While there I contacted three neighbors who were interested in buying the remaining forty acres originally designated for the retreat center. They each wanted to submit a bid and needed time to evaluate the price, so we headed out in the biggest truck U-Haul provides and a

U-Haul trailer behind the F-150. I drove the U-Haul truck and Jenny drove the F-150. Tod flew into Denver and took over the U-Haul truck while Jenny and I tackled Wyoming again in the F-150, arriving in Sisters very road weary from five days fighting the wind.

This time we were also greeted by our son Doug and his crew, who were visiting to help with the house-warming activities. With all that help we made short order of unloading. All that was left to make our portion of the house livable was to build an entire new kitchen. Oh, how I missed my good plumber friends, the Blockcolskys, from Kansas. I am passionate about trout fishing and Oregon has some great trout streams, but I spent the summer under the kitchen sink! Have you ever visited Someday Isle? There is great fishing there.

On the Road Again

With the kitchen completed and autumn in the mountain air drifting down from the snowcapped Three Sisters Mountains, we began to feel the excitement of taking a leisure tour across this beautiful country of ours one more time. We purchased a used Komfort travel trailer, hooked it up to our trusty Ford F-150, and headed east. The excitement for me was again marred by input from some evil source injecting thoughts like, *On this trip I will finally gain control and you will do what I have been telling you to do.* These thoughts plagued events that should have been pleasant. They caused me to stay on guard with little time to relax. But I have now reconciled myself to the mission of walking through enemy territory and recording the journey. With this in mind, our goal was to wind up in Florida for the winter so I could focus on writing this record.

This journey led through Manhattan, Kansas, then to West Virginia to visit family and treat our palates on good country cooking, and our eyes on the kaleidoscope of autumn color in the Appalachian Mountains. Turning south as the leaves began to fall, we sojourned with our son Doug and family in North Carolina.

The days with grandsons Luke and Logan on the skeet ranges were great. The nagging input about handling guns was scuttled by

Transforms. Levi, Doug and Connie's youngest son, enjoyed fishing, so he and I went to the lake near their house, and caught enough bass and crappie for a fish fry. Cleaning the fish and cutting off their heads with a fillet knife was unpleasant, but I welcomed the opportunity to use Transforms to cleanse the false-truth out of my mind. In this case, 2 Timothy 1:7 worked great: "For God has not given us a spirit of fear but of power and of love and of a sound mind."

The positive aspect of this issue is that I am no longer afraid to face the enemy head-on and am confident I will eventually learn the truth as I was promised in Vietnam at 0400 one morning. On that occasion, the spiritual enemy came and chilled out the room, but the Lord penetrated the fog and gave me this promise: *"You shall know the truth and the truth shall make you free"* (John 8:32). The offensive weapon against the forces of evil is the Word of God. I am gaining understanding of the warfare in which I am engaged.

The End of a Dream

We advertised TCN, our remaining forty acres in Kansas, and finally negotiated a price with one of the neighbors. The price was less than we had expected to receive and more than they had expected to pay. However, it was a consensus among our family members that it was time to close the Kansas chapter in our lives and move on. We closed the sale on December 20, 2011, and calculated the amount to pay Doug, Deb, and Lorena for their shares invested in TCN.

TCN had been more than just a beautiful spot in the rolling Flint Hills for more than thirty-five years. To me, it was at the same time a solace and a battleground. The most beautiful sunrises were the beginning of my winter dawns. The most awesome storms and fearsome cloud formations were frequent fare during the spring and summer. The rainbows were a frequent reminder the Creator honors His promises.

The battleground elevated my courage to a new level. Facing flying steel from an enemy's weapon in Vietnam paled in comparison to engaging the dark forces of evil in their own area of operation.

I had been trained in the conduct of battle against a visible enemy of limited strength. I entered the Invisible War against an invisible enemy of unknown strength relying only on OJT (on-the-job training). A journey that began four decades earlier with a dream of a place to share my overpowering sense of peace came to a fork in the road. And like Yogi Berra says, "When you come to a fork in the road, take it."

Chapter 14

Frontal Attack

Dream with no Vision

In September 2011, Jenny and I purchased a used travel trailer and headed east with the ultimate destination being Florida for the winter to mount a frontal attack on the past and focus on writing this book. We stopped to spend Christmas with Doug and his family. The sale of TCN was finalized December 20, and all property ties in Kansas were history. A dream of thirty-seven years never became a vision. I felt as if a part of me was buried on the hill that was TCN. So be it. The future is uncertain, but I have this consolation: "Some trust in chariots and some in horses, but we trust in the name of the Lord our God" (Psalm 20:7).

I remember waking up the morning after the sale of TCN feeling anxious about the drastic changes taking place in our lives. I dispelled the negative emotion with twenty-one repetitions of this Scripture Transform: "Peace I leave with you, My peace I give to you" (John 4:27).

My Personal Transform, which I also repeated twenty-one times, was: "I am wonderfully at peace as I see Jesus transmitting His perfect peace to me!" As I repeated the Transform, I also visualized waves of peace flowing from Jesus into my mind. That felt really great, but I did not prepare for an immediate assault.

Blindsided

Amazingly, after what appeared to be great success, Jenny and I had a severe conflict about what to do with the funds from the sale of TCN. She accused me of getting in her face, so I actually left the RV and spent the night in a motel.

While trying to calm down at the motel, I repeated numerous times, "I am crucified with Christ" (Galatians 2:20). "Lord, I can't do it. You alone know what the future is. But I also realize being crucified with You has not materialized in my life yet."

I thought about the storyline Jenny had selected for her devotional book for teenagers she was and is still planning to write. A husband commits suicide, leaving a note with a man he thought was a friend but who threw the note in the garbage. The story is about how the note finally gets back to the wife. So in my negative mood I thought, "Jenny subconsciously wants me gone and is fabricating a story that reflects that."

Then I considered George Bailey's plight in *It's a Wonderful Life*. George was going to jump in the river because he thought his meager life insurance policy was worth more than he was. My insurance policy would make up for the decrease in funds received from the sale to the TCN property by accepting a lower amount. I also sensed the enemy saying, *Yes, yes!* I discarded the thought, for that would be the ultimate disrespect toward my Creator.

I then reaffirmed my commitment to be crucified with Christ and began ingesting Galatians 2:20. I soon fell asleep, waking up about 0530. There was a Gideon Bible in the drawer, and I read about Jesus' trial and conviction and realized again how minute my suffering was, so I got in the truck and went back to the RV and apologized to Jenny for my faulty way of reacting the previous night.

The Birthday of the Savior

Sunday, December 25, 2011. Christmas with Doug, Connie, Levi, Logan, and Luke was a wonderful day with family, and Jenny and I began to resolve our conflict. We were beginning to wake up to the fact that we are waging a war with the enemy and blaming each other. It is interesting that the attack came at the end of the third day of fasting for Israel and the sale of TCN.

The boys got up about 0800. Doug carried on the tradition of reading the Christmas story in Luke and having a prayer of thanksgiving before opening gifts. It is so refreshing to have him lead his family in giving glory to the Lord for their abundance.

Jenny and I computed the amount we needed to redeem the shares in our corporation, Faith Enterprises, Inc., (FEI) owned by Doug, Deb, and Lorena. We first set aside a tithe on the gain on the land, then money for the car and savings.

Victory on the Rifle Range

The day after Christmas, my grandsons Luke and Logan and I went to the shooting range. It was great to enjoy target practice with thoughts of the past only faint memories.

On Tuesday, we all went to the Hibachi Hut for a mini celebration of selling the land in Kansas. We had a great time sharing and laughing about the good memories.

Jenny's best memories were the two baptisms in the lake in Kansas: Logan in December (*brrrrrrr*) and Levi in July.

Doug recalled that the property had resulted in one wife, three sons, and two baptisms. Connie laughed about her anxiety watching the boys driving the old truck when they could not even reach the pedals.

The boys shared several stories about adventure on the land when they came for visits, especially when they were younger. Luke remembered driving fence posts for the fence for his steer.

For me it was semisweet. I assume the Lord has managed this, but I felt like I may have failed by not getting the retreat center off the ground. Yet my growth indicates I was not ready for such responsibility.

Before turning in for the night, I dispelled the sad feeling with "The joy of the Lord is your [my] strength" (Nehemiah 8:10).

Onward and Upward

Jenny and I had a nice drive with the RV to Lorena's in Southern Pines on Wednesday, enjoying the new Garman GPS we got for Christmas. We had a good dialogue about our relationship and what to do with the proceeds from the sale of TCN.

"Lord," I prayed. "I really blew it last week. Thank You for forgiveness and another chance."

Jenny and I gave Lorena her check for her share of the proceeds from TCN. She was thrilled and hoped to use it to improve her house. We promised to help her when we returned from Florida.

I slept eight uninterrupted hours Friday night and went for a thirty-minute aerobatic walk Saturday morning with no cardiac reaction. I believe this confirms the irregular heart rate I have experienced in the past is the result of neurological fatigue caused by lack of adequate sleep.

With trial and error, I am learning to use Scripture Transforms to penetrate my thoughts and transform them from fleshly desires and fantasies to the mind of Christ. It does work, but with great effort of my will initially. It gets easier with practice. This is overcoming more than seventy years of habit.

Since war is inevitable, I choose to be on the winning team described in 2 Corinthians 2:14: "Now thanks be to God who always leads us in triumph in Christ and through us diffuses the fragrance of His knowledge in every place." In one of the classic sermons, Pastor Ron Dunn claimed the Apostle Paul was referring to the practice of the Romans to welcome their conquering general by diffusing a special fragrance into the air, alerting the populace that the general was on the way with the defeated general chained to his chariot. Pastor Dunn suggests that Paul was claiming that he had been conquered by Christ and was "chained to His chariot"[8] to always be led in triumph.

I have struggled with surrendering to the Lord. I perceive the reason has been the lie from Satan that God was going to use me as a judge against Jenny because she was keeping me from being a preacher! This is how distorted my life was in the rebellion. Incredible that I could entertain such a thought that Jesus wanted anything for me than to love Jenny as He loved the Church. This lie was planted in fear in 1957 and refined specifically in Lawton, Oklahoma, in about 1962. It was at that time that I experienced the torment of free falling through space and the first time I reached up my right hand to the Lord to save me.

Remembering can be very painful; the "black hole" incident in which I punished Greg for being afraid to sleep in his room came crashing into my mind. I stopped and wrote Greg another letter. The following is an excerpt:

> Greg, I am so very, very sorry! I have a hard time admitting that I was so cruel to you. It is incredible that God could forgive me. I know you have, but I have yet to forgive myself. My comfort comes from knowing you are safe and not afraid in the presence of Jesus. I look forward to seeing you and thanking you for all you did for your mother and me by absorbing the results of the ancestral sins of the fathers and mothers. I hope Jesus has rewarded you greatly.
>
> PS: Father, sometimes I don't think I can stand the pain of the memory of hurting my son. It doesn't seem fair that I should be forgiven. I think I understand why some people take their own life, but to do so only increases the evil already done.

I woke up the following morning with anxiety. I selected the following Scripture Transform and went for a walk:

> Be anxious for nothing, but in everything by prayer and supplication, with thanksgiving, let your requests be made known to God; and the peace of God, which surpasses all understanding, will guard your hearts and minds through Christ Jesus. (Philippians 4:6–7)

I now realize it will take time to erase the fear harbored for so many years. I woke up Friday morning at 0230 experiencing residual fear. I rebuked the fear and began repeating Isaiah 43:1: "Fear not for I have redeemed you; I have called you by your name, you are mine." I actually felt the spirit of fear leave. It was like the feeling after a deep sigh. Then I slept peacefully until 0600.

I am learning a lesson from Hezekiah, who was ill and about to die. It is written in 2 Chronicles 32:26–31: "Then Hezekiah humbled himself for the pride of his heart" and God blessed him with abundance and long life. Verse 31 is instructive: "God withdrew from him, in order to test him, that he might know all that was in his heart." God has done the same thing in my life and the nature of my heart was revealed, and it was not good. I went my own way and was angry with God. It has taken nine years for the anger to turn into a strong desire to be crucified with Christ. In all this, God has been faithful and kind. To Him be the glory. It matters not what I have accomplished so long as He is pleased.

Recon in Florida

My sister Norma invited us to spend the remainder of the winter at her retirement place near Bradenton, Florida. Since I was four years old, I had lived with fear from destructive thoughts and innuendoes lurking somewhere in my cognitive space and I was constantly on guard. While in Vietnam I operated without any fear from internal or external sources. I concluded the Lord had complete control of the destructive thoughts and innuendoes and the power for the permanent expulsion of them was contained in the Scripture Transforms. My goal for the next two months was an in-depth reconnaissance into spiritual enemy territory to determine the source of the random destructive thoughts. I was convinced these thoughts were not the real me, and I was going to find out their origin and expose the source, the tactics of the source, and the removal and recovery processes. I knew this required that I be totally transparent; four decades of fear of speaking or writing these thoughts had to be cast aside. I was initiating a frontal attack.

Armed with the Word of God, the most powerful weapon in existence, and taking the armor of God as fully as I understood it at that time, I turned on my computer and prepared to record the battle. I began by personalizing Isaiah 43:1–3 to fortify my belief that God has sent me on a mission through enemy territory and would guard me throughout the battle:

> Thus says the LORD God who created you . . . "Fear not for
> I have redeemed you; I have called you by your name, you are
> mine. When you pass through the waters I will be with you;

and through the rivers they shall not overflow you. When you walk through the fire you shall not be burned, nor shall the flame scorch you, for I am the LORD your God, the Holy One of Israel, your Savior."

Chosen for the Battle?

Scripture records that Satan roams to and fro upon the earth looking for someone to devour. "Be sober, be vigilant; because your adversary the devil walks about like a roaring lion, seeking whom he may devour" (1 Peter 5:8). Obviously Satan chooses individuals for the next battle site. In *The Invisible War,* Mr. Barnhouse suggests that God also chooses individuals for the battle and refers to the story of Job as an example. "The sufferings of Job began, not only by the permission of God, but by the direction of God."[9] The lessons from Job's challenge and eventual victory highlight the fact that Satan's power is limited by God and that a victory brings glory to God and blessings for the individual chosen for the battle. According to Dr. Barnhouse, "Such battles as that which was waged in the soul and body of Job are being fought in every part of the world every day."[10]

Rick Warren wrote in *The Purpose Driven Life* that God has a purpose for every person: "This . . . book is a guide . . . that will enable you to discover the answer to life's most important question: What on earth am I here for? By the end of this journey you will know God's purpose for your life."[11]

There have been many times in my life that I felt as if God could care less about me and my purpose. Warren would likely take that statement and say, "The problem, Richard, is that you are talking about *your* purpose and not God's purpose!"

After studying Warren's book, I began to learn that God's purpose has always been building His eternal kingdom and my part in this is to take Jesus to the marketplace. There is a battle going on in the marketplace, and one of the objectives assigned to me is to expose the nature of the enemy and the way this enemy engages human creatures in warfare and to contrast the nature of the Creator with His arch enemy. In order for that to happen, it was necessary for the Creator to permit Satan and

230 The Prodigal Road

his minions limited access to my life just as He did with Job. This would account for the peaks and valleys in my life.

It is interesting to note that God chose Job because he was "a blameless and upright man, one who fears God and shuns evil" (Job 1:8). If He chose me, it was out of my rebellion and disrespect for Him to show that He also loves prodigals.

Preparation for the Battle

Preparation for this battle included my twenty-three years as a soldier in an American uniform. I believe the principles of war I learned are applicable to the spiritual domain and the mission in which I am now engaged. Clarification that my calling has always been that of a soldier has made the transition from Army battle dress to donning the armor of God a natural progression.

It may even be that those years were just preparation for the spiritual conflict in which I am now involved. That would also explain the book handed to me by 1SGT Tolson as I boarded the plane in Vietnam in 1969, the master's course in bioenvironmental engineering in 1971–72, the *Investment in Excellence* course in Oklahoma City in 1987–88, developing the *Tools for Transformation* seminar and the process of devouring Scripture beginning in 1998, and the doctoral studies in strategic leadership at Regent University from 1997 to 2003. I now see this was not coincidental but systematic, progressive growth orchestrated by the Holy Spirit without my knowing what was happening.

This I know: I have not arrived. I am still tired and find myself always on guard, not yet fully trusting the Lord to protect me. But armed with the process to be transformed by the power of God's word, I march order my tent, douse the campfire until the ashes of the past are neutralized, and press forward to research the new life that may be just over that next mountain.

Spiritual Warfare and Groundwater Pollution

Research has been a fascinating and rewarding part of my career and, amazingly, the research in bioenvironmental engineering and the causes and correction of water pollution contributed to my grasp of mental and spiritual pollution. I recall my first day in the first biochemistry class at OSU. The professor showed slides of western Oklahoma, and I asked, "What are those mountains in the background?" After he figured out what I was asking about, he explained, "Those are not mountains. What you are seeing are huge piles of feedlot waste."

My next question was, "Why is that stuff not spread on the soil like we used to do in West Virginia?"

"I think you just identified your master's thesis topic," He said.

And so it was.

I learned the contaminants leaching out of mountains of manure piled around beef feed lots infiltrate the underground water sources. Medical research has revealed that expectant mothers who drink water from wells drilled into this contaminated underground water source sometimes give birth to babies with faulty heart valves.

The faulty valve results in lack of oxygen in the baby's blood stream, the baby's skin turns blue, and the baby is referred to as a blue baby. A more detailed discussion of this phenomenon is contained in my master's thesis, *A Comparative Study of Changes in the Soil* on file at the OSU library, and in an Internet article in 2013 that contained this statement:

> Excessive amounts of nitrogen, in the nitrate form, which is converted to the nitrite form in the body, will prevent oxygen from binding to hemoglobin in the blood. Infants are especially sensitive to excess nitrite and can suffer methemoglobinemia, or *'Blue Baby Syndrome.'*»[12]

My referenced master's thesis reported on the validation by laboratory research that the age-old process of properly distributed animal manure on cultivated cropland does have a positive, twofold effect: eliminating the concentration of pollutants and transforming the soil to enhance productivity and water retention of the soil to mitigate the stress of drought conditions.

So what is the connection between groundwater pollution and mental and spiritual pollution? The connection began to be apparent to me in 1971 while manually mixing aromatic, raw cow manure with soil test plots in the lab. I asked the virtual audience in the lab, "What am I, an electrical engineer, doing with my hands in this bucket of stinking stuff?"

The response I heard was, *I am preparing you to study the pollution of human minds.*

"That is good to know," I said. "But is there not a substance with a more pleasant aromatic content?"

Silence. Well, all right then!

I must admit this challenge gave the research project a different dimension, and it became a venture to find the comparisons between the effects of pollutants in the soil and pollutants in the mind. The first objective was to find what effects the addition of organic material had on soil that previously supported nothing but the most tenacious of weeds, then compare that to the positive effects of productive inputs on the human mind.

The comparisons of the pollutants is rather obvious. The nitrate laden contaminate seeping into the underground aquifer from which drinking water was being drawn is comparable to the negative information from culture and demonic activity that seeps into and pollutes the hearts, souls, and minds of humans. For instance, the heart, mind, and soul of children are often polluted by the contaminants of wrong values, neglect, and abuse. These actions by parents or culture, be it from mental or physical abuse, contaminate the child's heart, mind, and soul, causing skewed values, false beliefs about themselves, or scars of rejection.

Greg, Doug, and Debbie were recipients of just such contaminants, which I freely dispensed in their formative years. I believe inconsistency was one of the greatest culprits. They never knew what to expect from me. One day I was gentle; the next I was angry. Based upon what I have learned from the ongoing research, my heart, soul, and mind were polluted by the effects of the generational sin of anger. Reporting only as facts and not to cast condemnation on my dad, he preached love from the pulpit, but disciplined with explosive anger. I operated in the same generational sin of anger and other pollutants until the Lord stood me at attention and reset my life compass with positive counsel, deliverance, forgiveness, and love.

Various labels are used to describe the effects of this pollution, ranging from paranoia to mental illness to psychosis, accompanied by a variety of techniques to mitigate or remove the symptoms. The success of these techniques varies greatly as manifested by the admission by various agencies that mental health care in our culture is an abysmal failure. I can attest to this admission. I have been in and out of numerous counseling sessions with numerous practitioners with minimal success.

The positive effects of organic material on the soil are comparable to the effects of Thought Conditioners and Scripture and Personal Transforms on the human heart, soul, and mind. The Lord has blessed Jenny and me with the opportunity to learn and to be forgiven by our children. Now our greatest joy is to provide positive reinforcement to them along with unequivocal love. It has been a challenge to both them and us, but by the grace of God, life continually gets better.

Enemy Territory

In Vietnam, there were frequent opportunities to venture into enemy territory. I confirm that the enemy is desperate to hold claim to his territory and fights tenaciously with techniques that cause every step to be precarious. You kick an empty soda can on the trail and a dozen poisoned spikes slam into your chest, or your leg is shattered to bits by explosives packed in the can. My spiritual boot camp was a lot like that and I found the spiritual enemy just as ingenious in planting ugly and painful booby traps along the trail.

After a few virtual spikes in the solar plexus, it became obvious I needed to be armed with spiritual body armor and knowledge about spiritual warfare and the tactics of the enemy. I began a literature search and was surprised and gratified to find significant documentation on the personality and organizational structure of the spiritual enemy forces.

Pinning the Tail on the Donkey

The Medical News headline for April 13, 2013, read: "School shootings raise questions about adequacy, availability of mental health care."

Our culture appears to be stumbling around blindfolded, trying to pin the tail on the donkey when the problem may be that we have the wrong donkey. While the chaos of school shootings continues, our culture rejects the reality of demonic activity even though there is abundant historical, biblical, and empirical evidence that a complex network of militaristic spiritual beings does exist with a mission to cause as much chaos in humans as possible. This activity runs the gambit from pestering to possession. In the latter condition, the enemy spirit exercises various degrees of control over the host person.

Merrill Unger, in his book, *What Demons Can Do To Saints*, wrote: "The nature of the times in which we live calls for clarification of the precise role Satan and demons may play in the life and experience of a believer." Unger also argued that the action of demonic powers working to corrupt a person "may be of various degrees of severity, depending on the resistance the believer offers the satanic onslaughts (cf. James 4:7)."[13] Then the question, "Can a believer be indwelt by a demonic spirit?" Many theologians claim a demon cannot indwell a Christian, yet Mr. Unger cited several examples of Christians hosting demons and declared, "Clinical evidence abounds that a Christian can be demon-controlled as a carryover from preconversion (sic) days."[14]

Lester Sumrall, in *Demons: The Answer Book*, written after he had traveled to one hundred countries and visited more than one thousand cities, supports Unger's claim: "I began to understand that when a Christian goes into the devil's territory, unless to do battle and rescue lost souls, that a Christian becomes vulnerable to whatever Satan offers, even to being invaded by an evil spirit."[15]

It has been liberating to learn that other believers also have been hosts to evil spirits. My story that I was born again in Thailand in August 1969 and received deliverance from demons in 1970 has been questioned by those who believe a Christian cannot be indwelt by demons.

I have no need to convince others one way or the other. I rest in the assurance that Jesus Christ is my Savior and my Deliverer.

Psychiatrist Meets Exorcist

The late M. Scott Peck, renowned psychiatrist and author, perceived connectivity between mental illness and evil, and analyzed the relationship rationally and scientifically, "explaining the specific psychological mechanisms by which evil operates." In his book, *People of the Lie*, Peck briefly described two cases of demon possession he was involved with that convinced him that evil spirits do exist. Later, Peck wrote about these two instances in detail in *Glimpses of the Devil*. In his commentary on the first of two successful exorcisms, Peck wrote, "One of the goals of the commentary is to highlight the mystery of evil by clarifying areas where we are still in the dark. . . . I hope that the healers of the future will know better what they are doing than I did."[16]

But Scott claimed there is a body of knowledge regarding demonic activity: "Not a huge one, but certainly large enough to constitute the foundation of a new branch of science, enough to make demonology a respectable field of research and study."[17] In a small way, the objective of this record is to cite the application of Peck's findings in my own story.

Mr. Peck further wrote that his mentor for dealing with evil spirits was Malachi Martin, a Catholic exorcist. Martin claims he had long since desired to team up with a psychiatrist who was open to considering demonic activity as a cause of some mental disorders. In his book, *Hostage to the Devil*, Mr. Martin describes in detail the deliverance of five people from demonic possession.

Martin also wrote that in the 1990s there were more than eight thousand covens of Satanists—and the number was growing. He claims the reason for this growth is the desolation of culture that he lays at the feet of the clergy who no longer proclaim the truth about sin and salvation, claiming,

> [The] diminished belief among Christian churchmen . . . that
> he [Satan] does not exist at all is an enormous advantage that

he has never enjoyed to such a great degree. It is the ultimate camouflage . . . if your will does not accept the existence of evil, you are rendered incapable of resisting evil.[18]

I believe my encounter with a satanic worship pavilion in the cove below our house in Kansas was of this sort. Gerald's encounter with the giant snake wrapped around our house we were building explained the constant problems and setbacks we experienced until the very week after he effectively destroyed the spiritual serpent.

Game On

The names of the characters in the colossal warfare and their normal mode of operation are contained in the Bible. The name of the archenemy of God and the leader of all demonic forces was recorded in Isaiah 14:12: "How you are fallen from heaven, O Lucifer, son of the morning!" Barnhouse described the evolution of Lucifer from the son of the morning who rebelled against God as a rebel who was subsequently cast out of Heaven onto the Earth as Satan, also called the Devil:

> As we proceed with the ordered reading of the Bible, we come now to the first mention of the devil. When he appears, he is already a malignant being, hateful and hating, manifesting himself as the seducer. . . . He wished to detach man from God, but he also wished to attach man to himself.[19]

Lucifer's demise was also recorded in Ezekiel 28:13–17: "You were in Eden, the garden of God. . . . You were perfect in your ways from the day you were created, till iniquity was found in you. . . . Therefore I cast you . . . out of the mountain of God. . . . I cast you to the ground." The rest of the story of Lucifer's fall and destination, along with the angels that had joined in his rebellion, is recorded in Revelations 12:9: "So the great dragon was cast out, that serpent of old, called the Devil and Satan, who deceives the whole world; he was cast to the earth, and his angels were cast out with him."

Barnhouse further argues that Satan, having lost on all of his conquest objectives, set about to destroy as much of God's creation as possible by waging an invisible war using a militaristic organization:

> [I]t would appear that angels of every rank in both camps are constantly at war with each other . . . the victory or defeat is gained by the application of power and the withdrawal of the inferior force. . . . The importance of all this to believers in our day is that it can be demonstrated from the Word of God that the warfare in the invisible realm principally concerns individuals in the human realm.[20]

Know Your Enemy is one of the principles of war and dates back to the sixth century BC in China and Sun Tzu's classic book, *The Art of War.* Since this principle has survived twenty-six centuries of scrutiny, it seems appropriate to include it in this present spiritual conflict.

Knowing the Enemy

The tactics of Satan and his minions are predictable as recorded by various writers, such as Barnhouse, Peck, Unger, and Sumrall. Peck's description of four grades of demon activity is at Appendix B. Also included in this appendix are eyewitness accounts of direct intervention by Jesus as He cleared the battle sites of various invaders from the demonic forces. An example of Grade 4: Possession would be the example cited in Mark 5:1–13, when Jesus encountered a Gadarene who was indwelt by a "legion" of demons. There were enough demons dwelling in the Gadarene, when released by Jesus, to enter a herd of two thousand swine, causing them to jump into the lake and drown.

Afterward, the Gadarene was found "clothed and in his right mind." A common expression for his previous condition would be, "He was out of his mind." However, the correct statement would be, "The demons had complete control of his mind." Once they were removed by Jesus, all of the Gadarene's cognitive functions reset to normal.

This book in your hand is the story of one prodigal living in the real world where evil exists, but the book is not meant to be a textbook on demonology and mental illness. I leave that to the experts and return to the focus of my encounter with life and the victories promised in God's Word, which are received by ingesting His words as spiritual nourishment.

CHAPTER 15

The Journal of a Wandering Pilgrim

Pilgrim in Exile

The intensity of the battle definitely increased as I turned to face the enemy with a determination to learn to walk in the victory Christ has already won by His death, burial, and resurrection.

Obviously the enemy did not like the idea of being exposed as I began to seriously write this book and record the events in daily journals he literally threw his book of tricks at me.

Opening Pandora's Box

I recently shared some of my frustration with my daughter, Deb. Her response was to quote John Eldredge: "The story of your life is the story of the long and brutal assault on your heart by the one who knows who you could be and fears it."[21] I remember writing in my journal that day, At this point, I have no idea what I could be and this morning I have no interest in finding out. What does one do in exile?

War Zone in Florida

We arrived in Ellenton, Florida, on Tuesday, January 10, 2012, after driving more than seven thousand miles from Cattle Drive Road in Sisters, Oregon. We prayed: "Lord, we give You praise for the provisions and Your protection all across this great land. Now I join You in the battle!"

Thursday morning I woke up at 0527 dreaming we were involved in some sort of conflict. I was in charge of a small force and selected a female for a critical job because I knew she would complete the task.

Then, as I approached the battlefield, another woman came running and yelling, "We have to retreat! There are too many of them!" My response was to counter her panic and encourage her to go round up everyone she could find to come help. In the meantime I was determined to use any resources at hand to defeat the enemy that I had not yet seen. There was just me and one other person moving forward.

Was that reflective of the spiritual battle in which I was engaged? I woke up experiencing apprehension at the dire circumstances we were in. I spent several minutes repeating, "I can do all things through Christ who strengthens me" (Philippians 4:13). Soon the apprehension gave way and I enjoyed two hours of relaxed snoozing and focusing on Transforms.

Updating the Past

Friday was a beautiful day, so Jenny and I strolled to the workout room after breakfast and began a fitness program. On the way back to the house we walked leisurely around the small lake on the retirement property and listened to the frogs squeak as they splashed into the water. The lake was stocked with bass that were surfacing with slurping sounds to catch insects floating on the surface. It was a delightful morning with Jenny and our first quiet morning alone for several weeks.

When we arrived at the house, I reluctantly went inside and set up my desktop and pulled up the draft manuscript of this book that had been sitting there for several years. There were sixty-one pages in draft and I began to peruse the document to decide how to proceed. I felt the tension begin to seep into my soul and realized the battle had begun.

I ordered Mike Leehan's book, *Ascent from Darkness*, the story of his battle with demon possession and deliverance. Gerald Deaton and I were involved in his recovery. My involvement was very guarded because I was still not ready to submit all my life to the Lord, and the relationship between Jenny and me was not resolved. I also became keenly aware that I had always had a wayward heart and engaging in heavy combat would be dangerous to me as well as the person receiving ministry.

In his daily devotional, *My Utmost for His Highest,* Oswald Chambers wrote about having a "white funeral"[22] (dying to self). My daughter gave me a copy of *My Utmost* that has space for journaling. In 2006 I had written that I desired to have such a funeral. I was chagrined that six years later, as I began to write about my journey, so little progress had been made. No wonder God did not bless TFT!

One of the conditions inhibiting my progress is a divided heart in respect to Jenny. I have harbored in my heart memories of past relationships that were pleasant and recalled those memories to placate my feeling of rejection from Jenny. I now understand this is one area to be crucified with Christ. For instance, I dreamed last night I was at a place where a previous relationship was exciting and pleasant to recall. The scene was vivid and presented an opportunity and desire to spend the night with a woman from the past.

As I woke up, the Spirit challenged me with the opportunity to remove the stored memory from the *recall at will* file and place it in the *crucified file.* I presented the memory and the relationship to Jesus, asking Him to forgive me of the past and to put the memory in the proper file. I then spent almost an hour concentrating on the phrase, "I am crucified with Christ . . . and I crucify this adulterous memory from the past." The effects of the memory have not been totally removed, but the negative effect has been mitigated.

Forward March

A new phase of the battle started as I anticipated it would. Satan does not want this book written, and I am sure others writing similar records have experienced the same opposition. Well, the Lord created me to be a soldier, so as the song says, "Onward Christian soldiers!"

Wednesday, January 18, 2012, Ellenton. It is 0403. I woke up at 0338, not under stress, but with thoughts that are evil and I am pursuing to determine the origin. For years I have been afraid Satan would overpower me and cause me to react the way the man did in 1957 in the story Eldon Ross' father read from the newspaper.

Again I ask, "What is the origin of these thoughts? I have been born again and the Holy Spirit of God dwells in me and the blood of Christ has purified my heart. Therefore I conclude the destructive thoughts are coming from a satanic source masquerading as my own." Last night as Jenny and I were preparing dinner, I was using a knife to make a salad and I "saw" an image of me using the knife to hurt Jenny. There was no problem resisting the thought, but it is troubling that I should even have such a picture come to my mind. Another area to be crucified.

This is the closest I have come to writing about this for fear doing so would actualize it or, if anything ever happened to Jenny, I would be accused of being the culprit even though I may not even be in the area.

Okay, Commander, You knew all about this from the beginning. Now that I have started writing the book I am reliving this awful stuff. I don't want to do this, but just like I didn't want to go to Vietnam, if this is Your order for me to go through this painful stuff, so be it. I go with the assurance that You will protect me and those around me. I go "crucified with Christ so that I do not live but Christ lives in me." You were constantly confronted with Satan and descended into Hell and got the keys. You have already conquered Satan. In every encounter recorded in the New Testament, You were always the victor. So it will be now!

Battling the devil is nothing new. Martin Luther is said to have been pestered by evil spirits from childhood and, on one occasion while translating the Bible, threw an ink well at the devil. "Resist the devil and he will flee" (James 4:7).

In his daily devotional for January 18, Chambers wrote, "We are not sent to do battle for God but to be used by God in His battlings (sic)."[23] Hmmmm. "Used by Him . . ." Maybe I have been trying to escape the battlefield when He is using me in the battle. I have been assuming that I would bring glory to God by using Transforms to build strength to rise above the battlefield and out of the battle. What if the greatest glory for Him is attained in His battle on the battlefield?

The power of God's Word has drawn me into peace with Him, but it is not permanent. I have reviewed the period in Vietnam when I was totally at peace and wondered how that can be regained. So I began searching deep in my life to confront any demon or attitude that may still be there and force it to identify itself.

At one point in a fierce scrimmage, I thought, *If I could just take a gun and shoot the demon, it would be simple.* At that point I realized this may be what happens in murder–suicide cases. The demonic forces entice the person to commit the evil crime, then, because of conviction by his conscience, he turns on the evil spirit to destroy it, aims the gun at the demonic spirit in his head or body, and kills himself in the process. Of course, the bullet does no damage to the evil spirit, but destroys the body of the host.

As I began to record my journey in detail in 2012, I realized there were elusive demonic forces still accessing my cognitive processes. At various and random times, they attempted to entice me to perform some evil deed by counterfeiting a lie that it is the "right" thing to do. Sometimes, they also injected a feeling that it was the "right" thing to do. This immediately caused confrontation from the Holy Spirit living in me and my own knowledge and conviction of right and wrong. The evil intent of the demon was forestalled but not yet eliminated.

I was always on guard and not able to totally relax, even in the care and protection of Jesus. But I began to develop trust by ingesting His words such that the negative source of fear and fretting were replaced with the truth contained in His words. As I ingested Scripture, Galatians 2:20 became a reality. John declared Jesus is the Word, and as the Word came alive in me, I could say, "I no longer live, but He lives in me."

I believe this is true and writing about it has a positive effect. As a human being, I have the capacity to have a "wicked heart," but I now reject that I am an evil person for I have been cleansed by the blood of Christ and declared to be righteous. As the battle continues, according to Romans 8:15–17, I grow spiritually and am delighted that He has lifted me to become a joint heir with Him and by suffering with Him I will eventually be glorified together with Him! Let's roll!

Digging In!

I began having a tingling in the left side of my face and three episodes of sharp pain along the left side of my skull and three episodes in which my body went numb. Another time I was doing moderate exercises at the fitness center when I became faint. I checked my blood pressure on the center's monitor. It was 80/40. Normal for me was 120/60. I began claiming the promise in 2 Thessalonians 3:3: "But the Lord is faithful. He will establish you and guard you against the evil one." I walked to the house we were living and lay down. My blood pressure was normal within an hour.

Saturday, January 21, 2012 Ellenton. Beautiful day. I slept about 7.5 hours. There was some anxiety upon waking up, discharged with transforms. Jenny and I drove to Sarasota to test drive a Lexus and evaluate the various models. She decided she liked the ES 350 and the 2010 model was near the budget we set. Of course it has to be white. We had a very pleasant day today; Jenny said she had really enjoyed having me all to herself and had a great day.

Prepare to Move Up!

Crazy. I went through a period of feeling as if I were trapped in the spirit of my dad. Several years ago I was talking to a psychologist about the hand clamped over the top of my head. He surmised it was my dad's hand guiding me oppressively at every turn. Recalling this illuminated the fact that I had not forgiven Dad. So, I visualized facing Dad and saying, "Dad, I forgive you for the times you hurt me, and I ask you to forgive me for being such a stubborn kid!" Then I forgave myself for what I have done to hurt people, especially Jenny and my children. What a mess.

In preparation for a right-of-passage ceremony for one of my grandsons, I was reading the book *Raising a Modern-Day Knight* by Robert Lewis. He wrote about Jeffrey Dahmer, a serial killer, who was sentenced to 957 years in prison in 1992 for numerous murders. Jeffrey's father wrote a book in which he attempted to piece together the eerie events of his son's life. According to Lewis, the father identified three parental mistakes, which he claims often result in a son going astray, unnoticed:

1. I wasn't there.
2. He began to sink into himself.
3. He might be drifting.[24]

That story would have sent me into an emotional tailspin a few years ago. The impact was profound yet without the fear of doing a similar thing as a result of the story told to me in 1957 by my roommate's father. Although neither Lewis nor Jeffrey's father mentioned satanic involvement, I am convinced that the three parental mistakes listed by Lewis above open the door for satanic involvement. Satan is a hideous character.

However, the next morning I woke up feeling defeated and began reciting, "I can do all things through Christ who strengthens me." It seemed hopeless at first, but I persisted. After several repetitions of inhaling that verse, I felt a distinct release and immediately began to recover from the hopeless feeling. That's it! I woke up feeling hopeless! Is there an evil spirit whose name is "Hopeless?"

The Boat

Sometimes when I can't sleep, I join Jesus on The Boat and rest awhile. The Boat comes from the record in Mark 4:35–41. Jesus and His disciples were crossing the lake in a boat when a violent storm threatened to sink them. Jesus was asleep in the back of the boat and the disciples panicked and woke Him up. "Then He arose and rebuked the wind, and said to the sea, 'Peace, be still!' and the wind ceased and there was a great calm."

The Boat is my refuge. I have learned to visualize going to The Boat and lying down at His feet. Sometimes He reaches down and touches my shoulder gently and I immediately go to sleep.

Then, as I imagined joining Jesus on The Boat, hopefully to lie down and sleep, I sensed Him saying He has been with me throughout my life. To my amazement, He also commended me for joining Him in the battle against the enemy and being willing to walk through the world of darkness to conquer and expose the battle techniques of Satan and his minions!

Here is the strength: "Yea, though I walk through the valley of the shadow of death, I will fear no evil; For You are with me" (Psalm 23:4). I have been afraid because I tried to fight the battle myself. Now, "I am crucified with Christ and I no longer live, but Christ lives in me." I have no plans. I submit to be used in His plans. His approval for being courageous in the battle felt really good!

I realized I had been letting Jesus guard and rule in my heart and soul, but not my mind, for I have lived in fear that Satan would take control of my mind and force me to do evil things. Philippians 4:7: "and the peace of God, which surpasses all understanding, will guard your hearts and minds through Christ Jesus." So there is the challenge: trust the peace of God to guard my heart and my mind in Christ Jesus.

One great thing my dad taught me was responsibility. After the forgiveness exercise, I dreamed I was responsible for delivering lunch to some troops, and it was raining heavily and the road was flooded. I could not find my rain gear, so I walked the entire way in the rain in deep, rushing water, uncertain where my next step would land.

When I woke up, I felt an urgent need to pray for Doug. Reading *Raising a Modern-Day Knight*, I had been recounting many areas of my failure as a dad with our children. I had this feeling recently that I may have lost Doug's respect. However, this is purely subjective. He has honored me always when we were visiting in his home. He arranged for me to sit at the head of the table at dinner, while he sat at the side of the table. Nothing was ever said about it, but I know that was the case. And he always showed respect when I came into the room. *Anyway, Lord, we all belong to You, and I submit to You. I cannot erase the facts, but You can erase the effects.*

Tuesday, January 24, 2012, Ellenton. Very interesting morning. When I woke up at 0600 I was feeling dread and began to oppose the feeling with Philippians 4:13. There was mental resistance to this and I began to see all kinds of images floating around arguing that I was going to lose control as I get older. I persisted in opposition, then switched to Galatians 2:20. I know this is the answer; to be totally immersed in Christ and using Scripture to purge my mind of the negative storage from years of fear.

Reticular Activating System

Job wrote, "That which I greatly feared has come upon me" (Job 3:25). Here is what I began to understand: As the human mind focuses on an item or issue over long periods of time, something occurs in the mind to accept the item as being a "truth" and the device in the brain, called the reticular activating system (RAS), has the mission of ensuring that the truth happens even though it is false.

The RAS is a network of neurons found in the brain stem of the vertebrae that functions much like a cruise control in your vehicle; the cruise control will cause the car to travel at the number you set. The RAS is programmable and does not distinguish between the truth and a lie, which I call a false-truth. So here is my hypothesis: I have feared becoming insane for so long that insanity has become a false-truth, and the RAS is trying to bring it to pass. The truth is, "For God has not given us a spirit of fear, but of power and of love and of a *sound mind*" (2 Timothy 1:7, emphasis added). A practical discussion of the RAS and psycho cybernetics can be found at www.make-your-goals-happen.com.

I have learned that visualization adds effectiveness to the Transforms. The process is simple but requires discipline and tenacity. I pick a Scripture Transform and recite it twenty-one times, visualizing the Transform as a compact bundle of energy, like the core of a golf ball, drifting down into the center of my being. I then watch it expand and bring light to any dark places where the enemy may have residence or false-truth is stored. Then I do the same with a Personal Transform.

The battle then rages between the Truth that is living in me, i.e., the Holy Spirit, and the forces of evil that attempt to activate the mechanism of the RAS. But according to Hebrews 4:12, the truth is winning: "For the Word of God is living and powerful . . . piercing even to the division of soul and spirit, and of joints and marrow, and is a discerner of the thoughts and intents of the heart."

One more thought: When a person "snaps" and does evil things, I believe that person and Satan have been battling for control. The snap occurs at that point when Satan, or a minion, finally takes control. I used to be afraid to even say the word *snap*. Now, by the power invested in me by my Lord Jesus Christ, I am exposing these dark secrets of the enemy and am being opposed vigorously. I have strength, but not enough to stand against the devil except immersed in the power of Jesus and His blood. And He provides on-site help: "Are they not all ministering spirits sent forth to minister for those who will inherit salvation?" (Hebrews 1:14).

According to 2 Corinthians 4:8–10, "We are hard-pressed on every side, yet not crushed; we are perplexed, but not in despair . . . always carrying about in the body the dying of the Lord Jesus, that the life of Jesus also may also be manifested in our body."

Joy does not come from human relationships or activities or accomplishments, but from a life immersed totally in Christ. "The joy of the Lord is your [my] strength." These truths, like others described recently, are coming to the surface quietly, yet profoundly. I believe this is happening because the Word of God is penetrating the darkness in my heart, soul, and mind and bringing His light to my life. The hope of joy is to have my name written in the Lamb's book of life, to know the only true God and His Son He has sent, and to be known by Him. "Fear not for I have redeemed you, I have called you by your name; you are Mine" (Isaiah 31:3). My RAS is being reprogrammed!

Static

Friday, January 27, 2012, Ellenton. Today the input from an evil source has been constant. I was outside gazing into the star-studded heavens above Florida and asked the Lord what was going on. I received a typical one-word answer from the Lord: "Static." I responded in typical fashion, "Static. Is that all?" That was all.

Okay, I recalled how a radio works. Desirable information, such as music, is superimposed on a carrier wave at the broadcast location and a receiver in a radio deciphers the desirable information and the music as broadcast is heard from the speaker in the radio.

Undesirable information, such as lightning during a storm or an arc from an electric motor, can modify the carrier wave of AM radios causing irritating noise. If the storm is close with rapid lightning discharges, the static may overpower the desirable information. Static is interference from an outside source that has access to the carrier wave. That identifies the proximity of the static: Outside.

However, this means the enemy and his minions somehow have access to my mental carriers. While this is very irritating, and was at one time fearful, I am not asking the Lord to remove the static, but to give me understanding of its source and the means to resist and/or defeat the source.

I have been reluctant to write what the static thought is, but will do it. If I read of a murder, the static is, "That could be you." If I pick up a knife the static often is, "You could use that on someone."

I just took out the trash and the story of a kidnapping and the body found stuffed in a trash bag was vividly displayed on my mental screen! The ugly feelings I had when I heard of the details began to emerge, but I rejected it and challenged the source with, "Therefore if anyone is in Christ, he is a new creation; old things have passed away; behold, all things have become new" (2 Corinthians 5:17).

I recall hearing of an assassin who heard a dog tell him to kill another person. My hypothesis is that Satan, or some minion, used the dog to convey the command, and it was so overpowering the assassin followed the instructions. The basis for this is Genesis 3:1: "Now the serpent was more cunning than any beast of the field which the LORD God had made. And he said to the woman . . ." Of course it was Satan using the serpent. I have experienced frontal attacks directly from the enemy, but have not heard an animal or other external object speaking.

Amazing Love!

Saturday, January 28, 2012 Ellenton. Beautiful day. I called Doug and we had a wonderful discussion of the father-son issues. I am excited about his insight and discernment.

I have experimented with various Transforms to determine which one works best for a particular static. Philippians 4:13 worked best against the feeling of helplessness. Galatians 2:20 works best against static with sexual or negative emotion content. Isaiah 43 is a powerful counter to the spirit of fear. The combination of all these is powerful. *Thank You, Lord, for the power You store in Your words!* Hebrews 4:12 is confirmed.

Occasionally, I have a brief glimpse of what it will be like when I am free of the oppression. Then immediately the static will be interjected and clouds the peace. This snake is persistent! When this happens, I immediately rebuke the static as a lie of the enemy and grab a Transform.

The objective is to conquer regardless of the source. If it is RAS related, I replace the false-truth that I am evil with the truth that I am a forgiven prodigal and declared to be a Knight in the King's Army. My Personal Transform is "I am delighted to be an avid guardian of life!" To counter the fear of insanity, I imprint my subconscious storage area with, "In Christ, I am fearless!"

So now that I have written about what I feared to write about, the power of the enemy to work through this hidden false-truth is broken. The power of God's Word has penetrated the darkness and exposed the hiding place of the evil spirit. I do not act in my own strength, but I have been given the strength of Jesus. I act as He directs. I resist the devil and he does flee.

I have been vulnerable in this battle because I was deliberately sinning against the Lord and Jenny by entertaining fantasies about other women. I have renewed my covenant with the Lord to offer my body a living sacrifice and to slay the sin in my flesh. Therefore His power is again flowing in my life and I come against Satan and his minions because I am chained to His chariot. Victory is assured and I just walk in the victory He has already won.

"Amazing love, how can it be that You my King should die for me?" the song written by Billy James Foote asks. Recently, we were singing this song at church and I wept as I leaned against His side with the scar from the spear.

Oswald Chambers wrote in *My Utmost for His Highest* about the Law of Antagonism in the devotional for December 4: "Life without war is impossible either in nature or in grace. The basis for physical, mental, moral, and spiritual life is antagonism. This is the open fact of life." I no longer ask to be removed from the battle, but for strength in His battle, "chained to His chariot!"[25] Hallelujah!

Here are my marching orders: to love Jenny as Christ loved the church and gave Himself up for her. Yes, I see it. One avenue of access to my cognitive circuits came because I was angry at Jenny for not submitting to my every whim. This is the spirit of dominance, the evil of my flesh that I now crucify. The power of God is also at work in Jenny's life and I definitely feel her love for me. We are winning!

It is amazing. As soon as I wrote the paragraph above, the static came as a sinister whisper: *It's time to finish the job!*

I countered with, "If you have anything to say to me, talk to my Attorney!"

The whisper evaporated and I sensed I heard the Spirit say, *That is the way; stand up and be strong!*

There it is!

I have gone through the hard parts of the draft manuscript, and it has been cathartic. I hurt inside and sometimes weep, but still I carry on by His strength.

I took a short break and began scanning the Internet, and I noticed an ad for a Lexus in the right margin of the page. I clicked on it and read the ad. It was for a white 2010 Lexus, ES350, and the price was within the limits we had budgeted for her car. It sounded perfect. The car was at Larsen Motors in McMinnville, Oregon, where our friends, the Powells, lived. I called Richard. He checked the car out and gave it a clean bill of health. Tod and Deb then went over the next weekend and test-drove the car; splendid with all the bells and whistles. We paid for the car and Larson Motors stored it until we returned to Oregon. That was an exciting break, but the battle was not over.

Some Heavy Stuff

Ron Phillips described the demonic phenomenon as an oppressive operational aspect of Satan's organization. Phillips opines this is precisely what the Apostle Paul wrote in 2 Corinthians 11:14: "And no wonder! For Satan himself transforms himself into an angel of light." Even more distressing is that by reacting in fear of satanic input, I had to suspect that God is capable of directing me to commit an evil act that would cast an evil shadow across His character. This affirms the effectiveness of Satan's masquerade.

Then there was some lie about my eyes. There was a time when I was afraid to look at a plane in the air for fear I would cause it to crash. I had a fear that others saw in my eyes some evil, and I would hesitate to make eye contact. I had a fear that if I watched a football game I would cause my team to lose. When I looked at people's throats, I got some ugly feeling. I have wondered if that comes from my dread of butchering a pig because we had to cut its throat to drain the blood.

Wow, that was painful to write about!

I asked God to explain to me the origin of all these twisted thoughts and urges and fears. They seemed like the proverbial bucket of worms. Come to think of it, I used to have an occasional image of a large worm penetrating my heart. I eventually conquered the image with Psalm 51:10. "Create in me a clean heart, O God." My Personal Transform was: "I am excited about the clean, healthy heart God has given me." I repeated this twenty-one times while visualizing a clean heart that was beating strong and normal.

Well, I have opened Pandora's Box and written about fears kept submerged for a lifetime. Ron Phillips devoted Chapter 16, "The Strategy of Fear," in *Demons and Spiritual Warfare* to identifying and exposing satanic use of fear to hold people captive. Phillips wrote that "fear is a magnet to demons. Fear will draw in the enemy and will bring to pass the thing you have spoken out of your mouth."[26] Now I open up every area of my being to the cleansing power of the Word and the Holy Spirit. I marvel that with all this garbage in my life I have been able to function as well as I have. It is only by the intervention of the Lord that it has been possible. "Now to Him who is able to do exceedingly abundantly above all that we ask or think . . . to Him be glory" (Ephesians 3:20–21a).

CHAPTER 16

Time for a Break

Shades of Green

Jenny was delighted to hear me say I needed a break, and immediately made reservations at Disney World in Orlando, Florida, and the nearby Holy Land Experience. Doug called to say he and Levi would be at Disney World Thursday evening. There was vague static about that meeting with Doug and Levi. I rebuked the lie and commended my life to His hands.

Monday, February 06, 2012. We are at the Shades of Green Hotel adjacent to Disney World. We went first to The Holy Land Experience. The passion play was great and the tour of the history of the Bible was very interesting. I sat in a boat similar to the one Jesus went to sleep in during the violent storm. We enjoyed the ambiance. The last event was a praise and worship service. When the invitation was given for prayer, I went up and a young man prayed for me to be protected as I write the book.

The Shades of Green was really nice and we had a view overlooking the pool area. *Lord, You have been so very good to us. Thank You!*

The first night there, I woke up with a throbbing headache. I took one Tylenol and went into the bathroom and began praising the Lord and documenting the event. *Though He slay me yet I will trust in Him!* I wrote, Lord, I laugh at Satan and his minions who may be involved in this. You, O Lord, are worthy of praise for You conquered Death and Satan and he is powerless before You.

The headache was mostly gone by 0800, but I felt a little fuzzy. What a life! Yet I noticed the desire to be crucified with Him increase even in the midst of the pain.

Jenny and I spent the day at Epcot Center. The most enjoyable was the history of America and the boat ride showing all the new gardening techniques to grow food in a smaller space. During the display depicting the pain of growing America, I had the thought that nothing in this world comes to fruition without pain and sacrifice. So be it with regard to this book.

OK, so the enemy was not taking a break. I woke up again during the night fearful. Rather than react in fear, I turned to the power and strength of the Word of God and put on the full armor of God and began a frontal attack on the static and the enemy. Using the same technique as Jesus, I attacked the false storage that I would be overpowered by the enemy and declared, as it is written, "Therefore, if anyone is in Christ, he is a new creation; old things have passed away; behold, all things have become new" (2 Corinthians 5:17). As this declaration began to penetrate the storage area, I replaced the negative with love thoughts from Matthew 22:37–39, paraphrasing thusly: "Richard, love Jenny as Christ loved the church and gave Himself up for her."

Then I wrote a Personal Transform: "I am in Christ and in His strength I am an avid guardian of life!" I began to repeat this Transform numerous times while visualizing myself clad with the armor of God, walking right through enemy territory and observing the enemy scattering out of the way. I also visualized the Transform being written across my cognitive storage board in bold letters thusly: **"In Christ I am an avid guardian of life!"** I repeated this process several times to imprint the truth upon which my RAS operates. It worked. The static began to be like a memory without any energy.

Wow! I woke from a terrible dream that Jenny was having both legs amputated because of out-of-control diabetes. I felt helpless and began to cry out to the Lord for help. He reminded me that He has given me a spirit of power, a spirit of love, and a spirit of a sound mind. I was not to feel helpless, but to exercise protective and redemptive power on her behalf. So that is what I began to do. I then focused on Galatians 2:20 for several minutes and drifted into deep, peaceful sleep until 0700.

Doug and Levi came at 1730. Levi was thirteen and this was his right-of-passage outing. We had dinner at Shades of Green, then Levi invited me to go with them to Magic Kingdom. The first ride was a roller coaster in the pitch black. It bucked and jumped like a wild stallion! The effort to cope was enormous and in the dark I could not prepare for the next twist or turn. The exertion was great enough to cause an erratic heart rate, but I proved to my grandson how tough I was. They went again. I went for sodas. *Goodnight, Commander.*

Victory in Outer Space

The next morning we had breakfast with Doug and Levi. They headed for Disney World. We headed for Kennedy Space Center. The best part of the visit was a forty-five minute IMAX story of the construction and operation of the International Space Station. The pictures were so real! I was right there in outer space and not afraid (a little queasy, perhaps, when looking down the length of the platform at the small blue ball called Earth). But this was a great victory over the fear of my mind being trapped in outer space that began in 1958.

We also went on a simulated space vehicle liftoff mission. The person in charge of loading warned anyone with any heart condition to "please exit now." I thought about the erratic heart rate caused by the roller coaster and considered getting off. However, I decided it was time to face the fear head on. I enjoyed the rough ride. The victories continue one at a time. *Lord, You are my strength.*

I commended Jenny for braving the simulated launch, climbing the stairs up the observation platform, and watching the IMAX of outer space at Kennedy Space Center.

Back to the Front Lines

The first morning back at Ellenton, I was having quiet time and was querying the Lord regarding the origin of the static and asked, "Who am I, Lord, that Satan would want to destroy? I am nobody."

I heard the Lord say, *It is because I love you that he hates you.*

Then I recalled a comment I heard Dad make one time about losing his mind. It seemed that Dad was struggling with something that was causing him to doubt his sanity. I shared that with my brother John, and he said that Dad lived all of his life in fear, perhaps a generational spirit of fear. Apparently it was so pronounced that Mom had to hold him at times until he stopped shaking.

My Mother

Mom was a stable force in our family. She took everything in stride and could laugh at anything. She was truly a pioneer woman. From her bountiful garden, she fed her family so they never knew hunger. Her children were always dressed in clean clothes, many of which she had made from feed sacks and scrubbed clean every week on a wash board with lye soap she had made in the large cast iron pot over a wood fire. Mom loved flowers and any vacant spot was turned into a beautiful flowerbed.

One of the most special weeks of my life was spent with Mom in the summer of 1984, the year after my father died. I went to her home at Camden, West Virginia, and we spent the week working up apples to make apple butter in the fall. The apples were Early Harvest, and she decided we needed to gather a bushel to make applesauce. I climbed the tree and began to shake the limbs. I would ask, "Mom, is that enough?" She would reply, "Well, maybe just a few more." When she finally said, "Come on down, I think we have enough," we gathered up four bushels. We spent the remainder of the week sitting opposite each other on the back porch talking, laughing, coring apples, and transforming them into sauce with an aroma that permeated the entire house.

Mom was an outstanding cook whose unwritten recipes consisted of a "pinch of this and a dab of that." She could whip up a feast for unexpected guests in short order, and her kitchen was always the gathering place for the family. She was my anchor, and I know it was her prayers that convinced her Lord that I was worth rescuing. *Thank you, Mom. I still plant dahlias in your memory.*

Serpents in the Swamp

I was warned to back up my journal, but I was sleepy and the thumb drive was somewhere else, so I thought, "I will get it in the morning." Big mistake! My laptop would not start the next morning and my journal and the manuscript were stored there. Was this a purely mechanical failure or did the enemy attack the computer?

I began a new journal and three months later a friend was able to restore most of my journal and the manuscript of this book. I now back up to at least two thumb drives, frequently.

The static has been frantic at times, like the static generator realizes it's losing its grip on me. The static is normally vague with veiled threat. The most active static occurs when I am getting ready for a family gathering. *This would be a good time to finish the job*, or *It's time to do what I want you to do*. Sometimes when I pick up a knife to peel an apple, the static may be, *You could use this on . . .* Or *I know a good place to use that.* It used to be when I was handling a gun, the static would be, *Remember what you are supposed to do?* with apparent reference to the early morning story in 1957 at Eldon's house. If I were going to a movie, the static would be, *This would be a good time, while they are all together.*

Occasionally, the static would include a picture. Once a female clerk bent over, exposing a large portion of her chest, and the static was, *That would be a good place for a knife.* As I mentioned earlier, there were frequent images involving the throats of people or animals. The static caused me to react in fear at one time, but now as I write about it, it is more or less a memory to be erased. Much of the power of the static vanished after I shared with Jenny what was going on, especially after she has edited this book and still lives here! She didn't like the incident I cited that occurred one night as we were saying goodnight.

I said, "Jenny, I love you . . ." Before I could finish the sentence, the static input was, *I am sorry I have to do this to you.* It wasn't definitive what I was to do.

My fear of dying was so pronounced that I thought I would be dead by forty-five, so as I passed that point, the static frequently reminded me, *You know you are living longer than you were supposed to. You will not finish this book!* There were many variations of this static, especially when I was awakened at night: *You know all the men in your family die young,* or *You will die before seventy-five just like your dad.* To counter this static, I developed a Personal Transform based upon Psalm 139:16: "all the days ordained for me were written in your book before one of them came to be." I repeat this rhyme often: "I am alive at age eighty-five!"

Recently I had a very vivid dream. Dad, John, and I were walking up a steep hill. Dad was doing pretty well, and I thought, *He must be at least ninety by now!*

In the dream I took that as a good sign that I was released from the trap of having to die by seventy-eight.

What was that all about? Was the Lord telling me to get over being afraid that I was going to die early?

I will mention one more serpent. Recently, I was feeling bold and decided to investigate the weird feeling I had the evening on the hill above Auburn when I picked up the hatchet to chop firewood. I wondered if there was a demon named Hatchet. When I began to investigate the source of the sensation, it came at me with a fury of impulses and images. Man, that thing was evil!

"Lord," I prayed. "I ask You to intervene and get this thing off my back and out of my life! I follow Your exhortation to resist the devil and he will flee, so I resist this evil force in Your power."

The extent of the evil is so gross that this demon delights in the evil it perpetrates. I wonder if the beginning of this sensation in my life was when I was a small child and heard about the body in Grantsville they found in a bag. I recall a feeling of dread and did not want to go to Grantsville after that. Is there a demon named Dread?

Lord, I have no fascination with this demonic power, only repulsion that this spirit, which at one time had been on the Mountain of God, could be so unspeakably evil to delight in the destruction of one of God's creatures!

God created me with the freedom to choose. I choose LIFE!

Life Is about Choices

One of the most helpful lessons I have learned is that I have the choice whether to live with joy or with fear. The choice is mine. I have spent too much time focused on the enemy. Therefore, after documenting the actions of the enemy, I began to shift my focus to Jesus and choose to live in His joy. "As for me and my house, we will serve the Lord" (Joshua 24:15).

> **Tuesday, February 14, 2012, Ellenton.** Interesting day. I got so little rest last night. I did not work out this morning. I tried to nap this afternoon, but [was] unable to relax. Jenny and I went to Miller's Amish restaurant for Valentine's Day dinner. There were books for sale about spiritual warfare. It dawned on me that my task is not just to tell a story, but document the journey and balance it against existing research. That gave me a new perspective and I shared with Jenny, "I am no longer a victim, but a test platform."

Rwanda, Again?

In early February 2012, a request appeared on the Regent Alumni website for volunteer mentors to assist graduates from the Regent Center for Entrepreneurship (RCE) Business Development Center (BDC) course in Rwanda. I wondered if this would be another false alarm, but I filled out the application anyway. To my surprise, I was accepted. I called RCE and explained I would begin working on the project when we returned to Oregon. We had one more visit to make before leaving this battleground.

A Real Soldier

Bob and Judy Hicks live in Tampa. Bob is the 2LT who came to A Battery, 3/76 Artillery in Kitzingen, Germany, for his first assignment out of West Point Military Academy. He retired a few years ago as a major general. Judy was a jewel from the beginning. When Trey, their first child, was born, they asked us to be godparents to him. I didn't know what that entailed and didn't take it seriously for several years. But some time ago, I called Bob and Judy and ask for forgiveness and have prayed for Trey daily since. It was wonderful to finally meet Trey and his son Barrett (Bear).

The letter I had written to 2LT Hicks when we were notified he would be coming to Germany was in one of the albums they showed us that night. They spoke with pride about me being his first boss, and Judy said she was impressed with Jenny from the beginning and was grateful for the many things Jenny taught her about being an army wife. I am deeply honored to have played a small role in their early life. I regard MG(R) Robert Hicks higher than any other officer I served with. More than regard, I love this man and his family.

Change Station, March Order!

Our goal was to be in Sisters, Oregon, for Tate's birthday, March 18—a very optimistic goal. We cleaned up Norma's house in the retirement center, loaded the truck, took a deep breath, and sat for a moment contemplating the past two months. Our sojourn there was productive and a definite turning point in my life. I had opened my heart, mind, and soul and recorded my reaction and my understanding of the causes of those reactions. There were residual imprints to deal with, but I have learned to face them head on dressed in the full armor of God described in Ephesians 6:10–17.

I asked many times, "How is this stuff getting into my cognitive circuits?" I have learned it is because my shield of faith was porous and the enemy knew exactly where to aim the fiery darts. Beginning in Bangkok, my faith was strong. However, with Greg's death and my business failures, I began to doubt God, and holes began to appear in my shield. A major overhaul of my shield was mandated, and I became excited about the adventure of walking in His light!

"Thy Word is a lamp to my feet and a light unto my path" (Psalm 119:105, KJV).

Pit Stop One

We arrived at Doug and Connie's house in Goldsboro at 1530 after driving through some very heavy rain along the GA/SC border. Jenny was driving and forged ahead like a pro! She is an excellent driver. We had a great family time. We had pizza night, Luke and Logan reset cell phones and Bluetooth, and we test-fired Levi's potato gun and went to his baseball game. His team won!

We spent the night with Doug's family, and Luke loaned us his bed. I noticed a large folding knife on the head of his bed where we were sleeping. I just ignored it and went to sleep. *Lord, You are setting me free.*

Goodbyes again, schedule to meet, headed west.

Pit Stop Two

Jenny loves to drive, so I did research while she was at the controls. How do we know who God is? Well, howdy! There is the answer in Hebrews 1:3: "The Son is the radiance of God's glory and the exact representation of His being, sustaining all things by His powerful Word" (NIV). It's in the Book!

We arrived at Lorena's in Southern Pines, North Carolina, just in time for a delicious dinner with Lorena, Judi, Kayla, Joe, Loretta, Emily, and Nate. Before turning in for the night, I read about our amazing Father, Abba, and the extent of His love as recorded in Ezekiel 34:

> For this is what the Sovereign Lord says: 'I myself will search for my sheep and look after them...'" (verse 11). "I will search for the lost and bring back the strays. I will bind up the injured and strengthen the weak!" (verse 16). Then in verse 31, "You are my sheep, the sheep of my pasture, and I am your God, declares the Sovereign Lord." (NIV)

Commander, I am chained to Your chariot and walk in the victory You have already won! Hallelujah, what a Savior!

Pit Stop Three

We stopped in Ravenswood, West Virginia, to visit Jenny's sister, Edie. I woke up at 0445, and static was present like this: I looked at the clock and the static said, *It's a good time to do what I want you to do.*

I thought it was a good time to look deeper into this stuff. Here is a mystery: In Bangkok, the sludge in my life was emptied at the feet of the Presence of Jesus. I felt clean for the first time in my life. So, what was the stuff that had to be delivered in Lawton and the stuff that still fogged up my life?

OK, here is a possibility: In Bangkok, I finally accepted Jesus as my personal Savior, and He cleaned up my heart and forgave me of my sin of rebellion and the associated garbage. However, the demonic presence existed in my flesh, not my spirit, and He chose to clean this up through deliverance and using His Word to cleanse the false-truth stored in my subconscious.

Pit Stop Four

Saturday, March 03, 2012. 2228: *Now at Jane Lew with Jack and Norma [my sister]. Great dinner for us, the best cornbread in the world, stuffed peppers, mashed potatoes, carrots, cauliflower, and apple pie! I have a very special place in my heart for Norma; she provided my first travel adventure. When I was twelve, she invited me to stay with her in Jane Lew. Dad took me to catch the bus and I got off near her house. It was an exciting journey and I felt very special because she cared enough to invite me to come stay with her.*

Pit Stop Five

Friday, March 09, 2012, Manhattan, KS. *My sojourn on this planet is now seventy-seven years. We are parked in the Gifford's driveway. Ed and I had apple pie for breakfast then I went to the dentist who diagnosed an infection that will require antibiotics and a root canal when I get home.*

2222: As I was kissing Jenny goodnight, it was like she was not there. I went outside to speak to my Lord and rebuked the impression. The aggression from the enemy intensifies as I determine to be recklessly abandoned to Christ. So be it; I laugh at the enemy that has been overcome by Jesus and is totally subject to His power. "When He has tried me I shall come forth as gold" (Job 23:10, KJV).

I am turning away from the negative emotion toward Revelation 2:7: "To the one who conquers I will grant to eat of the tree of life, which is in the Paradise of God" (ESV). OK that speaks to me. The Lord is allowing me to be oppressed, to purge me, and bring to the surface the garbage I have suppressed for years. "OK, I am chained to your chariot."

We could not stop in Manhattan without visiting our dear friends, Vida Blockcolsky, Bob and Alma Buchanan, Hugh and Kaye Emrich, Robert and Linda Demmie who bought our house, Duane and Norma Benton who purchased TCN, and Sam and Verta Riniker, our Canasta partners every Friday night for years. I have to say it was tough to leave these folks, but Tate's birthday was closing in.

Then we had to decide how to get through the mountains. The shortest route was too windy. We looked at going through South Dakota, Montana, and Washington then down to Oregon. It looked as if there was a four-day window we could sneak through. Our goal was to get to Oregon in four days for Tate's eleventh birthday. *Lord, help!*

That night I dreamed I was watching a father and son interact. The son had done something expecting affirmation from his father, but his father pushed him aside. The boy's face got red, and he turned and walked away rejected. In the dream, I took the boy in my arms and held him until he could relax and smile. Was the boy me?

Billings, Montana—Disaster or Rescue Mission?

We pulled into Billings for a fuel stop. On the way to the filling station, we hit a drainage swale in the road that I did not see in the waning shadows. The Ford went up in front, then up in back, then down in back with an agonizing *crrrrrunch*! That did not sound good! We jumped out and went to the rear of the truck. I stood there aghast. They build Fords tough but not RVs. The tongue was still connected to the Ford, but it looked like a lazy U. The bottom of the U was about four inches off the pavement.

"Well," I said. "I came for fuel, so let's go."

Why should I be surprised that nothing surprises the Lord? When we pulled into Sam's for fuel, He was already working things out. One of the customers came over and asked, "Are you aware there is a Keystone dealer a few blocks away?"

Seriously?

"Yes, right over there," he said, pointing to the Keystone sign.

The people at the dealership just stared at the wounded A-frame tongue in disbelief. They could not repair the damage, but knew two machine shops that may. Each one dialed—one did not answer, the other said he was willing to look at it. So we limped through town to get there. When I turned into the welder's shop, there was a mountain man completely filling the door space. I thought, *He looks like a Marine.*

Tony, the welder, turned out to be a Marine! He took one look at the RV tongue and just smiled. "I can fix it if you will let me put the right size metal in the tongue. That metal is totally inadequate for a rig like that!"

I gave him the go-ahead and he said he would order the material in the morning and hoped to begin work on it by 1000. The estimated cost was one thousand dollars, and he could have it ready the next day.

Lord, for what purpose are we delayed here in Billings?

We called Deb to inform her we would be late for the party. She always has a positive spin. "That may have been in order to avoid a disaster later should something like that happen at highway speed," she said.

There had been an interesting set of events on this trip: My laptop crashed, Garman went south, and my cell phone died. Now the trailer broke. Did the enemy have permission to attack, or were these just things that happen? *In all things, give thanks!*

Tony completed the trailer repair, and it looked great and strong. However, the delay closed the window to get over the mountains before the storm hit. I was frustrated until I walked along the Yellowstone River and the Lord said, *Tarry.*

Tarry? I dumped my frustration on the river and began picking up colorful pebbles. I also picked up two larger stones that looked alike.

When I went to pay the bill, I had a great sharing time with Tony, including my experience with Jesus in Bangkok and invited him to let

Jesus in so we could spend eternity together. He said he would consider it. I believed he would because that tough Marine had tears running down his face.

Three days and several new friends later the weather cleared, and we watched Billings disappear in the rearview window. *Tate, we tried to make it to your party, but the Lord had a rescue mission for us in Billings.*

CHAPTER 17

Home at Last

Happy Birthday, Tate

Friday, March 23, 2012. Home at last after 13,070 miles on the great American highways since October 2011. It is great to be here with Tod, Deb, Anson, and Tate. They had a big sign to welcome us home. The trip from Billings was especially beautiful today with blue sky, billowy clouds, and the snow-covered Cascades. Snow-covered Mt. Jefferson pierced the azure sky and was our majestic companion for hours as we drove south from the Columbia Gorge on HWY 97. Jenny drove the last 3.5 hours and did a great job on the winding road.

We had a mini birthday party for Tate. Our gift is paint and labor for her room.

Summer in Central Oregon

In Billings the Lord said, "Tarry," and I asked Him how that was possible. I had a program of instruction to compile for Rwanda and a speech to write for the Veterans Memorial Day celebration in Sisters, not to mention the sparkling mountain streams teeming with trout!

I wrote Tony a Thank You letter for the excellent work on the RV and included it in a box with one of the two rocks I gathered at the Yellowstone River. I annotated the letter with a promise that every time I look at the other rock, which I placed on my desk, I would remember him in prayer.

I began exchanging emails with Patrice Habinshute, the entrepreneur I was to mentor in Rwanda. Patrice was a graduate of the very first cohort hosted by the Regent Center for Entrepreneurship (RCE) at their Business Development Center in Kigali, Rwanda. He had won a prize for his idea to organize entrepreneurship clubs in all the high schools in Rwanda. After several emails I still could not discern the extent of his idea, so we decided I was to go to Rwanda with a Regent University representative to learn more about what was going on there. Patrice requested I prepare a seminar for students to be presented to as many as twenty high school and college students during our visit.

Saturday, March 24, 2012, Sisters, OR. This has been an instructive morning. . . . The static began and I again asked the Lord to show me where this stuff is coming from. There was an immediate response that is difficult to explain in words. I felt a distinct shift within my cognitive circuitry. It was similar to the carriage shifting on an electric typewriter.

After I asked the Lord where this static is coming from, this thought came to mind, "Resist the devil and he will flee." Being cautious, I asked the Lord if I was to do this directly or only by asking Him to do it. This is my understanding: "The verse is instructive. Yes, directly, in power that I have made available to you." I addressed the evil spirit directly with, "Minion, you are an evil being, and a weakling. You attack children and people in their weakness." The response was, "But we have gotten along in the past, why are you acting this way now?" This is weird! This was not a voice, but a cognitive exchange.

It was as if the minion was sensing its demise and arguing for permission to stay, pretending it was not evil, to be a victim of circumstances and just following orders! To this I replied, "You are evil! You made a choice a long time ago to follow the rebellion. Even if you are just following orders now, you are evil and are responsible for your actions. Therefore I resist you in the Name of Jesus and in His power. You have no power over me."

The static vanished and I was no longer afraid and stood in the power of the Spirit. "Lord, I have long resisted getting involved in this warfare, but now I report for duty realizing that all truth and strength comes from YOU alone. I worship the Lord God Jehovah and Him only do I serve! Please protect this computer and this record."

Sunday, March 25, 2012, Sisters. *0500 came early this morning. I woke up feeling listless. The future seemed formidable and I lack the energy to conquer. This is a roller coaster life. Individual victories are temporary. There must be lingering footholds of evil or residual recordings in my cognitive storage that I have not overwritten with the truth of who I am in Christ. So I turned to the Word and began with Philippians 4:4 and 4:13: "Rejoice in the Lord always. . . . be anxious for nothing. . . . I can do all things through Christ . . ." Energy in the Word began to dispel the fog and I got up and shaved and prepared for the day.*

2243: *I rested in total peace this afternoon, but tonight the static has been constant with unpleasant images. I declare them to be foreign to who I am and I am going to lay down and sleep!*

I did sleep and woke up rested. Then Jenny and I drove to McMinnville, Oregon, and had lunch with Richard and Mildred Powell. After lunch we all went to Larsen Motors to pick up Jenny's Lexus. "Oh, it is so beautiful!" was Jenny's response when she saw it—a delicate pearl color with all the bells and whistles. We completed all the paperwork, bid our friends goodbye, and headed back over the Cascades with Jenny leading the way, happy as a lark!

On the way back home to Sisters, the static was initially persistent. I countered the static by praising the Lord, repeating chapters and verses of Scripture. The static vanished in the wake of the power of God's Word, and that night I slept peacefully for eight hours.

I began to realize that God chooses a unique path for each of us. David addressed this concept in Psalm 25:4, writing, "Show me Your ways, O Lord; teach me Your paths." This spoke to me about the race God entrusted to me and shifted my paradigm from victim to victor because He promised, "The one who conquers, I will grant him to sit with me on my throne" (Revelation 3:21, ESV). According to John 14:6, the beginning point for all of His paths is Jesus for He declared, "I am the way, the truth, and the life. No one comes to the Father except through Me."

Obviously my straying from the Lord in the 1990s was much more grievous than I have heretofore acknowledged. After all the Lord has done to rescue me, I turned away from Him. He would be justified to treat me as a hireling and not a son. But He has forgiven me and is chastising me as a son. He is amazing!

In his March 30 devotional, Oswald Chambers spoke of "reckless joy"[27] and that excites me. I will abandon to Him with reckless joy! The day was static-free and I was blessed with gentle peace.

Sunday, April 01, 2012, Sisters. "Lord, You are awesome and yet compassionate with this wandering prodigal." I slept almost nine hours; I attribute the rest to the power of God's Word penetrating the false storage areas and bringing light where there was darkness. I dreamed there were several of us walking through the woods. I was with the group, yet separate, walking by myself. I came across a bear cub that was friendly and I told the group to look out for the momma bear. I was in front and found her curled up asleep. I began to scratch her head and belly and she woke up and wanted me to continue.

1500: This morning in church we were singing and asking the Lord to open our eyes. I began to visualize seeing Jesus and I "saw" the enemy between me and Jesus. Is the Lord allowing this to test my faith and strength? I will walk right on through enemy territory; I will stand in the presence of the Lord, so help me God! "But The Lord is Faithful, and He will strengthen and protect you from the evil one" (2 Thessalonians 3:3, NIV).

It was now clear to me that my concept of God and Jesus has been grossly in error. I had been ashamed of Jesus as if He is weak. My concept was changing radically as the Word of God penetrated and altered the false-truth with the Truth, as it is written, "Sovereign Lord, you have made the heavens and the earth by your great power and outstretched arm. Nothing is too hard for you" (Jeremiah 32:17).

Thursday, April 05, 2012. Today is Deb and Tod's fifteenth anniversary. The day was like their wedding day: blusterous with sunshine, snow, sunshine, wind, and more snow. They are a great couple and wonderful parents!

"Lord, You have given me strength to stand and I am beginning to climb out of the valley of the shadow of death."

2302: A good day. The strong affirmations yesterday began a process of reversing the false-truth and blocking the input from the evil one. I cannot back off, but will pursue this double prong attack, resist the enemy, and reset my RAS, until I am free.

Good Friday, April 06, 2012, Sisters. Skiff of snow on the ground, bright sun glistening on the snow, herd of deer in our front lawn fearlessly nibbling on the clumps of green grass peeking through the snow. "Thank You, Lord, for the wonders of Your creation."

2216: The two pronged attack on the static is working. The static today has been minimal; I countered it immediately and set about to change the false-truth by absorbing Scripture Transforms and resisting the evil one in the Name of Jesus. I am declaring that I no longer fear going insane by paraphrasing 2 Timothy 1:7 and repeating it at least twenty-one times several times each day: "God has given me a Spirit of power, tempered with love and controlled by a sound mind."

We went to a Good Friday service at Sisters Community Church. We had communion as a Miller Family, including John and his family, as part of the larger crowd. We were given the opportunity to write on a card and go nail it to the cross. I wrote Galatians 2:20 and nailed that to the foot of the cross. As other people nailed their paper to the cross, the sound of the hammer on the nail was painful to me. I felt like every blow was my sin driving the spikes through His hands. As the hammering went on and on I wanted to yell, "Stop it!" Then I wept silently with tears of regret. "Lord, thank You for coming to rescue us."

I learned a profound truth at the Good Friday service from a neighbor. His wife had Alzheimer's and was in a senior care facility. He went to see her every day and he considered it the highlight of his day because he was giving her love. His statement was this: "Men are fulfilled by giving love not by receiving love." Scripture confirms that. Paul wrote three times in Ephesians 5:25–28 that husbands are to love their wives as Christ loved the Church. Men, we have had it backwards.

Easter Sunday, April 08, 2012, Sisters. I enjoyed a private sunrise service walking through the forest as the sun spread its warm rays through the giant ponderosas. He is risen! He is risen indeed!

Tonight Deb and Tod came down to visit awhile. At some point in our conversation, they mentioned a counselor who had worked with a friend of theirs. Apparently this counselor also is involved in deliverance ministry. This may be the answer to my prayer for someone to work with on the book and to find the source of the static in my life.

Grandson Anson competed today in acrobatic skiing; he was in the top half for the first event and in the top ten on the next event. "Lord, please protect Anson and the team."

Tuesday, April 10, 2012, Sisters. My meditation Transform before turning off the light last night was Proverbs 3:24: "*When you lie down, you will not be afraid; yes, you will lie down and your sleep will be sweet.*" My Personal Transform was: "I am fearless as I lie down and claim His promise of sweet sleep." And so it was. I hardly remember laying my head down and the dreams were pleasant; we were celebrating some achievement with bowls of strawberries.

2154: I called Dan Hicks, the counselor Deb and Tod spoke of, and made an appointment for tomorrow at 1000. Filling out the paperwork stirred up emotions and some fear of what happens tomorrow when I finally begin to tell my story. I hope Dan can be helpful in validating and adding credibility to the story.

Wednesday, April 11, 2012, Sisters. The meeting with Dan Hicks went well. He is a licensed professional counselor (LPC). I believe he is God's answer to prayer for a professional to work with. He gave me a website to enroll in a spiritual warfare seminar in preparation for deliverance.

Thursday, April 12, 2012, Sisters. As Dan Hicks alluded to yesterday, I see an alternate personality in me. There is the personality God created me to be and there is a personality attempting to emerge that is the personality of one or more operatives of the enemy assigned to discourage, to disrupt, to cause pain and other destructive initiatives.

I realize now that the long term effect of this oppression is that I have operated at a small fraction of my created potential because of the opposition of the enemy force and the energy it has taken to oppose this force on my own. It is incredible that I have allowed this to go on for so long instead of addressing it head-on long ago.

I just had the thought that the reason may be that I did not want to have my old nature crucified. "Lord, I am ready to turn the fight over to You and Your mighty power, and really ready to be done with my old nature."

Friday, April 13, 2012, Sisters. Friday the thirteenth; one of my favorite days. Many people are superstitious about the number thirteen, but on the morning of a Friday the thirteenth in 1984, I was without a job and owned two houses in Manhattan, KS. By evening that same day, I had a good job as an engineer and one of the houses had sold! I will rejoice and be glad in this Friday the thirteenth also, even though I woke up this morning from a frustrating dream.

In the dream, I had been doing menial work, like mowing the lawn for the business and my supervisor was displeased because I had used a military vehicle to go someplace. Then as I was waking up, I heard in the dream, "He is already dead!" What?! I woke up fretting and wondering who was already dead. Then I felt overwhelmed with tasks and I am not getting the most important ones done. I have not written on the book this week and I don't have any idea how to help Patrice in Rwanda. Neither do I have a clue about what I am to say at the Memorial Day celebration.

Again, as I was writing about the activity of satanic minions, suddenly my computer shut down before I could save the text so I have to start over.

One of the prevailing mysteries in this battle is, "How is the enemy gaining access to my cognitive transmitters?" As I was meditating and reading about the domain of Satan and his minions and their legal claims over humans, an interesting possibility surfaced. In the days when Jenny and I had such bitter arguments, we both had said, "Why doesn't the Lord just take one of us?" I recall fleeting thoughts that it would be nice to be free to pursue other relationships. In so doing, I was really asking God (I can't believe I would think this) to remove Jenny or me.

In essence, I had a divided heart and wanted God to be evil and "take one of us out of the world." Dare I claim I preferred the victim would be me? Of course not. The fact that I had feelings of being free shines a spotlight on the evil in my desire to prefer that He take Jenny. This may have given the enemy legal access to my thoughts and to reinforce the evil desire by encouraging me to be the executioner.

Wow, I have been afraid to write such a thought. But if my heart could desire such a thing, I need my heart purged and I come before the Lord and confess this evil and ask for cleansing. Instead of following the input from either the evil in my heart or evil input from the enemy, I follow the Spirit that is now in me, repent and pursue the path of loving Jenny as Christ loved the Church and gave himself up for her. I crucify this evil desire of a divided heart!

0933: While walking this morning after entering the journal entry above, I felt like my body from my waist down was numb, yet a nerve in my left foot felt as though I was stepping on a nail and it caused a similar pin prick in my left side. I continued to walk and considered what Dan Hicks said about multiple personalities. I realized I may have at least two personalities; the one God created me to be and the one the enemy is attempting to cause me to be.

I was repeating Psalm 139 out loud as I was thinking about the two personalities and suddenly my voice changed to a low, more confident tone and I felt more confident. Initially I got Psalm 27 and Psalm 139 confused, but as I walked the cognitive process became clear and I recited each one clearly. There is definitely a battle going on and victory has already been declared in Jesus Christ of Nazareth who came in the flesh and I am chained to His chariot!

2248: Quiet day free of static.

Saturday, April 14, 2012, Lafayette, OR. We came over today to visit with Richard and Mildred Powell. Richard had surgery Monday to correct a misaligned spine and crushed vertebra four, five, and six. He is in a rehab facility and the recovery time is beyond expectations, perhaps because of the spirit of despair that is so prevalent in this rehab facility. It is oppressive!

Tod's mom, Dot Ann Ricker, died last night. She is finally "home" after a forty-year battle with multiple sclerosis (MS).

Monday, April 16, 2012, Lafayette. Good morning, Jesus Christ of Nazareth who came in the flesh. Thank You for rest and protection. You are very much aware of the momentary concern I had last night when I knelt to pray with Jenny and one of the boys' large hunting knives was right there by my head. In the past that would have caused great fear and it did cause some concern, not that I would lose control and use it, but just the thought of it made me uncomfortable. I declared the thought evil and felt totally in control as I asked the Lord for clarification of the origin of the thoughts and the fear.

When I turned off the light and lay down to sleep there was an image of the knife and blood as if it were being used to stab someone. Again, I rebuked the thought in the Name of Jesus Christ of Nazareth who came in the flesh and began replacing the image with images of rivers and boats and was soon asleep. "Thank You for the progress on the journey to freedom and the complete victory coming soon."

2149: Vida Blockcolsky passed from this earth this morning. I will be going to Kansas on Thursday to assist with the funeral. I had momentary sadness, now joy that she is home with Jesus and Clark.

Richard Powell moved out of the facility that was saturated with a spirit of gloom into a different facility where the atmosphere is positive and hopeful. Now he is doing much better. That is Instructive.

Jenny and I drove home this afternoon. I called Mick Ricker to offer our condolences at the loss of his wife, Dot Ann. Jenny and I went up to share with Tod as soon as he had dinner. He is doing ok, but regrets he didn't get to tell his mom goodbye.

Friday, April 20, 2012, Riley, KS. The funeral of our dear friend, Vida Blockcolsky, at the Olsburg Methodist Church went well. I felt comfortable sharing my thoughts at the church and a brief farewell to Vida at the gravesite. She is beside her husband whom we buried last November. They were true warriors and now are both "home."

Wednesday, April 25, 2012, Sisters. I woke up at 0436. Today is Tod's birthday. We will celebrate when he gets home from memorial services and burial of his mother. It is amazing how much my emotions swing from day to day. Yesterday I was the Lord's friend, this morning I am blah.

The static was absent while I was back for Clark's funeral and again for Vida's funeral. It felt wonderful! In fact, at Clark's funeral, I felt the same peace I felt in Vietnam. Today I sensed a return of some of the static; it is easier and easier to rebuke and exercise control over it. So I conclude when it is necessary for me to perform exceptionally well, the Lord intervenes and orders the static vendors to back off. Then it must be that He is offering me the opportunity to grow spiritually by permitting the enemy to provide opposition in the same way tackling sleds provide opposition for football linemen. It is interesting that the static seems to be more vigorous when I am close to Jenny.

Monday, April 30, 2012, Sisters. A new Transform for today is Isaiah 51:11: *"So the ransomed of the Lord shall return, and come to Zion with singing, with everlasting joy on their heads; they shall obtain joy and gladness; sorrow and sighing shall flee away."* Amazing how this works; my emotions are now stable and I know, *"I can do all things through Christ who strengthens me."*

Now after just three repetitions of this verse, excitement of walking through enemy territory without fear prevails. I will continue for 21 times and then record the results.

Yes! I followed with a Personal Transform, "I am ransomed of the Lord and I come to Him with singing, with everlasting joy on my head!" The resistance has resulted in a minor headache. So I will just relax and let the sorrow and sighing drain out through my fingers.

Sunday, May 06, 2012, Sisters, 0616. "Thank You, Jesus of Nazareth, for rest and strength and joy." I turned off the light about 2230 and woke up at 0530; I was eager to get outside in the bright morning, so at 0615

I went for a walk around Cattle Drive Rd. That is a fifteen-minute walk through our housing addition nestled in a Ponderosa Pine forest alive with mule deer, wild turkeys, squirrels and a myriad of birds.

When I rounded the curve at the end of our road and turned west, I was awed by the snowcapped Three Sisters Mountains sparkling in the early dawn. The road undulates through the forest giving rise to an elevated heart rate that refreshed my muscles with fresh oxygen as I inhaled the crisp mountain air! It is also exhilarating to recite Scriptures such as Psalm 139, Isaiah 51:11 and Nehemiah 8:10 personalized, "The joy of the Lord is my strength."

I experienced the joy of the Lord beginning to return to a parched soul! This exciting morning lends confirmation that the Personal Transform constructed from the Scriptures just listed is producing positive results. The Personal Transform is "I am filled with joy and strength from the Lord!" I ingest this transform by reciting it at least 21 times and imagine it as a compressed capsule drifting slowly down into the pool of my life, then opening up to disperse joy and strength to my heart, soul, and mind like a time-lapse photo of a beautiful, fragrant rose.

"Lord, Your brilliant handiwork and creative energy You inject into Your words attest to the magnificence of Your creative genius! Thank You for the time with You on the trail."

These are the promises I am claiming from the Lord: ". . . I will restore to you the years that the locust hath eaten" (Joel 2:25, KJV). "Restore to me the joy of Your salvation, and uphold me by Your generous Spirit" (Psalm 51:12).

2242: Beautiful, static free day. Jenny baked Tod a chocolate cake with peanut butter icing for his birthday; his favorite. Delicious.

Monday, May 7, 2012, Sisters. Tate just came down to say, "Good morning." She is like a ray of sunshine on a cloudy day! She is my Little Angel of the Dawn.

Psalm 18:2–19 (ESV) records the incredible reaction of Father Abba to one of His children. I recite it and am refreshed.

The Lord Is My Rock and My Fortress. . . . The cords of death encompassed me; the torrents of destruction assailed me; the cords of Sheol entangled me; the snares of death confronted me. In my distress I called upon the Lord; to my God I cried for help. From his temple he heard my voice, and my cry to him reached his ears. . . . He rescued me from my strong enemy and from those who hated me, for they were too mighty for me. . . . He brought me out into a broad place; he rescued me, because he delighted in me.

1955: Another beautiful day, clear, crisp with breezes. Doug called today and we talked for a long while about his eye and the issues he faces as a commander. He has the correct orientation and I commended him for his courage to take actions he believes are correct. I affirmed him and really am pleased with his perception and courage. He believes that exercising choice is the ultimate act of faith. We shared Scripture verses that promise acquisition of the peace Jesus left for us, such as John 14:27 and Isaiah 51:11.

Deb blessed me by sitting down and chatting with me today. We talked about healing in our family and agreed with Isaiah who wrote: "He gives power to the faint, and to him who has no might He increases strength" (Isaiah 40:29, ESV).

Friday, May 11, 2012, Sisters. The day of remembrance of Greg's birthday. "Son, I miss you and have learned to focus on all the good memories we made together. I look forward to seeing you soon."

2414: Wonderful day, no static. "Good night, Lord. Thank You for a beautiful family and delightful day."

Saturday, May 12, 2012, Sisters. I slept soundly until 0815. What a great dream! I was confronted by a group of terrorists and the Lord gave me such great strength that I subdued them all. When one tried to strike me with a sword, it glanced off my bare arms. Even in the dream I was aware the Lord was giving me strength and wondered, "What is the reason God is blessing me so much after the way I have grieved Him?" Jehovah is incredibly compassionate and forgiving. *"The Joy of the Lord is my strength."*

2200: Another beautiful day, clear and about 78F. Tate and I painted and installed a gutter under the roof over the patio to keep the water from dripping on the new concrete. She is a joy!

John and I walked about four miles. His health is improving. We talked about sins of the fathers and what that means in our lives. He said he was delivered of a spirit of anger and felt it lift off his shoulders. We are learning to rejoice in His provisions. "These things I have spoken to you, that in Me you may have peace. In the world you will have tribulation; but be of good cheer, I have overcome the world." (John 16:33). "In everything give thanks; for this is the will of God in Christ Jesus for you" (1 Thessalonians 5:18).

Sunday, May 13, 2012, Sisters. Mother's Day. We went to Suttle Lake with Deb, Tod, Anson, and Tate for Mother's Day dinner; serene.

Tuesday, May 15, 2012, Sisters. Lord, this is a strange morning. It is 0441, I am sleepy, but can't sleep. Several times in the past year I have felt as though my mind is working, but not getting traction. Yesterday as John and I walked I had that sensation; I was fully cognizant, but not feeling the impact of being totally present. I wonder if this is part of the process I am going through with upcoming deliverance and am being oppressed by some demonic spirit. Or is it the medicine the cardiologist prescribed? Or perhaps it's the beginning of dementia?

I was dreaming I was in the military again and several of us were given a certain gas that was being tested and even though I was a little confused, I was the only one who could function in that environment. I was escorted into the commander's office. "Sir, Captain, er, I mean Colonel Miller reporting." The others laughed at my stumble. I was confused because the officer I was reporting to was a major. "Why am I reporting to a major?" I woke up laughing at myself!

Thursday, May 17, 2012, Sisters. Last night was one of the most pleasant times for a long time. I felt peaceful anticipation of what the Lord is doing in my life. There was no static.

Monday, May 21, 2012, Sisters. Doug passed the check ride with flying colors. Bob Maxwell, the speaker for the Memorial Day event in Sisters, is in the hospital and I am the backup!

Thursday, May 24, 2012, Sisters. As I woke up I perceived I am to focus on two points at the Memorial Day celebration: God's intervention in our military, and that the American soldier has always been America's most effective ambassador.

Saturday, May 26, 2012, Sisters. Jenny's birthday. "Lord, I thank You for Jenny. Help me to appreciate her more and more and to love her as You love the Church and gave Yourself for Her. Teach me what that means."

2309: Deb and Tod prepared breakfast for Jenny. Then Jenny went to Redmond for the day and I worked out a draft by 1530 and rested until 1615, then Jenny and I went to Outback in Bend for her birthday dinner. Tod, Deb, and Tate came down to say goodnight.

Monday, May 28, 2012, Sisters. At 1100 we had the Sisters Memorial Day service that went really great. The music, poems, and reading the names of the fallen veterans with the tolling of the bell was very moving; some people had tears in their eyes.

Regarding my part, I felt the presence of the Lord, and He just took over. Jenny said it was the best speech I have ever made. Many folks came by to thank me and some especially appreciated me mentioning Jesus and God's role in America. "Thank You, Lord. I hope You were pleased."

There was an excellent article in the local newspaper about the Memorial Day ceremony. It was very accurate and quoted some of my speech.

Saturday, June 2, 2012, Sisters. I woke up with the realization that it has been several days since there has been any significant static. There have been transient thoughts when I see a knife or a gun, but these thoughts were easily dispatched with a declaration that these thoughts are not who I am. The diminished frequency and strength of the static began to occur after I committed to focus on rejoicing in the Lord.

2255: Target date for Rwanda is August 13–24.

Friday, June 15, 2012, Sisters. "Lord, the power of Your words is amazing!" This morning I woke up at 0450 and felt overwhelmed by the tasks before me and regretted I had volunteered for the Rwanda mission. But I chose three Transforms and began to focus on them in this order: Psalms 51:10, "Create in me a clean heart O, God . . ."; Galatians 2:20, "I am crucified with Christ . . ."; then Philippians 4:13, "I can do all things through Christ who strengthens me." I had thought to spend forty-five minutes focusing on these in turn, but before I got halfway through the first, I was eager to get up and get started. I wrote a brief paper about Span of Control for Patrice.

"We the people are the rightful masters of both Congress and the Courts, not to overthrow the Constitution, but to overthrow the men who pervert the Constitution."—Abraham Lincoln

Today Jenny and I celebrate fifty-two years of "Bliss and Blisters," a term coined by Lorena for our fiftieth anniversary celebration. She had T-shirts printed for all of us with that slogan printed on them. The recent years have been mostly bliss for Jenny and me. We will celebrate by going to the Oregon Gardens on the west side of the Cascade Mountains. "Thank You, Lord, for Your love of us and thank You for Jenny. I know she is the one You selected for me from the beginning although I didn't act like it sometimes. Now it is obvious."

Friday, June 22, 2012, Sisters. Awake at 0335, dreaming someone was ramming a big sharpened rod into a man who was screaming. I countered with Galatians 2:20 and Galatians 5:1: "Stand fast therefore in the liberty by which Christ has made us free, and do not be entangled again with a yoke of bondage."

Today we are all going to the Metolius River to camp. The enemy is doing his best to steal my joy of going. This is typical when I set out on an adventure. When I packed the ax and hatchet there was a recurrence of the strange feeling and I thought maybe I wouldn't take them. However, I now have authority over the enemy and declare, "Rejoice in the Lord always; again I say Rejoice!" I have learned to immediately counter the thought, identify the lie, and refuse to be controlled by it and the associated fear. I still don't know the origin, but am confident I will soon. This promise came in Vietnam before I even knew where it was: "You shall know the truth and the truth shall make you free."

2119: Doug had the eye exam today and is now grounded and will not deploy with his unit. The retinopathy has returned.

Rain all day as we were setting up camp at the Metolius River Pioneer Ford Campground. It has been interesting to watch the attempt to inject static into my thoughts. I declare myself free of fear and claim His promise that He has called me by my name.

I was concerned we would not see our family on this trip because they would be totally involved with the others. So where did everyone eat dinner? At our table! There were eleven of us in our camper dining room and Jenny cooked hamburgers for everyone. Deb and her crew slept in our trailer and that worked just fine with the three bunk beds and a full bed out of the dining table. "Thank You for the rain."

Wednesday, June 27, 2012, Sisters. Awake at 0630, initial heavy anxiety about the nearness of death and poor health that I won't get everything done. I flushed the emotion with, "*I can do all things through Christ who strengthens me.*" Immediately the fog began to lift and I am now eager to get on with the tasks for the day. It is amazing the power of God's Word and the strength from it.

This thought came to me last night: "God determines the length of my life; I determine the quality of it." The reference to the length of days is found in Psalm 139:16 "*. . . all the days ordained for me were written in Your book before one of them came to be*" (NIV). This is a great mystery: God knows the time yet grants freedom to choose. It is only in the mind of God that this apparent inconsistency is totally consistent.

2211: Beautiful day. Spent most of it editing my journal entries for inclusion in the book; not very pleasant. I worked in the yard a little at noon. Tonight Jenny and I went to Redmond for dinner.

Anson came back from Fellowship of Christian Athletes camp this evening. He was beaming. "I rededicated my life to Christ and I left a lot of baggage there!" he exclaimed. Jenny and I both noticed a very different countenance than when he went to camp on Monday. "Thank You, Lord, for revealing Yourself to Anson."

Saturday, June 30, 2012, Sisters. Awake at 0650. That's about eight hours of sound sleep. There was no anxiety this morning and I dreamed I was giving a patriotic speech in a church and ended with singing a patriotic song. Peace is wonderful!

2204: Interesting day, beautiful clouds. Tod, Deb, Anson, Tate, Jenny, and I worked on the yard planting flowers and hauling trash to the dump, buying more compost for the garden and such. It was great working with the crew. It has been a good day with no static.

Wednesday, July 4, 2012, Sisters. On Independence Day, 1776, they gave us a Republic; are we going to keep it? Here is the basis for our nation: "Now the Lord is the Spirit, and where the Spirit of the Lord is, there is FREEDOM" (2 Corinthians 3:17, NIV, my capitalization).

Friday, July 6, 2012, Sisters. A perfect morning, 48F, a gift from a perfect Creator. Awake at 0615, eager to get on with the day. This afternoon I completed the edit of the remaining journal entries to date; now to enter the home stretch working with Dan Hicks.

This evening we picked up John (Kathy is in PA taking care of a friend who is ill) and the three of us went to dinner at Lake Creek Café nestled between Lake Creek, a delightful mountain stream that ripples past the dining patio, and the powerful Metolius River that comes out of the mountain as a small river, then gathers momentum as it consumes the many tributaries along its course through peaceful meadows and roaring gorges.

After a delicious meal, we meandered to a quiet place by the Metolius and enjoyed a perfect evening listening to the babbling river and watching the frisky trout feed on the latest insect hatch. Jenny stood by the river, took a deep breath to inhale pine-scented air and exclaimed, "This is the most perfect evening I have experienced, ever!" It was truly a delightful day of joy and freedom. I know the battle will never be totally over in this life, but the good days are more frequent.

Sunday, July 8, 2012, Sisters. Awake at 0400 with anxiety because of all the tasks to be done in a short period of time. I trusted the tasks to the Lord believing He will give me strength for all He has asked me to do and repeated Philippians 4:13 about twenty-one times, then went back to sleep until 0600; repeated Philippians 4:13 again and by 0630 actually sensed a positive challenge of so many tasks!

There were three very inspiring quotes in an email from a friend:

"Life isn't about waiting for the storm to pass. It's about learning to dance in the rain." — *Vivian Greene*

"The task ahead of us is never as great as the Power behind us." — *Ralph Waldo Emerson*

"The Will of God never takes you to where the Grace of God will not protect you." —Church sign

2158: Made reservations for Rwanda at a cost of three-thousand, five-hundred dollars.

Monday, July 9, 2012, Sisters. Here is a wonderful test. It is 0522. The stress last night was so pronounced it tasted like copper under my tongue! I began reciting, "*I can do all things through Christ who strengthens me.*" I also recalled the powerful anointing by the Spirit the night Paul Pettijohn invited me to go with him to Rwanda. Again I declare, "Lord, You and I make a perfect team. You are perfectly strong, I am perfectly weak!"

After experiencing the joy all over again, I visualized being with Jesus on The Boat and asked Him to touch me so I could rest. Then it was morning and I had slept peacefully. "Thank You!"

To God be the glory. John 14:1 and 27: "Let not your heart be troubled" and "Peace I leave with you, My peace I give to you."

2202: Busy day, got lots done, stress low. **No static.**"

Tuesday, July 10, 2012, Sisters. Jenny drove alone to the Portland airport to pick up Connie and the boys; Doug comes Friday. Good day!

Wednesday, July 11, 2012, Sisters. 2214: Great day with the family; we went to tour the volcanic mountain, then Proxy Falls. Grandson Logan led all the grandchildren on a venture up the mountain on the other side of the falls; worry? Nah, they beat us back.

Thursday, July 12, 2012, Sisters. 2230: Great day with the grandsons working on the garage. Luke and I purchased lumber and supplies, then

Logan, Levi, and Anson all helped put down the plate and began installing the studs. They all worked eagerly and when I had to leave in the evening, they continued installing studs and did a great job.

Friday, July 13, 2012, Sisters. 2156: Doug flew into Portland. I picked him up at the airport. We had a serious discussion about this book and the process I am going through. We also discussed his possible assignments and the impact of the leak in his left retina. I shared my theory that his eye problem may be rooted in stress generated from a void in his subconscious from lack of affirmation from me in adventurous situations. He is considering that possibility.

Saturday, July 14, 2012, Sisters. 2255: We completed the rough framing for the garage. I finished one section of the Spiritual Warfare seminar in preparation for the deliverance session with Dan Hicks. The goal of deliverance is two-fold: for personal freedom from the influence of demonic spirits and to record the journey to glorify the Creator and to expose the techniques and strategies of the evil one. To do this I have begun a literature search and have found my experience is not unique.

Paul E. Billheimer prefaced his book *Destined to Overcome* this way: "The Christian life is indeed a warfare. Unless we view it as such and learn the techniques of overcoming the adversary, we are going to live a life of defeat."[28] In characterizing contemporary culture, Billheimer claims that, "Humanity is beset by a host of self-conscious evil spirit personalities called demons who are responsible for much, if not most, of the personality difficulties . . . and the aggravated forms of evil that characterize our modern social order."[29]

The literature search has brought comfort and hope to me by describing the experience of others who have also been traumatized by evil spirits. According to Billheimer, "Many believers have been so tyrannized and dominated by Satan and the prevailing theology of Satan's power and invincibility that, like me, they would never dare speak directly to him, even in the name of Jesus."[30]

Billheimer's quote describes my life; there has been a raging battle with demonic personalities and I have been held captive by fear of speaking or writing of it. For more than six decades, except during the period of deliverance and counseling in the early seventies in Lawton, Oklahoma, I have waged a silent battle. Now the power in God's Word is giving me the courage and strength to face the enemy head-on and to record the results.

"Lord, I see how You have been with me all the while, even when I was grieving You. I now submit to You and 'take refuge under Your wings' (Psalm 91) and go to sleep."

Monday, July 17, 2012, Sisters. Doug and Connie's twenty-fourth wedding anniversary. We went to the McKenzie River falls where the boys wanted to do daring feats over the torrential river by walking across a log that spanned the frightening space. If one had fallen in, the Lord only knows where he would have come out, if at all. This is the kind of ventures Doug tried as a boy and for which I scolded rather than affirmed his bravery. This time I asked the boys to wait until Doug showed up and I said to him, "You are in charge. Do as you see fit." He did not hesitate, but went across himself to check the slippery log out, then led them across the log and back safely. I commended Doug profusely!

CHAPTER **18**

Amazing Journey with Jesus

Rebellion Identified and Deleted

Deliverance, July 17, 2012. It was amazing! I was expecting to be uneasy during the night in anticipation of the deliverance session today: with Licensed Professional Counselor Dan Hicks. However, the Lord blessed me with undisturbed sleep.

Jenny and Doug went with me. Dan assigned Jenny to pray and Doug to record. During the session, Dan had me first hold the sheet upon which I had checked all the sinful activities I had ever been involved in, confessed them without naming them individually, and then asked for forgiveness for them all.

The objective was to get me in the background to permit Dan to address the demons who would use my voice to speak. I was to say the first thought that came to mind assuming that would be the demon speaking. Portions of the record kept by Doug are copied below.

Dan initially addressed the head demon who said, "I have nothing to say to you."

Dan declared the demon uncooperative and began administering punishments by destroying his cadre and eventually sent the demon to God for final punishment.

The second in command stated, "My name is Rebellion and I don't want to talk to you!"

"I know you don't," Dan said. "But you either answer my questions or you will be sent for final punishment. What was your interaction with Richard?"

Rebellion said, "I visited him when he was three or four. He is confused."

But then the second in command became uncooperative. More of the cadre was destroyed and eventually the second demon was sent out for final punishment. The third demon (D3) in command was more cooperative.

Dan: "What is your mission?"

D3: "My mission is to destroy him, cause him to be confused about who Jesus is."

Dan: "How are you to do this?"

D3: "Fear of all kinds, of the dark, death, dying, going insane, being punished by God, falling, crashing a plane, killing somebody."

Dan: "How did fear keep him from Jesus?"

D3: "He couldn't get there through all the fear; kept him from trusting Jesus. I sent a person to show him things he should not see."

Dan: "You mean sexually?"

D3: "Yes. Caused him to focus on wrong things and not on Jesus. Made him afraid of the Bible. Didn't want him to know the truth because he would be free, made it hard for him to read, memorize, pray. Made up voice of God to bring judgment on his wife.

Dan: "What was the result?"

D3: "Did not work. God put angels to protect him, sent a spirit of truth. He began to recognize the lies. Jesus rescued him. He loved him. Mother was praying for him too many times, made job hard, but Big Man would punish me if I gave up."

Dan: "What are your techniques to do your job?"

D3: "Give away my secrets? Will you let me go if I tell you? He hated what his father was preaching, I used his father's anger to cause him to hate so he will not know the truth about who Jesus was, and I lose my grip on him.

Dan: "What you are doing is evil."

D3: "I just did my job! Led him to believe he was saved when he wasn't. Jesus Christ sent a Spirit of Truth."

Dan: "The Holy Spirit cleaned that up?"

D3: "Not at this time. I sent a spirit of homosexual against him, but didn't stick."

Dan: "Anything more?"

D3: "No. I want to hit you!"

Dan: "Are you telling me the truth?"

D3: "Yes. I already told you. Wanted him to feel he was not in control, I was. I tried to beat him up."

Dan: "Did you affect his sleep?"

D3: "Yes fifty-three percent demonic, forgetfulness ninety percent." [D3 seemed confused].

Dan: "Ninety percent?"

D3: "Yes. Tried to give him a tumor. Jesus removed it."

Dan: "Is there more?"

D3: "Sure. I attacked his nervous system—don't let him sleep, kicked him off a roof, caused accidents in his life. I'm afraid you will remove me and I won't be able to finish my job."

Dan: "What was your primary job?"

D3: "He was supposed to kill someone."

Dan: "Is that true?"

D3: "Yes. I lied to him, told him he had killed his little friend, told him he wasn't worth much to destroy him, keep him from Jesus. I was behind violent thoughts."

Dan: "How did Jesus feel about him?"

D3: "He loved him from very beginning."

Dan: "What was his gift to be?"

D3: "Prophesy, loving, giving, teaching, empathy, bold, brave, figuring things out. After today? Warrior for Jesus. His calling: loving, warrior, warrior, warrior! It was my job! Tied him up in knots emotionally, suicidal thoughts, rejection to keep him away from people."

Dan: "True?"

D3: "Yes. Made him feel unloved by those close to him, keep him isolated, not—on Jesus, tell him lies, learning stuff before he was—to keep him distracted. Gave him spirit of anger for destruction. Twisted gift of warrior to be one for me. I just want out of here!"

Dan: "That is good because you are through here. Get out of Richard's life."

With that command, I felt a sudden release and new freedom! It was not an emotional feeling, just peaceful. We mutually agreed the session was productive and terminated the formal part of the session.

Doug was glad he was involved and desires to follow along the process. Mr. Hicks cautioned that the enemy would probably try to reconnect. "If that happens," he said, "rebuke the demon in the Name of Jesus Christ of Nazareth who came in the flesh. There were other people named Jesus, but only one Jesus of Nazareth, so let the enemy know that you know the correct source of power."

This process was another milestone along a long journey that included severe suffering that affected not just me, but also other people with whom I had contact, especially my family. This brings to mind a man's thoughts after suffering much more severely: "For I consider that the sufferings of this present time are not worthy to be compared with the glory which shall be revealed in us" (Romans 8:18). Some sufferings are ordained, others are self-generated.

John Wayne remains my favorite patriot and actor, and *The Sands of Iwo Jima* (1949) is a favorite movie because of the bravery of the young Marines who won one of the bloodiest battles in World War II. In the movie, Sergeant Stryker, played by John Wayne, admonished his men, "Life is tough. It's even tougher when you're stupid!"[31] I have been stupid.

After the Dance

Following the deliverance session, I slept eight hours and woke up without anxiety. I felt as if a great load had lifted, and I was in control. I found it interesting that the possibility of an evil spirit that may be vacillating between Jenny and me was not addressed.

Then on Friday, I took Anson and his friend to see the midnight showing of *Dark Knight Rising*, a violent episode of Batman and a far cry from the first Batman and Robin movie I enjoyed fifty years ago. For me, it was an affirmation that the power of Scripture absorption into my heart, soul, and mind and the sequence of deliverances were having a very positive outcome.

However, a couple days later I reverted to another facet of my old nature and unloaded on Deb because Anson was playing instead of helping with the projects we had agreed upon. Even as I was verbalizing, I actually had a mental picture of my dad saying it the way I said it and, in fact, I felt like it was Dad speaking!

I felt awful all day after the encounter with Deb. I asked Deb for forgiveness and she forgave me, but the pain in her face grieved me. She asked to visit soon about our living situation. I don't attribute my action to an evil spirit, but more likely a result of sins of anger passed on from previous generations. It is possible I may have opened myself up for demonic action as warned by Mr. Hicks. I immediately repented of my anger and repented of all the sins of the fathers and declared myself and my children cleansed of the ancestral sins.

On Guard

Sunday, July 22, 2012, Sisters. I was restless during the night with regret for succumbing to the old pattern of behavior with Deb. When Tod tried to address the state I am in, I rejected his counsel that was offered as a fellow traveler. Later we had a good conversation and agreed we have each other's back.

John Eldredge claims every man has a deep, triad longing in his heart. He wrote, "Deep in his heart, every man longs for a battle to fight, an adventure to live, and a beauty to rescue."[32] I welcome the battle for truth, I am excited about the adventure, and Jenny is my beauty to rescue. I vow to take my place as Jenny's spiritual head and protector in a different mode, letting Jesus bear the burden of spiritual forces.

I called Doug to share my awaking to the fact that God created me to be reckless but the enemy had stolen my heart. He had some great insight into the battle and we have covenanted to join forces in the Name of the Lord Jesus Christ of Nazareth who came in the flesh! I went through our house and claimed victory for all of us. "Lord, Your blood has cleansed us! Thank you."

Tuesday, July 24, 2012, Sisters. Awake at 0600, eager to get started!

2220: Beautiful day, high 80°F. I worked on the garage with Deb, Anson, and Tate. Deb and I talked about fear. She has been afraid since we came here, not sure why. We agreed to pursue this further, and it was great to share with her how much I regretted hurting her last week and to be forgiven. She is a good carpenter.

Thursday, July 26, 2012, Sisters. As I was praying this morning asking for help with the seminar for Rwanda, I sensed the Spirit say, *I will help you, just don't leave Me out of the seminar.*

I sense a new power and peace since the deliverance session with Dan Hicks. There is an attempt occasionally for the enemy to inject static, which I immediately counter with rebuke and Scripture Transforms.

Tuesday, July 31, 2012, Sisters. Wow, Lord, this is a real battle! The enemy and my own self-talk are telling me I am going to blow this training in Rwanda big time! I woke up at 0455, lots of anxiety about being ready for the seminar. It is not complete and I have less than 10 days to get ready! "Lord, You are the only One who can make this happen. Here I come before You, weak and fearful. You are strong and powerful! I give this whole thing to You."

Thursday, August 2, 2012, Sisters. What a night! I dreamed several of us had been exposed to some fatal disease and the only way to keep it from spreading was to die ourselves. Hugh Emrich and I and another man drank the drug that was to kill us and then if the disease were eradicated we would live again. So we waited for the drug to take effect, but it was delayed and I kept waiting to feel the effects of dying. Finally, I felt as if I were going to sleep, then nothing for a little while. Then I was alive again and feeling fine. Next, we began to build a house and I woke up. What was that all about?

Last night Jenny, Deb, Tod, and I had a meeting to discuss our living conditions. Deb explained that she has had a knot in her stomach since we moved in thinking we were always disappointed in her actions and she is afraid she will offend us if she goes anywhere for fun without us. We asked for forgiveness and assured her that we want her to live a joyful life. *Dear God, what a terrible way to live! Please forgive us and set her free!*

Rwanda presentation completed by 2100. I am amazed at the comprehensive understanding I was granted of the concepts of self-efficacy from Bandura's book, which I will be summarizing in Rwanda.

Tuesday, August 07, 2012, Sisters. When I woke up I felt emotionless, low efficacy. I began to recite Transforms such as Galatians 2:20, Proverbs 3:5, and Philippians 4:13 until 0625. I sensed this was a good test of the process. By 0625, I was ready to get up and begin working on the presentations. The Transform that seemed most effective was Proverbs 3:5: "Trust in the Lord with all your heart and lean not on your own understanding; in all your ways acknowledge Him and He shall direct your paths."

When I opened my Bible, my eyes fell on these words: "Behold, I send My messenger before Your face, who will prepare Your way before You" (Matthew 11:10). I realized this was spoken about the Lord, a quote from Malachi 3:1, and fulfilled by John the Baptist, yet it came alive for me also. I believe out of His great tolerance for a prodigal and His love for Rwanda, He has sent a messenger before me to Rwanda to prepare the way for me to share what He has given me to share. *Thank You!*

I was reading a devotional on the Internet yesterday in which the writer used a term "devil static" to describe input from the enemy that sounds very similar to the static I have been experiencing. I resolutely repel the static with the Word of God.

Wednesday, August 08, 2012, Sisters. Jenny is really going through a valley, no energy, no hope, no joy.

Rwanda, for Real

Saturday, August 11, 2012, Kigali, Rwanda. Arrived at 1900 local time, after two days and a total of twenty hours in the air. All flights were great, on time, no incidents, even my luggage showed up. On the flight from Amsterdam to Kigali, after crossing the Mediterranean Sea, there was desert for a long way, then jungle for the remainder of the trip. I saw no signs of life for hours. I leaned back and closed my eyes and attempted to get in touch with my feelings; it's as if I was somewhere in time on a mystical journey into a place I have only dreamed of. I let the dream loose and images of adventure clicked through like a terrestrial PowerPoint presentation.

At some point I drifted into a relaxed slumber for a couple hours; there was no other sleep for two days. I am tired, but no negative effects and great freedom to fly without fear. "Thank You for a wonderful trip and the messenger You have sent before me." Now to sleep; perhaps when I awake it will be real.

Sunday, August 12, 2012, Kigali. Asleep at 2300 local, awake 0520, amazingly rested. The Lord has given me strength. I woke up with eustress (beneficial stress that draws) and began finalizing what to share with Patrice and crew today at 1600. I began to imagine being crucified with Christ and as we rise, my new life is radiant with His presence. I then set a Transform, "Operating in the strength of Jesus of Nazareth who came in the flesh, I am a dynamic facilitator sharing important information with important people!" Then I imagine standing before the group with confidence and strength to share what I have learned that will benefit them.

I believe this is the most important thing I have done in my life. I have had a sterling day. I had breakfast on the patio overlooking a large section of Kigali. Breakfast consisted of hot milk, tea, coffee, hard boiled eggs, pastries with butter and honey, and a wide variety of fresh fruit, all excellent.

After breakfast I went to church at Christian Living Assembly, an English-speaking church with ninety percent Rwandans and lots of joyful praise and worship. The church was packed at five hundred or more.

At 1600 I met the four members of the SEN team for more than two hours to learn about their program. Patrice, Bernard, Anaclat, and Maria Louise are their names that I can pronounce. We mapped out the week of travel and the training for next week. I am really impressed with these four people. I have had a full, productive day.

Dr. John Mulford just came in. He is the one who organized the Regent Center for Entrepreneurship (RCE) and the Business Development Center (BDC) here in Rwanda. We had a good discussion about the program.

Lord, I am here. Thank You that You were already here.

Monday, August 13, 2012, Rwanda. I received an email from Jenny that she did not sleep well. I was awake at 0430 so I prayed and sent Jenny Psalm 138:1–3 and read it myself: "I will praise You with my whole heart. . . . In the day when I cried out, You answered me, and made me bold with strength in my soul."

2000: Wonderful day traveling to Rilima High School and visiting with the entrepreneur teacher there and listening to the Entrepreneurship Club members share their ideas for businesses. This is a great initiative. I spent several minutes trying to learn what motivates the students to want to work. Is it fear of starving or aspirations to be successful? Their answer was "I have this idea I want to make work."

Rwanda is located in Central and Eastern Sub-Saharan Africa, and is bordered by the Democratic Republic of Congo to the west, Uganda to the north, Tanzania to the east, and Burundi to the south. Rwanda is sometimes referred to as "The Land of a Thousand Hills." The hills are steep yet have a patchwork of micro-farms. The elevation is between 1,000 meters (3,282 feet) and 4,500 meters (14,780 feet). Consequently the temperature is mild, ranging from sixteen to twenty-six degrees Celsius (sixty to eighty degrees Fahrenheit), despite being two degrees south of the equator. Rwanda is about the size of the State of Maryland and has a population of about eleven million people. The population consists of three ethnic tribes: eighty-five percent Hutu, fourteen percent Tutsi, and one percent Twa.

Tribal rivalry increased dramatically in the 1950s when Rwanda gained independence and the Hutus began to express contempt for years of subservience to the Tutsis. The Hutus began a series of massacres that climaxed in 1994 with the genocide of nearly a million Tutsis in a ninety-day period while the world stood by paralyzed. The movie *Hotel Rwanda* is a reasonably accurate portrayal of this horrific event. The genocide ended when General Paul Kagame organized the Rwandan Patriotic Front (RPF) in Uganda among refugees that had fled because of the Hutu persecution. The RPF invaded Rwanda and took control of the government. Paul Kagame is now the elected president of the Republic of Rwanda.

President Kagame's first emphasis was to eliminate registration by ethnic groups and began the process of repatriation, thus eliminating the tribal divisions. He then began implementing entrepreneurship education and processes, especially among the youth of Rwanda, many of whom were orphans because the adults in their families were slaughtered in the genocide. I find it amazing that the scars from the genocide have healed sufficiently for Rwanda to rise out of the horrific cultural disaster. According to the Heritage Foundation, "Rwanda's economic freedom score is 64.9. . . . Rwanda is ranked third out of forty-six countries in the Sub-Saharan region, and its score exceeds the world average."[33]

In 2010 Regent University Center for Entrepreneurship (RCE) opened a Business Development Center (BDC) in Kigali, the capital of Rwanda, and began teaching a fourteen-week course in Entrepreneurship with the objective of teaching students to transform their ideas into small businesses. More than three hundred Rwandans have completed this training and more than fifty percent of the graduates have started their own small businesses.

Patrice Habinshute was a graduate of the first class and won a prize for his idea of organizing Entrepreneurship Clubs in every high school in Rwanda. Patrice, with Bernard, Anaclet, and Maria Louise, formed a group that is now called School Entrepreneurship Network (SEN) and began organizing clubs in high schools in each of the Provinces of Rwanda.

SEN's mission is to teach Discipleship and Entrepreneurship to young people and to recover a 1946 dedication by King Mutara III, who dedicated Rwanda to Christ the King. On Sunday, October 27, 1946, in Nyanza, King Mutara III, kneeling at the foot of the altar, prayed this prayer:

> Lord Jesus, King of all men and all nations, I, Mutara Charles Leon Pierre, I bow to you. . . . I acknowledge that You are the sovereign Master of Rwanda, the root from which all power

[comes]. Lord Jesus, You who have shaped our country. . . . Now that we know You, we acknowledge publicly that You are our Master and our King. Lord I give you my country and myself.[34]

Tuesday, August 14, 2012, Kigali. 0229. I went to sleep last night at 2130, now 0230 and I am wide awake and writing an introduction item for the training. Today we go to two high schools. My Scripture Transform is Philippians 4:13: "I can do all things through Christ who strengthens me." My Personal Transform is "Operating in the power of Jesus, I am an excellent facilitator sharing His message with the important people in Kigali!" Then I visualize myself facilitating the SE and TFT training and enjoying it immensely!

2011: Beautiful day in the hills of Rwanda. We went to two schools in the northern district and met students and faculty. I am still wondering what role the Lord has for me.

Email from Jenny, she says she is doing fine. *Lord, please protect Jenny. She obviously is bearing a heavy emotional burden of me being here in Rwanda for three weeks.*

On Wednesday we traveled to a high school in the western-most province of Rwanda; fourteen hours driving time round trip. The high school is in a picturesque setting on the banks of Lake Kivu, the largest of Rwanda's lakes. Lake Kivu shares coastlines with Rwanda and The Republic of Congo. The school is wonderfully clean and neat. Students and faculty expressed their appreciation for our visit and support. The Entrepreneurship Club talked about their project and proudly showed us the rabbit pens they have constructed on campus.

Only twenty-five percent of Rwandans have electrical power, but Internet access is available in all the schools. We also saw wild chimpanzees in the national forest we passed through, and we stood at the origin of the Nile and Congo rivers. A very good trip.

On Thursday we went to the Northern Province and visited a private school. The students were building a pig house for a school project.

Another eleven students were combining their resources for a goat-raising project and each are contributing two thousand Rwandan francs (RWF). I asked them where they would get the money. They said they would earn it by the time school started. I was impressed because these folks have limited financial resources but are rich in hope and ideas. I matched their contribution with twenty-two thousand RWF (about thirty dollars). They responded as if I gave them a gold nugget.

Friday we visited a high school near Kigali, a vocational training center, an art museum and the Rwandan king's palace with thatched roofs. This Palace was used until 1931 when Belgium built the king a modern house. There were pictures of the tall, handsome King Mutara III Rudahigwa, who reigned between 1931 and 1959 and dedicated Rwanda to "Christ the King" in 1946. I find this amazing that I could be a small part of working to fulfill that dedication!

I slept for more than eight hours Friday night, and then began studying for the presentations to begin on Monday. While studying I searched for the Scripture "As a man thinks in his heart" and found it at Proverbs 27:3. I found a link to a book written in 1903 by James Allen, titled *As a Man Thinketh*. This book contained great wisdom, such as the quote listed below that affirms what I am teaching with TFT:

> The soul attracts that which it secretly harbors, that which it loves and that which it fears. It reaches the height of its cherished aspirations. It falls to the level of its unchastened (sic) desires—and circumstances are the means by which the soul receives its own. . . . As the physically weak can make himself strong by careful and patient training, so the man of weak thoughts can make them strong by exercising himself in right thoughts.[35]

This quote is congruous with Job 3:25: "For the thing I greatly feared has come upon me, and what I dreaded has happened to me." But Allen also affirmed it is possible to change.

I concluded from Allen's posits that my prolonged and unchallenged fear of insanity could have eventually become reality. However, the Lord has rescued me and set me on the correct path, and by persistent use of Scripture as Transforms, the fear has been chastened with right thinking and the "inevitable" will never come to be! Praise the Lord. There is great resistance to erasing more than fifty years of lies and turning the destructive cognition train, but God made me tenacious and, with His strength, I am turning the train around!

It seems we have two positive guides and two negative guides: The Lord and our thoughts, and Satan and our thoughts. The Lord is always correct and positive; Satan is always a liar and negative. Our thoughts can be either positive or negative. We have a choice. As Doug suggested, "Exercising choice is the ultimate act of faith." I like it.

Saturday. I went to visit the SEN office. Patrice asked for fifteen minutes to discuss how we are doing. They said a lot of nice things and said they now consider me, not as a mentor, but as their dad! They are in their twenties or early thirties. Then they presented me with a sixteen-inch portrait of me painted from my picture on Facebook! It was their way of saying thanks, as they said, to "an old man who acts like he is young." Actually, I look better in the painting than in the mirror. What a surprise! I was speechless. These people barely have enough for food and they pay an artist to paint the portrait. I shall treasure it for all of life because of their sacrifice. Now they are trying to convince Mum Jenny to come to Rwanda.

On Sunday I went to church then rested and studied. Chef Jean Marie, the chef at the Solace compound where I was staying, prepared a special dinner: the best Cordon bleu since Germany! It was truly a meal fit for a king.

Monday, August 20, 2012, Kigali. I went to bed at 2130, up at 0500. I recited Transforms. There is opposition and attempts to cause me to think negative thoughts about the class. However, I rebuke the liar and confirm that I am a new creation in Christ and that His light now shines in my life giving light to those in this class. This is my Personal Transform: "Operating in His power, I am an efficacious facilitator sharing His message with those who come."

Lord, I commit my life to You today for Your glory.

1849: First day of class. The participants were mostly high school students and the concept of self-efficacy is totally new to them.

I noticed static this morning as I was talking one-on-one with some students; I was being bombarded with destructive thoughts regarding the students. I was listening and countering the thought at the same time. The bombardment ceased and did not occur once I began teaching. The class went very well.

"It is done! I am the Alpha and the Omega, the Beginning and the End. . . . He who overcomes shall inherit all things, and I will be his God and he shall be My son" (Revelation 21:6–7). I definitely am being challenged to move from fear to taking on the battle with the power given me from His Word.

Wednesday, August 22, 2012, Kigali. I feel a little timid in sharing the biblical perspective of the heart, mind, and soul, so I counter with this Personal Transform: "I am bold and stouthearted and I am blessed to share the truth with the class this morning."

2015: *God gave me boldness to pursue the TFT as written. The class members are for the most part listening and inquisitive. In answer to my request for the Lord to guide me, He gave me the idea of giving each student one thousand RWF with a challenge to see how much they can earn with entrepreneur initiatives and report on their progress in class on Friday.*

Tonight I went to monitor the BDC training. As I was leaving, Bernard, from the SEN team, was outside planning to come hear what I was telling the group, thinking I was going to speak. We walked up the street together, and he spoke great words of encouragement that I am doing God's will and doing the hard work instead of retiring. He was very complementary. *Thank You, God, for sending him. I believe You are confirming that I am correctly teaching the TFT as written. I know You love me.*

Thursday, August 23, 2012, Kigali. My Personal Transform was: "I am stouthearted and I present the seminar boldly and with passion!"

1933: Warm today. The class went very well, and I shared about the process of being born again and showed on the board how the Word goes through the mind into the heart for value comparison; then when belief occurs, the mouth speaks, confessing the belief.

I have to admit to the Lord that I am still a little timid about sharing the gospel with this class. This is now my Personal Transform: "I am bold and excited to share Jesus with this class!"

Friday, August 24, 2012, Kigali. As I woke up this morning I had negative thoughts that none of the students will have anything to report about the challenge I gave on Wednesday.

2205: The Lord has blessed me with strength and boldness as we completed the training today and graduated twenty-four students. Their entrepreneur assignments were spectacular! The negative thoughts this morning were totally bogus. To my surprise and utter joy, all but two or three invested the one thousand RWF and made a significant profit. The lowest profit was fourteen percent; some made two hundred fifty percent! Their entrepreneur ventures included buying and selling bananas, avocadoes, bubble gum, drinking water and acquiring investors in a teen magazine. Delightful!

When the final presentation was concluded, I cited the parable from Jesus, who rewarded the ones who invested wisely, and I rewarded those who participated in the challenge with an additional one thousand RWF and let them keep their initial "loan." The best investment I have made recently. The students were thrilled!

Now I can rest and enjoy the afterglow of praise and thanksgiving from a grateful group. *Thank You, Lord, for YOUR strength.*

We learned to sing, "Rejoice in the Lord always, again I say rejoice," as a round. They really got into it!

Saturday, August 25, 2012, Kigali. I slept eight uninterrupted hours last night. The first true peace I have had since I knew I was coming to

Rwanda. *Thank You, Lord, for Your peace! It is evident You sent a messenger before me.*

Sunday, August 26, 2012, Kigali. I went to sleep immediately when I lay down about 2220 and slept until 0640. That's more than eight hours of sound sleep! I woke up a little sluggish and began reciting Isaiah 43:1–3 and affirming that God does love me even when I don't feel lovable. Isaiah 35:4 "Say to those who have an anxious heart, 'Be strong; fear not! Behold your God will come with vengeance, with the recompense of God. He will come and save you'" (ESV).

Tomorrow I leave for home. Ah, there is a lingering static thought that I believe is from the years of fear that implanted a false-truth. Now I will erase the fear and renounce the origin of the static.

I have not heard from Jenny in two days and am concerned about her. "The Lord works out everything for his own ends" (Proverbs 16:4).

2133: A very interesting day. Jenny wrote a nice note; she is OK. At 1230 Patrice, his fiancée Anastasia, Bernard, and Damascene picked me up and we went to the stadium for the annual day of "Thanksgiving to God" for all His bounty. It was a wonderful time of praise and worship. The soccer stadium was filled and there were numerous choirs that sang gospel hymns in their language with gusto. Even the Rwanda Army Band marched and played familiar hymns. They are calling for a national holiday to celebrate God. It was an incredible day. I feel like I am back in colonial days when America was grateful to God and set aside special days to celebrate.

We got back at 1800 and I went to say goodbye to a couple I had met earlier. They were going to dinner and invited me to go. So we walked to a nearby restaurant and had dinner and enjoyed chatting. I had not had an American-style salad since coming here and a salad at the next table looked so refreshing that I forgot to be cautious. I had been warned not to eat raw vegetables, but the restaurant was upscale . . I had been warned not to eat raw vegetables and I ordered the salad. After dinner we walked to Solace in the rain. The dry season is over.

Tuesday, August 28, 2012, Amsterdam, 0700. Arrived at the Amsterdam airport from Kigali at 0622 and am now waiting on a flight to

Portland, Oregon. It was good to settle in the seat and take a deep breath. The past two weeks have been an incredible experience. Patrice and Damascene took me to the Kigali airport and wanted pictures with me so they would never forget me. In two weeks I have made more friends than any time in the past several years. *Lord, please draw these to You and bless them as they grow. Now I look forward to seeing Jenny and Deb's family today.*

The experiences of the past seventeen days are surreal. I can still see myself in the simple classroom with the twenty-four students sharing what God has taught me and feeling their warm friendship.

Working with Patrice, Bernard, Anaclet, and Maria Louise was a real pleasure. They were so eager to learn and to help. When we went anywhere they carried my briefcase and camera bag. They took all the pictures and gave me the place of honor in the vehicle, which is the center place in the back seat. When we had a long drive, they let me ride in the front seat so I could take a nap.

Jean Marie, the chef at Solace, was magnificent. He prepared three meals for me that were the best I have had the pleasure to savor. The last evening he prepared cheese puffs as appetizer, then salad, then cordon bleu with sliced carrots and peas, oven baked potatoes, and the best gravy ever. Then for dessert he prepared crepes around ice cream and spread with hot chocolate. Out of this world! I gave him a double tip. He gave me two bear hugs! I got the better of the deal.

Now, I make the transition back to a totally different world and hold these memories as precious pieces of mental gold. *Thank You, Lord, for this wonderful experience!*

Wednesday, August 29, 2012, Home in Sisters, OR. Have spent the day resting and recovering from a sore throat and serious digestive problems. It hit just as I got off the plane. The raw salad the last day was good, but lethal! Next time I will avoid green, enticing salads on my last days on foreign soil.

Thursday, August 30, 2012, Sisters. Magnificent morning sky. I went to sleep immediately after laying down at 2230 and slept almost eight hours. I am now proceeding on the premise that the static is from the false-truth that came by the years of fear that Satan would take control of my life. Now with the deliverance session and the power of God's words that I have assimilated through the years, my mind is strong, I know who I am and the false-truth is the antithesis of who I am. This is now my Scripture Transform: *"Therefore, if anyone is in Christ he is a new creation; old things have passed away; behold all things have become new."* Personal Transform: "I am a new creation in Christ and my heart is gloriously filled with love for my Creator, for Jenny and all of life!"

When I woke up I was charged with energy and eager to get up and begin processing the goals I perceive He has for me. The first goal that comes to mind is to be recklessly abandoned to Jesus such that Mark 11:24 becomes a reality in my life: "Therefore I say to you, whatever things you ask when you pray, believe that you receive them, and you will have them."

I received the following email from Patrice the week after I returned home:

> Subject: Update
>
> Dear Richard, Thank you for your update, and we are pleased to hear that you enjoyed Rwanda during the wonderful 16 days, and that you arrived home safely from Rwanda. . . . Dad, we are very thankful for all you have done for us in the 16 days. We wished you stayed with us but this has not been possible. It is ok that you went home, because we know you are there for us: "Rwanda rising, together we can!"
>
> Greetings to our Mum Jenny and the family (Deb and Tod, Doug and Connie, as well as their children: Anson, Tate, Luke, Logan, and Levi). Mum Jenny, your sons and daughters in Rwanda miss you too much."

That was my first of three trips to Rwanda; the next was in 2013 and another in 2014. During the 2013 visit, the Lord called Patrice, and he accepted the challenge to claim Jesus as Savior. He has become a warrior for King Jesus. Notice that in addition to adopting me as Dad, they have adopted Jenny and call her Mum Jenny. The story of this wonderful people and the experiences we have had together is a book in itself, which I shall pursue as the Lord gives me strength. Patrice, Bernard, Anaclet, and Maria Louise have started businesses of their own. In addition to being co-owner of the Business Development Center in Kigali, Patrice is completing a Master's degree online with Regent University and making exceptionally high grades. We stay in touch via email, telephone, and Skype, and I offer advice as appropriate. I love these people and long to return to Rwanda.

CHAPTER 19

Wrapping It Up

Lessons Learned

It is indeed time to bring this record to conclusion. Jenny and I have continued to grow closer in our relationship. The Lord has blessed Jenny and me with the opportunity to spend quality time with our children; after four years of wonderful healing time with Deb in Oregon, now we have moved to spend time with Doug in North Carolina. We are enjoying time with Doug and his family, attending ball games and cross country meets and continuing the healing process with Doug. We have been given a rare second chance to do it right, to bless our children and to be blessed by them!

I am no longer on constant guard and am normally relaxed when not actively involved in some project. I believe the deliverance sessions, coupled with the intensive assimilation of Scripture Transforms, have productively replaced the false-truth from the past with the Truth. The persistence of the evil imprint has been agonizing, but the penetrating power of God's Word is doing its mighty work. The Truth has reset my Reticular Activating System (RAS). I know we will always be in a battle in this life and I face the enemy head-on with the Sword of the Spirit and a refurbished Shield of Faith.

The research also continues with a shift in focus away from the nature and tactics of the enemy to the magnificent provisions of recovery provided by our awesome Creator and Redeemer. When we visited Lorena at Thanksgiving, her daughter Judi shared with me the research of Dr. Caroline Leaf, suggesting it seemed to be similar to what she knew of my TFT seminar. I immediately ordered two of Dr. Leaf's books, which are referenced herein. I found her research extremely fascinating. I believe there is in her brilliant documentation the scientific validation of my own longitudinal study on the nature of our creation and cause and effects of environmental inputs on our personhood.

Beginning with what I now know to be the Lord's voice in 1969 when He said, "You shall know the truth and the truth will make you free," followed by Dr. Norman Vincent Peale's Thought Conditioners in 1970, the power of God's words have penetrated the darkness of my life to indeed set me free. After reading Dr. Leaf's books, I understand the scientific reasons the positive power in His words have renovated my heart, soul, and mind and corrected negative physical impacts caused by repressive thought and belief patterns.

Leaf's research illuminates my understanding of my perceived heart condition. The prolonged fear of a heart attack produced physical reactions and could have eventually caused a heart attack. Here is what she wrote regarding past trauma:

> Thoughts of the painful act will cause fear in the amygdala (the library for emotions), which causes stress chemicals, raises levels of stress hormones and increases blood pressure and heart rate. . . . [If not resolved] the stress response stays active, making those sick mentally and physically.[36]

In electrical terms, this seems to mean these toxic experiences somehow activate a pulse generator that produces the "fight or flight" energy at the subconscious level as background static. According to Leaf, unless the toxic conditions are resolved, the person continues to experience the effects on all their thoughts all their life without even knowing it:

> For example, have you ever become ill in the wake of a traumatic time in your life? You may not have made the connection, just chalking it up as coincidence, when it was more likely to have been the result of toxic thoughts taking their toll on your overall health.[37]

Dr. Leaf further claims that for every memory, there is a corresponding emotion that is stored in the brain and records her claims thusly: "These emotions are very real and link your thoughts to the reaction in your body and mind . . . called the psychosomatic network. They can surface even years after an event has occurred, when the memory of the event is recalled.[38]

This could also explain Jenny's sudden elevated heart rate each time I was preparing to travel to Rwanda. This likely resulted from a subliminal fear initiated in childhood that she would be abandoned. Now she feared I would not return and she would be left alone. Consciously, she was brave, strong, and supportive of my mission to Rwanda. Our relationship is the best it has ever been and getting better all the time. On the surface there was no visible or rational reason for her heart to suddenly start beating at more than two hundred beats per minute because there was no conscious fear. However, as Dr. Leaf's research shows, "the patterns for adulthood are laid down in childhood, so an excessively stressed child could be prone to life-long stress-related illnesses."[39] (Jenny's journey is a book in itself and reserved for a separate record.)

In Part Four of *Who Switched off My Brain*, Caroline Leaf identified The Dirty Dozen: "let's meet the Dirty Dozen—twelve areas of toxic thinking in our lives."[40] As I have studied each of these toxic patterns, I can identify with each one at some point in my life. The amazing grace from a forgiving Father and the mutual repentance and forgiveness between Jenny and me confirms in real life: when you make the commitment to stand and fight, positive change begins to happen.

I found it fascinating that Leaf proposes a twenty-one-day regimen for conquering the Dirty Dozen. As recorded earlier in this record, when I made the commitment to memorize and internalize Norman Vincent Peale's Thought Conditioners, it was after a dedicated effort for twenty-one days that change was definitely taking place. On the morning of day twenty-two, I suddenly realized I was no longer afraid to leave the house! I stood in the open door in amazement that I was eager to get out into the world to do what I loved to do: serve as a soldier for my beloved America!

Dr. Leaf's "21-Day Brain Detox Plan" is contained in her book *Switch on Your Brain*, a fascinating and instructive compilation of research findings and analysis. In this volume, Leaf focuses primarily on the mind. She posits, "We can even predict the seeming elusiveness of the main functions of the mind—that of thinking and choosing—through quantum mechanics."[41] The functions she describes as "thinking and choosing" are highly correlated to the functions of the mind contained in the TFT that was an extension of my doctoral work from 1998 to 2003.

The synopsis of TFT is contained in Appendix A of this book and describes the functions of the mind as "the center of logic and cognition. Logic is defined as the science of reasoning. Cognition is the act, power, or faculty of apprehending, knowing, or perceiving." The similarity of the terms should not be surprising since both are guided by the Creator who spoke into being this complex and wonderful component of the human anatomy. Leaf's derivation is based upon extensive scientific research, whereas my conclusions were based upon objective use of a simple engineering process called "best fit" analysis.

It is especially intriguing when Leaf writes, "You are able to stand outside of yourself, observe your own thinking, consult with God, and change the negative, toxic thought or grow the positive, healthy thought."[42] I believe she is precisely correct. In order for us to control our heart, soul, and mind, God has ingeniously created in us a control center that resides above and separate from the building blocks, just as He resides above and separate from His creation. My hypothesis is that the control center is above and linked to our Zone of Congruence as shown in the Connectivity Diagram contained in the TFT synopsis. The mystery of how our Creator activated this link is similar to the mystery of how He connected our spirit to our body with a switch that releases our spirit at the moment of physical death.

What an exciting adventure life is when we are surrendered to our Creator!

Purge Me with Hyssop

*OK, Lord, I see it. In Your kingdom, to which I aspire, there cannot be **any** rebellion or defiance. There are things in my life you have tolerated in the past that you are now saying must go. The stubborn spirit must be transformed into "Spiritual Tenacity."* Oswald Chambers wrote about tenacity in the devotional for February 22:

> If our hopes are being disappointed just now, it means that they are being purified. . . . Tenacity is more than endurance, it is endurance combined with the absolute certainty that what we are looking for is going to transpire. . . . Tenacity is the supreme effort of a man refusing to believe that his hero is going to be conquered.[43]

I shared with Jenny the struggle I am having with so little progress and even more intense opposition from the enemy and my flesh as my desire to be recklessly abandoned to Jesus increases. She retrieved an article from *Our Daily Bread* for February 21, 2015, and shared it with me. A portion of the article is included below:

> Approaching God. It used to bother me that the closer I drew to God in my walk with Him, the more sinful I felt. Then a phenomenon I observed in my room enlightened me. A tiny gap in the curtain covering my window threw a ray of light into the room. As I looked, I saw particles of dirt drifting in the beam. Without the ray of light, the room seemed clean, but the light revealed the dirty particles. What I observed shed light on my spiritual life. The closer I approach the Lord of light, the clearer I see myself. When the light of Christ shines in the darkness of our lives, it exposes our sin—not to discourage us, but to humble us to trust in him.[44]

I thanked Jenny for her observation and her strength. I receive the perceptive observation contained in the *Daily Bread* article as being from the Lord. I rejoice that He cares enough to clean me up!

Light always displaces darkness. I have learned that release and recovery from the erroneous thought patterns takes time and persistence, so I don't anticipate perfection in my heart, soul, and mind. However, being willing to confess the dark side of my heart has provided increased authenticity to my life and I have a renewed determination to complete the reprogramming of my RAS with the truth of who I am in Christ.

It is amazing that God often provides a window of confirmation to what He knows is a true desire to change. Soon after the confession mentioned above, I was focusing on a Personal Transform, declaring twenty-one times that "I am a dedicated guardian of life!" I was visualizing standing between a person and some danger and I "heard" another person who was observing the action say, "When Richard is near, everyone is safe!" Perhaps that was confirmation that my commitment to reset my RAS with the truth of who I am in Christ is in fact working.

I also notice a major shift in my attitude about God the Father and Jesus, His only begotten Son. I once feared God, but now I rejoice to go into His presence as Abba, my gracious and approachable Father. Jesus is not only my Lord—He is also my best friend. At the beginning of this journey, I greatly feared death and distrusted Him. I have learned to trust Him explicitly and am excited about the adventure of crossing over from this earthly kingdom to the eternal Kingdom Jesus is now preparing.

I also understand the purpose of this period called "time." It is not to achieve greatness in this life, but to respond to God's invitation to spend eternity with Him. To accept His invitation means to rule and reign with Him in His eternal Kingdom. To reject His invitation means to be eternally condemned and suffer His just punishment. But His demonstrated desire is summed up in this verse: "For God so loved the world that He gave His only begotten Son, that whoever believes in Him should not perish but have everlasting life" (John 3:16).

Jesus Christ, Begotten Son of the Most High

In John 1:1–14, the apostle explains the mystery of creation and salvation; John declares that all things were spoken into being by the Word of God, "And the Word became flesh and dwelt among us . . . the glory as of the only begotten [Son] of the Father." Therefore it was Jesus who created the physical universe and gave life to all forms of created beings. It was also Jesus who came to the earth in the flesh to rescue fallen humanity and "as many as received Him, to them He gave the right to become children of God." In the language of our corporate world, God's Kingdom is a privately held entity. God as the Founder has delegated to Jesus the role of Chief Executive Officer (CEO), given Him complete authority over everything pertaining to His Kingdom, bestowed upon Him all the characteristics of Himself, and elevated His name above all other names.

Cruden's Concordance, in continuous publication since 1737, lists one hundred ninety-eight names for Jesus. The two names that have the most significance for me are Christ—the Messiah, the Anointed One—and Emmanuel, which means "God is with us." This amounts to unfathomable grace and love! Think about it: the Creator of the universe, estimated to contain as many as one hundred seventy billion galaxies, enters into the body of a human and permits men weighing less than two hundred pounds, and standing less than six feet tall, to pull his beard, spit in his face, and shred His flesh with a cat-o'-nine-tails without vaporizing them! That is infinite restraint. But that is not all. I snubbed my nose at this "weakling" and said time and again, "No! I will not!"

What was His response? He set limits for the enemy and pursued me as "the Hound of Heaven" described in a poem by English poet Francis Thompson (1859–1907) and orchestrated a forty-four-year journey. He met me in Bangkok, Thailand, and there He greeted me, not with a whip, but with "Richard, I will forgive you." And He has forgiven me many times. Now I sit leaning back in an easy chair listening to Amadeus Mozart's Thirty-third Symphony in B-Flat Major, remembering the events of my life that could have ended in chaos! But here I am at eighty-one years old, healthy enough to carry a thirty-pound backpack and climb three miles up a mountain for an overnight campout with Tod, Levi, and Tate.

Jesus is everything to me! He has loved me, guided me, healed me, chastised me, laughed at and with me, and out of the morass of my early life provided me with a beautiful, strong companion who even has the strength to edit this book! I am of all men most blessed.

If I were a great writer, I would write volumes of compelling stories about Jesus. If I were a composer, I would compose a great symphony of praise. If I were a poet, I would write verse after verse of His virtue! Since I am none of these, I, like the Little Drummer Boy who played his drum for Him, offer Him what I have: this record of His majestic Person and the power of His Word.

Afterward

The Apostle Paul wrote, "That I may know *Him and the power of* His resurrection, and the fellowship of His sufferings . . . forgetting those things which are behind . . . I press toward the goal for the prize of the upward call of God in Christ Jesus" (Philippians 3:10–14).

We just welcomed in year 2016, and this is a time for me to press on toward my calling. I am learning to walk in the victory already won by Jesus of Nazareth. John Eldredge, in his introduction to *A Guide Book to Waking the Dead*, declares:

> There is more. . . . [N]o matter how precious your life with God has been to date . . . there is more available with God. . . . Now in this life. . . . But to discover that "more" we must launch out into deep waters, leave what is familiar, search for new shores . . . we must learn to live life spiritually, and we must take seriously the fierce battle for our hearts. We *must* get our hearts back.[45]

And that is exactly my mission, not only for me, but for every reader of this book! I have permitted the deceiver to steal my dream and contaminate my heart. I am energized by the fact that I am getting my whole heart back, and I accept Eldredge's challenge to launch out from my comfort zone on a journey to become recklessly abandoned to Jesus Christ!

Opa's Vette

Jesus has a great sense of humor. When we sold the last RV, I no longer needed the Ford F-150, and our garage is too narrow for two large vehicles, so in early 2016, I sold the truck. Jenny and I were planning to live nine months in North Carolina and three months in Sisters, Oregon. I had planned to purchase an economy car for our summers in Oregon and another car for the winters in North Carolina. Then I began to feel the power of spiritual freedom, and that began to spill over into my search for a vehicle that Doug and I could enjoy working on together. I have always enjoyed sports cars, but after selling the MGA in 1960, I have purchased family cars for economy.

Doug has always dreamed of owning a Corvette, but also has focused on economical family cars. When we returned to North Carolina from Oregon last fall, Doug and I began a search, with prayer, for a "fun" vehicle. Lo and behold! A sleek C5 Corvette with several thousand dollars of engine and drive-train enhancements showed up on the "lemon lot" at the Air Force base where he is stationed. We looked at it and looked at it and talked about it and prayed about it. Then it was gone! *Okay, Lord, that was not Your choice for us.*

Doug sent a text to the owner. It was not sold, but they had a man coming from out of town to look at it the next day. I began to pray that the owners, a Christian couple, would receive the full price for the vehicle. The following day I received a call from the owner. The man from western North Carolina was delayed a day because of heavy rain. "If you are still interested, you can have it." The amount he offered was the same amount I had set as my final offer, so in February, 2016, Doug and I agreed I should purchase the 2000, modified C5 Corvette with an exhaust system that lets both exhaust gases and the associated noise of combustion escape freely.

Doug, Luke, Logan, and Levi truly enjoy driving the "Vette." Luke, twenty-one in July, came home for Spring Break. After driving it for the first time, I asked him what he thought of the Vette. Without hesitation he said, "It epitomizes the Miller motto: 'Drive fast and take chances!'"

The law sets the upper limit of speed on the highway, but it does not limit the rapidity with which one gets there! Right? The Vette is a physical manifestation of my spiritual goal: "Recklessly abandoned to Jesus Christ." I have also learned a lesson about the proper use of power, both of the Vette and the Holy Spirit. The Vette engine has 411 break horsepower. I can use it or abuse it. The Holy Spirit has unlimited power and I can learn to use it or abuse it. I think Jesus just chuckled.

Doug was flying again. He just completed four years as a squadron commander and recently returned from a deployment to a place with lots of sand and where war games are for real. In March of 2016, he called and said, "I am deploying to England for two weeks. You and Mom want to go with me?"

YES! Since I am retired military, Jenny and I are permitted to fly on military aircraft as space is available, referred to as "Space A." So Jenny and I flew with him to England for two weeks in April 2016. He invited me to sit in the jump seat behind him as he executed a perfect takeoff. Then he invited Jenny to sit in the jump seat for the landing in Mildenhall, England. Jenny and I spent twelve exciting days visiting various places in England, Scotland, and Ireland. Life is good!

God, Who Are You?

The veil has been lifted from my eyes and I see God's provision and protection afforded me unto this very day, even when I was in rebellion. I marvel that the Lord directed my life and rerouted my journey to always bring me back to the path He ordained for me. The reason God cares for me is a mystery to me, but it is this trait of God and His enabling strength that granted me a reasonably productive and exciting life.

Recently I shared with Abba, my Father, that I did not understand Him or know Who He is. A few days later I was reading Hebrews 1, and the words of verse 3 were literally emboldened to my sight: "He [Jesus] is the radiance of the glory of God and the exact imprint of his nature" (ESV). Then I asked the Holy Spirit to clarify for me why I should be eager to glorify Jesus. The next morning I woke up feeling totally alone and ugly. For two hours I lay on the floor weeping as my true nature was projected on the screen of my soul. It was horrible! I kept crying out, "I am unfit, I am unfit!" As I lay there exhausted and waiting quietly for enough energy to get up, I heard, "Yes, unfit, but forgiven." Then the weeping turned to tears of joy. Unfit, yet forgiven, is now my status.

There is no greater evidence of God's gracious intervention than in our family. By His grace, Jenny and I are enjoying the best years of our life. We have been blessed with three wonderful children. Greg is waiting to welcome us at "Home." Even with my abuse of a wonderful boy, God confirmed to me via Madam Sheik that Greg was, in fact, "with Jesus."

Debbie, a wonderful mother, has a gifted husband, Tod, and they both are excellent counselors and mentors. They have two exceptional children, Anson and Tate, and all their "names are written in Heaven."

Doug, an exceptional US Air Force pilot, says the best thing that came from living in Kansas was his wife, Connie. She is a gifted teacher and excels in every teaching position. They have three handsome, reckless sons and their "names are written in Heaven."

Our most precious physical possession is a large oil portrait of Greg, Deb, and Doug, the last portrait by a very talented artist in Germany with a unique form of splatter painting, which she did while on her knees.

Anson's Miracle

Anson has a passion for skiing. He especially likes the challenge of performing all kinds of tricks and often competes in slope-style competitions. On January 8, 2017, Anson was practicing for a slope-style contest at Waterville Valley, New Hampshire. He was trying a trick off a jump structure that was fifty feet long. He had never tried that trick before and became disoriented in the jump. He stopped his rotation in a vertical, head-down position. He landed on his head, on ice, from about twelve feet in the air. The ski patrol hauled him off the hill in a toboggan with a neck brace on.

Anson was released to a mountain clinic and they evaluated him and took x-rays that did not go far enough down his spine and showed no significant injury. They sent him back to the condo with no neck protection. He was in a lot of pain, but happy that nothing else happened in the crash. He did not sleep that night and any movement caused severe pain.

Anson was staying in a condo with another skier and the skier's mother. The mother became concerned and called his parents to get permission to take Anson to the hospital. Permission was granted and thirty hours after his accident, after two car rides and a long night on the sofa, Anson walked into Spear Memorial Hospital. They did an MRI and found that Anson's neck was broken between C7 and T1 vertebras. His spinal cord was deformed into an S-shape. The doctor who examined Anson sent him by helicopter to a neurosurgeon at Dartmouth-Hitchcock Medical Center in Lebanon, New Hampshire.

The team of surgeons who examined Anson were amazed that Anson was not already paralyzed and scheduled him for immediate surgery that lasted nine hours. The surgery required entry to the injured area from multiple directions. A steel plate was installed to bridge the space between C7 and T1 vertebras. Dr. Bauer reported that the surgery went well and he was very hopeful of Anson's full recovery. An hour after they rolled Anson out of recovery, he was able to wiggle his toes and squeeze his hands. There were shouts of joy in the room and on Facebook! A halo was installed to hold his neck rigid. He walked two days later!

In retrospect, it is easy to see that our loving God responded to the prayers of many people and not only protected Anson during those thirty hours of wandering around with a broken neck and severe concussion, but orchestrated a myriad of logistic details. Tod was able get to the hospital before Anson went into surgery, on tickets provided by a friend. When Tod arrived, Anson said, "Dad is here—everything is going to be all right."

Deb traveled later on tickets provided by a friend. A family member provided a rental car. They were able to stay at David's House, a house set up for parents and children receiving treatment at the hospital, for free. A predicted Nor'easter on a travel day produced only wind and rain.

Anson stayed in the hospital six days and in the recovery house seven days. The halo was removed after nine days and a neck brace installed. A friend postponed a trip in order to provide Anson and family first class tickets for the ride home so Anson would have more space. Then westerly winds predicted to be 150 mph did not happen and the flight was four hours instead of the scheduled five, which was a great relief for Anson.

Now after five months, recovery continues and Anson has resumed activities that do not require lifting or pulling. He drives a car and hikes in the mountains. The steel plate is already partially covered with new bone. When asked about future skiing plans, Anson responds with, "I will ski again. I will wait and see what kind."

Our miracle-working God is alive and well. Those who asked Him for a miracle are now praising Him for His powerful response!

Halfway from Hell

The journey has been painful, but I am learning to celebrate pain as one of God's pruning instruments. The completion of my sojourn on this Small Blue Marble as seen from outer space is anticipated with eager expectancy.

Out of the Ashes

God is creating a New Life for both Jenny and me. He has chosen His own process to accomplish what He has promised to complete. This process is reflected in my journal entry as follows:

Saturday, August 24, 2013, Sisters. Beautiful sunrise. I am reading *Glorious Freedom* by Richard Sibbes. This morning I read about the freedom in sanctification and in particular about the battle that continues therein:

> In sanctification, *we are liberated from slavery to sin. . . . We must understand this spiritual liberty in sanctification. It is not a liberty freeing us altogether from combat and deadness and dullness. It is a liberty . . . enabling us to combat, to fight the battles of our Lord against our own corruptions.*[46]

After describing hindrances to liberty, Sibbes amplifies the reason for the struggle in sanctification: "[W]hile we live here there is sin in us, but it does not reign . . . the spirit of Christ maintains a perpetual combat and conflict against sin. . . . God chooses to humble us while we live here and exercise us with spiritual conflicts."[47]

This assertion is profound and enlightening to me since I have been in a fierce battle with the corruptions in me from my rebellion that gave Satan legal access to my life. My reaction to the fear of punishment for my rebellion and refusing God's invitation to be forgiven was choosing to continue to live in fear rather than be a preacher. Those years of fear imprinted corruption in my cognitive system and distorted my RAS such that it was doing its job by attempting to bring about, "that which I greatly feared."

The Lord has progressively led me to understand the doors I have opened to Satan and his minion. A friend recently sent me a link to Robert Morris' series of fifteen sermons entitled *Free Indeed.*[48] I now understand that my rebellion, unresolved fear, and jealousy of Jenny and my roommate in 1957 opened the door and gave satanic spirits legal access to my life. When my roommate's father read the newspaper story about a man who went berserk and killed his family, those same spirits that drove the man to commit that evil act entered my life and began to try to convince me to also commit acts of violence. Although there was a terrific battle for several years, the Lord protected me and eventually set the stage for my deliverance beginning in 1972 in Lawton, Oklahoma.

I also understand that the major cause of the struggle between Jenny and me has been the battle between two sinful or demonic forces: a spirit of domination in me clashing with a spirit of defiance in Jenny. This conclusion is based upon Ephesians 6:12: "For we do not wrestle against flesh and blood, but . . . against the rulers of the darkness of this age, against spiritual *hosts* of wickedness in the heavenly *places.*" Although we still have disagreements, they are resolved without the anger that was so prevalent in the past.

The Lord has intervened, has totally forgiven me of my rebellion, and now has provided the means and methods of reversing the RAS setting by the power contained in His words. He would have been justified in permitting one or both of the fears to become reality or He could have corrected the imprint immediately. But as Mr. Sibbes wrote, He chose to use the conflict as exercise for my spiritual growth.

"I can do all things through Christ who strengthens me" (Philippians 4:13). By His strength I conquer my flesh and its corruptions. Through His strength I resist the devil and his minions! From His strength I acquire strength to answer His call to "Come on up!" The battle is now purposeful. The climb exhilarating. The vista magnificent!

One may wonder which calling is nobler: to accomplish great feats of science or to cast a ray of light onto the path of a fellow traveler. This writer can say, "I have dreamed of the former," then concludes, "If perchance I am a means to the latter, I shall not have lived in vain." To Him be all honor and glory now and forever!

Jenny—God's Choice for Me

Jenny is the exact person God knew I needed in my life. She has traveled this journey with me step by step, side by side, while experiencing all the "bliss and blisters" along the way. Looking back over the years of our life, I agree with her analysis that I have often sided with the children or others and not supported her. It is not a case of supporting her because she was always correct, but my lack of strength to react toward her in a correct manner even if she were acting improperly. I was unable to separate my love for her from the pain of rejection I often felt from her. The dilemma was that we both had a huge wound in our self-image that was more powerful than our ability to show our true love for each other.

I recall that I often said I was a perfect husband while I was traveling, but crash-landed when I got home. As the power of God's words have penetrated my heart, soul, and mind, the plank has been removed from my eye and I am able to see more clearly our relationship and separate my love for Jenny from the pain of rejection. There is great resistance for me to write this record, but now I have the tools and presence of the Holy Spirit living in me. Just think of it: "You are of God, little children, and have overcome them, because He who is in you is greater than he who is in the world" (1 John 4:4).

It is amazing that in the middle of all this there were times that I call "windows of Heaven." I remember one such window in Manhattan, Kansas, when Jenny and I were struggling with our identities and it looked as if our relationship was crashing on the barriers. I was fasting and praying for her and in response God gave me a glimpse of her as He created her. He made her beautiful! And that image sustained me through some very troubling times.

Jenny was the one who made the greater sacrifice for me to travel to Rwanda. Fear of being abandoned in childhood reared its ugly head from its submerged hiding place, resulting in nighttime terror and racing heart rate. It was after the third trip to Rwanda that we realized what was happening, yet she toughed it out for me to complete the mission in Rwanda. She is amazing! It is fitting that I dedicate this book to her and ask her to close this chapter of our lives with her thoughts.

Epilogue

By Jenny

After reading Dick's story, I have to admit I am surprised to find I didn't know as much as I thought I did about this modest, giving, and very complex man I have been married to for over fifty-five years. Let me make it very clear: my husband has never carried through on any of the demonic-induced thoughts or impulses revealed in the pages of this book. Not with me, or anyone else he knows or who knows him. Quite the contrary, he is known as a quiet, unassuming, gentle man who would give you the proverbial shirt off his back if you asked for it.

Lest you think he has been the 'perfect' husband, father, or friend, I'm here to set that record straight also. Our marriage has been a roller coaster ride almost from the minute we said "I do" until this very day. We have had our share of disagreements (some, VERY disagreeable), temper tantrums, and, yes, fights, none of which came to blows. Dick used to keep his anger bottled up for unbelievable periods of time. I, on the other hand, generally fly off the handle at the first sign of conflict. Somehow, our personalities and emotional makeup have not served us well in practicing good communication while in the heat of anger and tends to spill over into all areas of our relationship. We carry the excess baggage with us to the next confrontation, and before we know it, the snowball effect is in play and recovery becomes slower to achieve.

Although our marriage may have been on the bottom side of "average," I believe most couples will be able to identify with the wide range of disagreements and pitfalls that have plagued us—conflicting priorities for our assets, be it finances, talents, accomplishments, ambitions, or goals. Very few marriages escape all of these, and it doesn't seem to matter whether the people involved are Christians or not. It's true, those who have a good foundation in Christ will have the added benefits available to them through the help of the Holy Spirit, and often that is the ingredient that can make a difference in the critical and very weak link of staying together or ending the marriage. I can tell you it made the difference for us. At the most vulnerable time when one word spoken could have broken every vow we took in 1960, we made the choice to grab hold of the rope and start climbing. The rope we grabbed hold of was *forgiveness*!

It was absolutely amazing! When I was able to "see" my need for and receiving forgiveness from Dick, life took on a whole new dimension. I didn't look beyond that need. I realized divorce could still happen. I didn't care. I was sick at heart, confused, and unable to function mentally or physically. I knew that I had to release this burden of unforgiveness, and it made no difference whether Dick felt the need for my forgiveness or not.

Matthew 5:23–24 says: "Therefore if you bring your gift to the altar, and there remember that your brother [husband] has something against you, leave your gift there before the altar. . . . First be reconciled to your brother, and then come and offer your gift."

What a deep, deep cleansing I felt at that moment when I released my pent-up anger and said the words that washed all the negative feelings away! Years and years of what I thought were "justified grievances" dissolved in that moment, and I was free to enjoy the peace that "passes all understanding."

Is that the Cinderella story, "and they lived happily ever after"? No. We will continue to work on this marriage until one or both of us depart this world. However, we see all things from a new perspective now. Divorce is not in our vocabulary and doesn't enter my thoughts. We have been able to sort out what counts and what doesn't count in our relationship, what will survive through eternity and what will not. Bill and Gloria Gaither nailed it in a song on their show in 2012: "sweeter as the days go by." It was intended to express our relationship to the Lord, but it also now applies to our marriage relationship. *To God be the Glory!*

Appendix A

A SYNOPIS OF *Tools for Transformation* © SEMINAR
(All Scriptures from NIV)

God's ultimate purpose for every believer is "*to be conformed to the likeness of his Son, that he might be the firstborn among many brothers.*" (Romans 8:29). God's purpose in conforming every believer to the image of Jesus is for His own glory. "*For from him and through him and to him are all things. To him be the glory forever!*" (Romans 11:36).

Tools for Transformation seminar is based upon three foundational Scriptures: The first, "*Be transformed by the renewing of your mind*" (Romans 12:2). The second is Jesus' teaching in John 6:51: "*I am the living bread that came down from heaven . . .*" Our spiritual bread is the Word of God. The third is Hebrew 4:12: "*The Word of God is alive and powerful . . .*" The power contained in the Word and directed by the Holy Spirit, penetrates the believer's heart, soul and mind, breaking down barriers to produce a congruous, Christ-centered life.

This victorious life is not automatic. The new birth event re-establishes the relationship that was broken when Adam disobeyed. This relationship is a partnership between the Creator and the re-created human spirit.

This partnership established by the Holy Spirit has a new objective. Paul wrote about this in Philippians 2:12–13: "*. . . Continue to work out your salvation with fear and trembling . . .*" God's purpose for believers is to be conformed to the image of Christ. He has provided the tools and the instructions. He expects us to use them with diligence, because of the awesome privilege and responsibility to become "*like living stones . . . being built into a spiritual house to be a holy priesthood, offering spiritual sacrifices acceptable to God through Jesus Christ*" (1 Peter 2:4–5).

TOOLS FOR TRANSFORMATION ©
TABLE OF CONTENTS

Synopsis of the Seminar Program 2

Segment I – BLUEPRINT DESIGN 3

    Module 1 – Need for Transformation 8

    Module 2 – Definitions and Important Concepts 5

    Module 3 – Definitions, Functions, and Connectivity 7

        Session 1- Definition and Function of the Heart 7

        Session 2 – Definition and Function of the Soul 12

        Session 3 – Definition and Function of the Mind 16

        Session 4 – Definition and Function of the Spirit 19

        Session 5 – Connectivity of the Building Blocks 21

Segment II – SITE PREPARATION 26

    Module 4 – The Process of Being Born Again 27

    Module 5 – Human Response to Being Born Again 31

    Module 6 – God's Purpose for Being Born Again 32

Segment III – CONSTRUCTING THE TRANSFORMATION . . 34

    Module 7 – Overview of Transformation 34

    Module 8 – Self-Evaluation, Constructing the Life Graph 42

        Session 1 – Critical Areas of Spiritual Maturity 42

        Session 2 – Self-Evaluation, Life Graph 44

    Module 9 – Transforming the Building Blocks 48

    References 68

Tools For Transformation© Beta Test Results

The data presented below are the results of a pre- and post-test of the *Tools for Transformation* (TFT) © seminar. TFT was presented to twelve members of Sedalia Community Church one night per week for a period of six months. The instrument used to measure spiritual maturity was the *Christian Life Profile* (CLP) developed and validated by Creative Leadership Ministries, an extension of Pantego Bible Church in Arlington, TX.

Participants completed the CLP before the seminar began and the same assessment after the seminar was completed. The percentage change in the average scores is shown in Table 1 below for each of the six categories. The changes were all positive, ranging from 3.85 percent to 21.23 percent, indicating there was positive spiritual growth during the six-month period.

Table 1. Spiritual growth resulting from TFT beta test

Variable	Before	After	Percent Change
Love God Benefits (LGB)	93.40	97.00	+3.85
Love God Practice (LGP)	75.73	9.89	+18.70
Love God Virtues (LGV)	71.44	80.33	+12.44
Love Neighbor Beliefs (LNB)	86.67	94.78	+9.36
Love Neighbor Practice (LNP)	68.00	82.44	+21.23
Love Neighbor Virtues (LNV)	74.07	84.89	+14.61

Correlation Data from TFT Beta Test – Sedalia

The following data was obtained from a correlation study using the *Christian Spiritual Participation Profile* (CSPP) as the measuring instrument. The twelve members of Sedalia Community Church also completed the CSPP questionnaire before and after the six-month period. The character traits measured by this profile are shown below:

SE = Spiritual Efficacy; AW = Awareness of God;
LO = Love; JO = Joy; IP = Inner Peace;
PG = Patience/Gentleness; FA = Faith;

KG = Kindness/Generosity; SC = Self-Control;
FO = Forgiveness; GR = Gratitude; CO = Compassion.

The correlation of Spiritual Efficacy (SE) with each of the eleven character traits is presented in Table 2 below. The top row, Pre, is the magnitude of the correlation of each of the character traits with SE for the participants prior to the six-month beta test. The Row 2 is the confidence level of the correlation. The third row, Post, is the magnitude of correlation of each of the character traits after the six-month seminar. The Row 4 is the confidence level of the correlation between SE and each of the character traits evaluated.

The number before the back slash / is the magnitude of the correlation and can be between minus one (-1) and plus one (+ 1). The number below the / is the confidence that a correlation actually exists. A high confidence exists when this number is between .05 and .00. The smaller this value, the higher the confidence, with .00 being extremely high confidence, as in Post: SE with AW being .79 magnitude, which is very good with confidence being .00, which is extremely high confidence.

Another example: In the Pre: SE with SC the magnitude is .44 but the confidence is .08 meaning there is low confidence that there is a correlation between SE and SC prior to the seminar. However, after the seminar the magnitude increased from .44 to .78 with a confidence increase from .08 to .00, an extremely high confidence that a very positive correlation exists between Spiritual-Efficacy (SE) and Self-Control (SC).

Table 2. Correlation of Self-Efficacy and eleven character traits

TEST	AW	LO	JO	IP	PG	KG	FA	SC	FO	GR	CO
Pre-Test											
Row 1	.52/	.52/	.59/	.34/	.51/	.55/	.44/	.44/	.65/	.10/	.39/
Row 2	.04	.04	.02	.20	.04	.03	.09	.08	.01	.71	.14
Post- Test											
Row 3	.79/	.80/	.74/	.56/	.71/	.74/	.71/	.78/	.83/	.54/	.79/
Row 4	.00	.00	.01	.06	.01	.01	.01	.00	.00	.07	.00

<u>Conclusion:</u> The power of God's Word assimilated by the participants penetrated barriers between the various character traits resulting in a significant increase in congruity among the traits evaluated.

Excerpts from the TFT Seminar Definition Modules

Definitions of Heart, Soul, Mind

Module 3 of the TFT Seminar explores the definitions and functions of the Building Blocks Jesus identified in Matthew 22:37 as being Heart, Soul, and Mind: "*Jesus said to him, 'You shall love the LORD your God with all your heart, with all your soul, and with all your mind.'*" Since Jesus identified these three components with the greatest commandment, it seems reasonable to conclude that these three components are the non-reducible building blocks of our human, eternal structure. Since Jesus distinctly identified these three components with which we are to love God, there is no other component with which we can love the Lord and these three components are unique and always distinct in definition and purpose.

The detailed derivation of the definitions and purposes of the heart, soul, and mind is included in the full TFT seminar and is available upon request. This may be one of the areas in which the Creator has intentionally hid a matter to challenge us to search it out as recorded in Proverbs 25:2: "*It is the glory of God to conceal a matter, but the glory of kings is to search out a matter.*" The summarized definitions and purposes of heart, soul, and mind are as follows:

<u>HEART:</u> The heart is "The center of Value" and where the comparison of values occurs. Notice in Romans 10:10 Paul declared: "*For with the heart man believes . . .*" Therefore it must be in the heart that value is processed and sanctioned or rejected.

<u>SOUL:</u> The center of identity, relationships, and emotions. Identity: Luke 1:46: "*My soul magnifies the Lord . . .*" Relationships: Leviticus 26:30: "*My soul shall abhor you . . .*" Emotions: Matthew 26:38: "*My soul is exceedingly sorrowful . . .*"

MIND: The center of logic and cognition. Logic is defined as the science of reasoning. Cognition is the act, power, or faculty of apprehending, knowing, or perceiving. Cognitive process is a process that originates with a specific cognition. Romans 12:2: *"And do not be conformed to this world, but be transformed by the renewing of your mind that you may prove. . . ."*

According to Jesus, the ultimate tribute to our Creator is to love Him with all our heart, with all our soul, and with all our mind. The love Jesus was speaking of is not romantic love in a human sense. Rather it is aligning the functions of our heart, soul, and mind in total congruence with those of the Father. Our response would then be:

HEART: Since my heart is the center of values, I love God with all my heart by totally assimilating His values. *"I delight to do Your will, O my God, and your law [word] is within my heart"* (Psalm 40:8).

SOUL: To love the Lord with all my soul is to totally identify with Him such that my identity is encased within His identity. *"I am crucified with Christ and I no longer live, but Christ lives in me"* (Galatians 2:20). With Christ living in me, my relationship with Him is congruent and His emotions and my emotions are synonymous.

MIND: To love the Lord with all my mind results when His thoughts become my thoughts. *"How precious also are Your thoughts to me, O God! How great is the sum of them"* (Psalms 139:17). His logic is the basis for all my decisions: *"You will guide me with Your counsel, and afterward receive me to glory"* (Psalm 73:24).

Connectivity of Heart, Soul, and Mind

There is obvious interaction between the heart, soul, and mind as indicated in such Scriptures as Psalms 10:6: *"He has said in his heart . . ."* Speaking is a cognitive function controlled by the mind. The heart as the center of value does not interact directly to the external world as shown by Romans 10:9–10 that declares the heart believes but it is the mind that channels the message to the heart and announces the belief to the world.

Likewise in Psalm 16:2: "*O my soul, you have said to the Lord . . .*"The soul is the center of identity but it is the mind that instructs the mouth to speak. One possibility of interconnectivity is shown below. The area in which the heart, soul and mind overlap is labeled the Zone of Congruence; it is in this area that the heart and soul and mind interact.

Figure 1. Connectivity Diagram of the Heart, the Soul, and the Mind

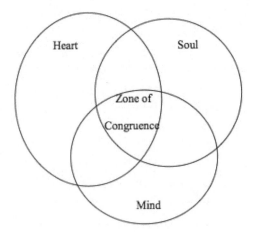

In the perfect case, as with Jesus, the Zone of Congruence would encompass the entire area of the heart and the soul and the mind with total congruity between all three.

Appendix B

Spiritual Warfare

Satan Exposed

Fear has been the great deterrent in my life. Fear of death, fear of insanity, fear of being overpowered by demons, fear of flying, fear of jumping out of an airplane-—without a parachute—and fear of important people. In his book *Slaying the Giants in Your Life*, David Jeremiah called fear the "Ultimate Enemy" and wrote: "There is no feeling quite like the icy grip of fear. And it comes in so many varieties." [49]

One of the examples Jeremiah cited was very similar to my fear of opening the emergency door of an airplane and jumping out or crashing the small plane I was flying:

> I've also read about a young truck driver whose route takes him across the Chesapeake Bay Bridge every day. The thought entered his mind that he just might feel compelled to stop the truck, climb out, and leap from the bridge to his death. . . . He finally asked his wife to handcuff him to the steering wheel so he could be fully assured that his deepest fear wouldn't come true. [50]

It was never necessary for me to be chained to the seat of the plane, but the urge was often very strong. Ten years after I resigned from the Army flight school, I decided to face the fear and proceeded to earn a commercial pilot's license. The first day I soloed, my flight suit was soaked with perspiration when I finally landed. Using the processes described in this book, not only have I overcome the fear of flying, but it is my favorite mode of travel. David Jeremiah outlines a similar process in Chapter 1 of *Slaying the Giants in Your Life*.

Characters in the Spiritual War

Paul Billheimer (1982) claims that God initially gave man the dominion of this earth, citing Genesis 1:26: "And God said let us make man in our image . . . and let him have dominion over . . . all the earth." Billheimer further argues that when Adam disobeyed in the Garden, the earth legally became Satan's domain. However, Christ recaptured the dominion of the earth and gave dominion of the earth to His Church. Billheimer, citing Matthew 16:18–19, wrote:

> Calvary was indeed a victory . . . but the enforcement of Calvary's victory was placed in the hands of the church. . . . The fact that Satan seems to be having his way is no reflection upon the genuineness of Christ's victory over Satan at the cross. It means only that the enforcement agency has failed.[51]

Every battle has winners and losers. The winning characters in the spiritual war are God, the Father; Jesus Christ, the Son; the Holy Spirit; angels on assignment; and believers empowered by the Holy Spirit (Acts 1:8). We are to put on the armor of God and take up the sword of the Spirit, which is the Word of God (Ephesians 6:17). According to Hebrews 4:12, "The word of God is alive and active. Sharper than any double-edged sword, it penetrates even to dividing soul and spirit, joints and marrow; it judges the thoughts and attitudes of the heart." Empowered by the Spirit and armed with the sword of the Spirit, we go forth to battle.

According to Revelation 12:7–9, the main enemy of God is Satan, also called the devil: "So the great dragon was cast out, that serpent of old, called the devil and Satan, who deceives the whole world; he was cast to the earth, and his angels were cast out with him." Therefore the war that began in Heaven continues on earth: "For we do not wrestle against flesh and blood . . . but against the rulers of the darkness of this age, against spiritual host of wickedness in heavenly places" (Ephesians 6:12). Paul Billheimer argues that "heavenly places" refers to "the atmosphere surrounding the earth":

> Evil spirit personalities under the direction of their ruler, the god of this world, swarm the earth in an attempt to foil God's government and control earth's inhabitants; they are constantly inciting them to rebel against God. . . . The war that began in heaven when Satan was expelled merely changed locations and now continues on earth.[52]

According to Daniel 10:13 Satan's angels are assigned territories for the angel of the Lord speaking to Daniel said: "But the prince of the kingdom of Persia withstood me." Also when Jesus encountered an evil spirit in Mark 5:10, "He begged *Him earnestly that* He would not send them out of the country."

Matthew 25:41 identifies the final disposition of God's enemies: "Then He will also say to those on the left hand, 'Depart from Me, you cursed, into the everlasting fire prepared for the devil and his angels.'"

Conclusion: The losing characters in the spiritual warfare are Satan (the devil) and a myriad of minions, called evil spirits, who harass and may indwell humans.

Levels of Demonic Activity

Scott Peck identifies four grades of demon activity:

> Grade 1: Temptation. I perceive my temptations as being a natural part of the human condition. . . . [Others] are inclined to see the devil behind even the simplest of temptations.
>
> Grade 2: Demonic Attack: Here the individual is either being tempted on many fronts simultaneously or else is experiencing characteristic paranormal phenomena such as inexplicable coldness or bad odors.

On two distinct occasions I have experienced a sudden and drastic drop in the temperature in the room. First in West Virginia as a young child, then in Vietnam in 1969. Both incidents were accompanied by intense fear.

> Grade 3: Oppression. Here the demonic has obtained a foot-hold within the person but not yet a presence of sufficient strength to encase the victim's soul totally.
>
> Grade 4: Possession. This was perfectly described by [one of Peck's exorcisms] when she drew the picture of her soul represented by a fetus completely surrounded by demonic fluid to such a degree that the soul could no longer communicate with the outside world.[53]

There are numerous books and websites that now address spiritual warfare, such as www.bible-knowledge.com. This site describes levels of demon activity and the avenues by which the demon(s) gain access to people. Click on Bible Topics, scroll down to Spiritual Warfare.

Examples of Deliverance from Demons by Jesus in Scripture

1. A man with a spirit of an unclean demon (Luke 4:31–37).
2. He cast out a variety of demons (Mark 1:34).
3. The unclean demons fell before Him and were cast out (Mark 3:10–12).
4. He cast demons out of many people (Luke 4:40–41).
5. He removed a demon who tried to drown and burn a boy (Mark 9:25–27).
6. He cast out a demon that prevented a man from speaking (Luke 11:14).
7. He removed a spirit of infirmity that was crippling a woman (Luke 13:11–13).
8. He ordered a legion of demons out of a man into two thousand pigs (Mark 5:1–16).

References for the Believer's Authority over Evil Spirits

1. Jesus gave the twelve disciples power to cast out evil spirits and to heal all kinds of disease (Matthew 10:1–8; Mark 3:15).

2. Jesus gave authority to believers to cast out evil spirits (Mark 16:17).

3. Jesus gave his disciples authority over all evil (Luke 10:19–20).

4. Phillip cast demons out of many people (Acts 8:6–8).

5. Paul ordered a spirit who told the future out of a slave girl (Acts 16:16–18).

6. Handkerchiefs from Paul delivered from demons and healed the sick (Acts 19:11–12).

Tables and Figures

Listed on the next three separate pages are the two Tables and one Figure contained in the text:

Table 1. Spiritual growth resulting from TFT beta test

Variable	Before	After	Percent Change
Love God Benefits (LGB)	93.40	97.00	+3.85
Love God Practice (LGP)	75.73	9.89	+18.70
Love God Virtues (LGV)	71.44	80.33	+12.44
Love Neighbor Beliefs (LNB)	86.67	94.78	+9.36
Love Neighbor Practice (LNP)	68.00	82.44	+21.23
Love Neighbor Virtues (LNV)	74.07	84.89	+14.61

Table 2. Correlation of Self-Efficacy and eleven character traits

TEST	AW	LO	JO	IP	PG	KG	FA	SC	FO	GR	CO
Pre-Test											
Row 1	.52/	.52/	.59/	.34/	.51/	.55/	.44/	.44/	.65/	.10/	.39/
Row 2	.04	.04	.02	.20	.04	.03	.09	.08	.01	.71	.14
Post-Test											
Row 3	.79/	.80/	.74/	.56/	.71/	.74/	.71/	.78/	.83/	.54/	.79/
Row 4	.00	.00	.01	.06	.01	.01	.01	.00	.00	.07	.00

Figure 1. Connectivity Diagram of the Heart, the Soul, and the Mind

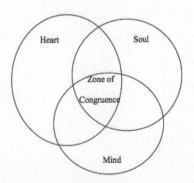

Bibliography

Bandura, Albert. *Self-Efficacy: The Exercise of Control.* New York: W. H. Freeman, 1997.

Barnhouse, Donald G. *Man's Ruin: Romans 1:1–32.* Grand Rapids, MI: Eerdmans, 1962.

Barnhouse, Donald G. *The Invisible War.* Grand Rapids, MI: Zondervan, 1965.

Benson, Herbert. *Timeless Healing—The Power and Biology of Belief.* New York: Fireside, 1997.

Billheimer, Paul E. *Destined to Overcome.* Minneapolis, MN: Bethany House, 1982.

Bottari, Pablo. *Free in Christ: Your Complete Handbook on the Ministry of Deliverance.* Lake Mary, FL: Charisma House, 2000.

Bunyan, John. *Pilgrim's Progress.* Poultrey, England: Ponder, 1678.

Cahn, Jonathon. *The Harbinger.* Lake Mary, FL: Charisma House, 2011.

Cetas, Anne, Joyce Dinkins, Tim Gustafson, J.R. Hudberg, Alyson Keida, and Becky Knapp. Eds. *Our Daily Bread.* Grand Rapids, MI: Our Daily Bread Ministries, 2015.

Chambers, Oswald. *My Utmost for His Highest.* Uhrichsville, OH: Barbour Books, 1963.

Eldredge, John. *Waking the Dead.* Nashville: Thomas Nelson, 2003.

Eldredge, John, and Craig McConnell. *A Guidebook to Waking the Dead.* Nashville: Thomas Nelson, 2003.

Eldredge, John. *Wild at Heart: Discovering the Secret of a Man's Soul.* Nashville: Thomas Nelson, 2011.

Festinger, L. *A Theory of Cognitive Dissonance.* Stanford, CA: Stanford University Press, 1957.

Gray, Benjamin. "Hidden Demons: A Personal Account of Hearing Voices." *Schizophr Bulletin* 34(6) (Nov 2008): 1006–1007.

"Animal Feedlots as a Source of Drinking Water Contamination." http//www.extoxnet.orst.edu/faqs/safedrink/feed.htm.   (April 12, 2013).

Jeremiah, David. *Slaying the Giants in Your Life.* Nashville, TN: W Publishing Group, 2001.

Jeremiah, David. *Agents of Babylon.* Carol Stream, Illinois: Tyndale Publishers, 2015.

Leaf, Caroline. *Who Switched off My Brain.* Nashville, TN: Thomas Nelson, 2009.

Leaf, Caroline. *Switch on Your Brain: The Key to Peak Happiness, Thinking and Health.* Grand Rapids, MI: Baker Books, 2013.

Lee, Jill E. (2013). http://fcaresources.com/devotional/2013/04/12/run-toward-roar#sthash,12S2e3kb.dpuf.

Leehan, Michael. *Ascent from Darkness.* Nashville, TN: Thomas Nelson, 2011.

Lewis, Robert. *Raising a Modern Day Knight.* Carol Stream, IL. Tyndale House, 2007.

Martin, Malachi. *Hostage to the Devil: The Possession and Exorcism of Five Contemporary Americans.* San Francisco: Harper, 1992.

Metaxas, Eric. *Miracles.* New York: Penguin Group, 2014.

Miller, Keith. *Habitation of Dragons.* Waco, TX: Word, 1970.

Mumford, Bob. *The Purpose of Temptation*. Alachua, FL: Bridge Logos Publishers, 1997.

Newman, Bob. *Everything the Bible Says About Angels and Demons*. Minneapolis, MN: Bethany House, 2012.

Peale, Norman V. *The Power of Positive Thinking*. New York: Simon & Schuster, 1952.

Peale, Norman V. *Thought Conditioners*. Pawling, NY: Foundation for Christian Living, 1951.

Peck, M. Scott. *The Road Less Traveled*. New York: Simon & Schuster, 1978.

Peck, M. Scott. *People of the Lie*. New York: Simon & Schuster, 1983.

Peck, M. Scott. *Glimpses of the Devil*. New York: Free Press/Simon & Shuster, 2005.

Phillips, Ron. *Everyone's Guide to Demons & Spiritual Warfare*. Lake Mary, FL: Charisma House, 2010.

Pierson, Arthur T. *George Müller of Bristol*. Old Tappan, NJ: Revell, 1899.

Piper, Don. *90 Minutes in Heaven*. Grand Rapids, MI: Revell, 2004.

Prince, Derek. *They Shall Expel Demons*. Ada, MI: Chosen Books; Reprinted edition, 1998.

Rotter, J. B. *Social Learning and Clinical Psychology*. Upper Saddle River, NJ: Prentice-Hall, 1954.

Ruth, Peggy J. *Psalm 91—God's Shield of Protection*. Midland, TX: The 1687 Foundation, 2009.

Sheikh, Bilquis, and Richard H. Schneider. *I Dared to Call Him Father*. Southampton, England: Jeremy Books, 1978.

Sibbes, Richard. *Glorious Freedom*. Carlisle, PA/Edinburgh, GB: Puritan Paperbacks, The Banner of Truth Trust, 1639

Sumrall, Lester. *Demons: The Answer Book*. New Kensington, PA: Whitaker House, 2003.

Thayer, J. *Assessing Participation in the Spiritual Development Modes: Construction of the Christian Spiritual Participation Profile*, 1996.

Tice, Lou. *Investment in Excellence for the 90s*. Seattle, WA: The Pacific Institute, 1992.

Unger, Merrill, F. *What Demons Can Do to Saints*. Chicago: Moody Publishers, 1991.

Unger, Merrill F. *Biblical Demonology*. Grand Rapids, MI: Kregel Publications, 1994.

Veith, G. E. *Postmodern Times: A Christian Guide to Contemporary Thought and Culture*. Wheaton, IL: Crossway Books, 1994.

Vines, W., ed. *Vines Expository Dictionary of Biblical Words*. Nashville, TN: Thomas Nelson, 1985.

Ward, Gary. *Living Free from the Shackles that Bind*. Apopka, FL: Reliance Media, 2011.

Warren, Rick. *The Purpose Driven Life*. Grand Rapids, MI: Zondervan, 2002.

White, Alasdair A. K. *From Comfort Zone to Performance Management*, Kindle Edition, 2009.

Woodbridge, J. D. *Renewing Your Mind in a Secular World*. Chicago, IL: Moody Press, 1985.

Notes

Chapter 7

1. Norman V. Peale, *Thought Conditioners* (Pawling, NY: FCL, 1951), 2.

Chapter 10

2. Donald G. Barnhouse, *The Invisible War* (Grand Rapids, MI: Zondervan, 1965), 137.

3. Don Piper, *90 Minutes in Heaven* (Grand Rapids, MI: Revell, 2004), 23.

4. John Burke, *Imagine Heaven* (Grand Rapids, MI: Baker Books, 2015), 27.

5. Ibid, 69.

Chapter 11

6. M. Scott Peck, *The Road Less Traveled* (New York: Simon & Shuster, 1978), 18.

Chapter 12

7. David Jeremiah, *Agents of Babylon* (Carol Stream, IL: Tyndale Publishers, 2015), 293.

Chapter 14

8. Ron Dunn, "Chained to the Chariot," Ron Dunn, accessed June 21, 2017, rondunn.com/chained-to-the-chariot.

9. Barnhouse, *The Invisible War*, 142.

10. Ibid., 153.

11. Rick Warren, *The Purpose Driven Life* (Grand Rapids, MI: Zondervan, 2002), 11.

12. "Animal Feedlots as a Source of Drinking Water Contamination."(url:http//www.extoxnet.orst.edu/faqs/safe-drink/feed.htm), 1.

13. Ibid., 56.

14. Ibid., 150.

15. Lester Sumrall, *Demons* (New Kensington, PA: Whitaker House), 120.

16. M. Scott Peck, *Glimpses of the Devil* (New York: Free Press/ Simon & Shuster, 2005), 97.

17. Ibid., 249.

18. Malachi Martin, *Hostage to the Devil* (San Francisco: Harper, 1992), XII-XV.

19. Barnhouse, *The Invisible War*, 83.

20. Barnhouse, *The Invisible War*, 83.

Chapter 15

21. John Eldredge, *Waking the Dead* (Nashville, TN: Thomas Nelson, 2003), 37.

22. Oswald Chambers, *My Utmost for His Highest* (Uhrichsville, OH: Barbour Books), Jan 15.

23. Ibid., Jan 18.

24. Robert Lewis, *Raising a Modern-Day Knight* (Carol Stream, IL: Tyndale House), 33.

25. Chambers, Dec 4.

26. Ron Phillips, *Demons & Spiritual Warfare* (Lake Mary, FL: Chrisma House, 2010), 107.

Chapter 17

27. Chambers, Mar 30.

28. Paul Billheimer, *Destined to Overcome* (Minneapolis, MN: Bethany House, 1982), 11.

29. Ibid., 21.

30. Ibid., 41.

Chapter 18

31. great-quotes.com/quotes/author/John/Wayne.

32. John Eldredge, *Wild at Heart* (Nashville: Thomas Nelson, 2011), 9.

33. "Rwanda Economic Freedom Score," *2012 Index of Economic Freedom*, 351–352, http://www.heritage.org/index/pdf/2012/countries/rwanda.pdf.

34. Jean I N Kanyarwunga, "Lithuania/Rwanda: Jesus Christ, inducted King of the Countries," *History of Africa Otherwise*, Oct 22, 2011, http://historyofafricaotherwise.blogspot.com/2011/10/lithuania-rwanda-jesus-christ-inducted.html.

35. James Allen, *As a Man Thinketh* (goodreads.com/author/quotes/8446.James_Allen?page=2).

Chapter 19

36. Caroline Leaf, *Who Switched off My Brain* (Nashville, TN: Thomas Nelson, 2009), 109.

37. Ibid., 21.

38. Ibid., 22.

39. Ibid., 31.

40. Ibid., 80.

41. Caroline Leaf, *Switch on Your Brain* (Grand Rapids, MI: Baker Books, 2013), 22.

42. Ibid., 39.

43. Chambers, *My Utmost for His Highest*, Feb 22.

44. Anne Cetas, et al., *Our Daily Bread* (Grand Rapids, MI: Our Daily Bread Ministries, Feb. 21, 2015), np.

45. John Eldredge, *A Guide to Waking the Dead* (Nashville: Thomas Nelson, 2003), vii.

46. Richard Sibbes, *Glorious Freedom* (Edinburgh, GB: Puritan Paperbacks, 1639), 36–38.

47. Ibid., 39.

48. Robert Morris, *Free Indeed*, YouTube playlist, from sermons given at Gateway Church starting on September 21, 2013, posted by "gatewaychurchtv," September 25, 2013, https://www.youtube.com/playlist?list=PLFgcIA8Y9FMDXa4LKQ_AdiiilReifMy56.

Appendix B

49. David Jeremiah, *Slaying the Giants* (Nashville, TN: W Publishing Group, 2001), 2.

50. Ibid., 3.

51. Paul Billheimer, *Destined to Overcome* (Minneapolis, MN: Bethany House, 1982), 35.

52. Ibid., 73.

53. M. Scott Peck, *Glimpses of the Devil* (New York: Free Press/ Simon & Shuster, 2005), 120.